WHYBELIEVE?

ANSWERS TO LIFE'S QUESTIONS

Gwendolen Adams

Christopher Blum

Tim Gray

Daniel McInerny

Randall Smith

Edward Sri

VOLUME 2

Augustine Institute

Greenwood Village, Colorado

2019

Nihil Obstat: Tomas Fuerte, S.T.L., *Censor Librorum*
Imprimatur: Most Reverend Samuel J. Aquila, S.T.L., Archbishop of Denver, Denver, CO USA
June 6, 2019

Editors
Christopher Blum, General Editor
Tim Gray, Associate Editor
Daniel McInerny, Associate Editor

Contributing Authors
Gwendolen Adams
Christopher Blum
Daniel McInerny
Randall Smith
Edward Sri

***Why Believe?* Staff**
Kathleen Blum, Editorial Consultant
Jonathan Brand, Editorial Consultant
Ben Dybas, Creative Director
Jane Myers, Graphic Designer

Augustine Institute
6160 South Syracuse Way
Greenwood Village, CO 80111
Information: 303-937-4420 or WhyBelieve@AugustineInstitute.org
AugustineInstitute.org
FORMED.org/whybelieve
ISBN: 978-1-7327208-3-1

Printed in Canada

Contents

CHAPTER 1

1

Rich in Mercy

Now the tax collectors and sinners were all drawing near to hear [Jesus]. And the Pharisees and the scribes murmured, saying, "This man receives sinners and eats with them." So he told them this parable: "What man of you, having a hundred sheep, if he has lost one of them, does not leave the ninety-nine in the wilderness, and go after the one which is lost, until he finds it? And when he has found it, he lays it on his shoulders, rejoicing. And when he comes home, he calls together his friends and his neighbors, saying to them, 'Rejoice with me, for I have found my sheep which was lost.' Just so, I tell you, there will be more joy in heaven over one sinner who repents than over ninety-nine righteous persons who need no repentance.

Or what woman, having ten silver coins, if she loses one coin, does not light a lamp and sweep the house and seek diligently until she finds it? And when she has found it, she calls together her friends and neighbors, saying, 'Rejoice with me, for I have found the coin which I had lost.' Just so, I tell you, there is joy before the angels of God over one sinner who repents."

And [Jesus] said, "There was a man who had two sons; and the younger of them said to his father, 'Father, give me the share of property that falls to me.' And he divided his living between them. Not many days later, the younger son gathered all he had and took his journey into a far country, and there he squandered his property in loose living. And when he had spent everything, a great famine arose in that country, and he began to be in want. So he went and joined himself to one of the citizens of that country, who sent him into his fields to feed swine. And he would gladly have fed on the pods that the swine ate; and no one gave him anything. But when he came to himself he said, 'How many of my father's hired servants have bread enough and to spare, but I perish here with hunger! I will arise and go to my father, and I will say to him, "Father, I have sinned against heaven and before you; I am no longer worthy to be called your son; treat me as one of your hired servants."' And he arose and came to his father. But while he was yet at a distance, his father saw him and had compassion, and ran and embraced him and kissed him. And the son said to him, 'Father, I have sinned against heaven and before you; I am no longer worthy to be called your son.' But the father said to his servants, 'Bring quickly the best robe, and put it on him; and put a ring on his hand, and shoes on his feet; and bring the fatted calf and kill it, and let us eat and make merry; for this my son was dead, and is alive again; he was lost, and is found.' And they began to make merry.

"Now his elder son was in the field; and as he came and drew near to the house, he heard music and dancing. And he called one of the servants and asked what this meant. And he said to him, 'Your brother has come, and your father has killed the fatted calf, because he has received him safe and sound.' But he was angry and refused to go in. His father came out and entreated him, but he answered his father, 'Behold, these many years I have served you, and I never disobeyed your command; yet you never gave me a kid, that I might make merry with my friends. But when this son of yours came, who has devoured your living with harlots, you killed for him the fatted calf!' And he said to him, 'Son, you are always with me, and all that is mine is yours. It was fitting to make merry and be glad, for this your brother was dead, and is alive; he was lost, and is found'" (Lk 15:1–32).

Bartolomé Estaban Murillo, The Return of the Prodigal Son, *1667–1670, Oil on canvas, National Gallery of Art, Washington, DC, USA.*

The parable of the prodigal son is a mini-drama recounting the spiritual history of the human race.

The parable of the prodigal son is among the best-known and most beloved stories in all of history. We can see why. Jesus is a master story-teller; like a painter who can bring a picture to life with a few strokes of his brush, he has told a vivid tale with only a few words. We can easily imagine and sympathize with the different characters and their states of mind: the younger son who wants freedom and who views the world as his playground; the change of mind he experiences as he faces the hard realities of life; his determination to creep back home and acknowledge his guilt; the father's joy and generosity in seeing his lost son now coming home again; the abashed surprise and delight of the returning son (not explicitly mentioned but evident in the way the story unfolds); and the jealousy of the older son who cannot understand his father's eager reception of his wayward brother.

It is clear from the context that Jesus is not merely telling an isolated story about one person's experience or giving a lesson in good family relations. He is telling in short form the tale of humanity. He is providing us with a mini-drama recounting the spiritual history of the human race. The father in the story is, plainly enough, God himself. The younger son is the human race as a whole. The older brother represents God's chosen people, the Jews. This is a story that belongs to each of us. It shows us important things about who God is and who we are, about God's heart toward us, and about what we need to do to find our way through life.

The Good News

The most important truth to be gained from the parable of the prodigal son, and the quality that has most riveted the world's attention and consoled its suffering people, is what the story tells us about God. It can be easy to have a grim and forbidding idea of God. We know that he is all-powerful, which can be a little frightening. We know that he is perfect in goodness, and we, who are nowhere near perfect, can feel uneasy around him. We cannot see him, so his power and goodness can seem distant and mysterious, and therefore alarming. The picture of God that many people carry in their minds is a stern policeman who sees everything and disapproves of most of what he sees and whose presence gets in the way of enjoying life. Jesus, God himself among us, completely explodes that wrong-headed and reduced notion of God. In this parable, Jesus gives us a very different picture of who God really is: a loving and devoted father who desires good things for his children, who is eager for their happiness, who is quick to forgive and forget their faults and sins, and who is overjoyed to see them do well.

The parable of the prodigal son makes clear why the message of Jesus has always been called the "Gospel," the Good News. What the news announces is overwhelmingly good. It tells us that we have a Father who loves us and knows our name. It reveals that we have a home and an inheritance, a future that has been planned for us by one who loves us. It means that even when we have "squandered our inheritance" by behaving foolishly or very badly, our Father in heaven is not only prepared to forgive us and to overlook our sins, but is waiting to embrace us with joy and to set heaven dancing as we return to him. It is no wonder that tax collectors, prostitutes, and all kinds of sinners drew near to Jesus. They saw themselves in the story he told, and they were given bright hope by the father's joyful words: "Let us eat and make merry; for this my son was dead, and is alive again; he was lost, and is found!"

Rohingya refugees from Myanmar waiting for food aid in Kutupalong refugee camp near Cox's Bazar, Bangladesh.

The Difficult News

So the good news of the Father's loving heart toward the human race is at the core of this parable. Yet there is another message in the tale, a truth that was taken for granted by most of those listening to Jesus and for that matter by most people who have heard the story through the centuries, but one that has been getting lost among us more recently. The father in the parable joyfully announces that his son has been found and is alive again. But good news of this kind assumes a more difficult reality: that his son had been lost, that he had been dead. We are a lost and dying race: this is the truth about the state of humanity that our modern world has found increasingly difficult to accept.

We certainly do not think that everything is right with the world. We are aware of serious problems all around us: injustice and unfairness, poverty, physical suffering, armed conflicts, and environmental damage. We also recognize that individuals often face severe personal challenges, whether in their relationships with those close to them or in sorting out their own emotional and psychological lives. Yet we tend to see all these problems, whether personal or global, as due to a flaw in the system and as external to ourselves. Jesus has a different view. In everything he teaches and does, he assumes that we are suffering from a deadly moral disease, a disease that often gets expressed in societal problems of various kinds, but whose root is in the individual human soul. Jesus saw the deadly disease of sin eating its way into every person's heart; he understood that the whole of the human race was infected, lost, and dying. He came among us to heal the sickness that was destroying those he loved.

Jesus sometimes spoke of himself as a physician, a helpful analogy for understanding his mission to us. In drawing out the analogy, we might imagine a highly competent and conscientious doctor, who cares very much about his patients. Imagine that a serious epidemic has broken out and is spreading through the populace, infecting everyone in the town. Wherever the doctor goes, he sees his patients, his friends and members of his family, falling sick and dying. A characteristic of this strange illness is that it does not show its worst symptoms at first, so a person could be deeply infected for a long time without fully realizing it. The doctor has spared no pains, working long hours in his laboratory to find a way to battle the epidemic, and he has discovered medicines and a regimen that can cure the disease. He is now taking his cure among the people of the town, offering his treatment at no cost to whomever wants it. We can imagine three possible responses to the doctor as he brings his medicine to the sick and dying.

The Lord is like the doctor, taking his cure among the people of the town, offering his treatment at no cost to whomever wants it.

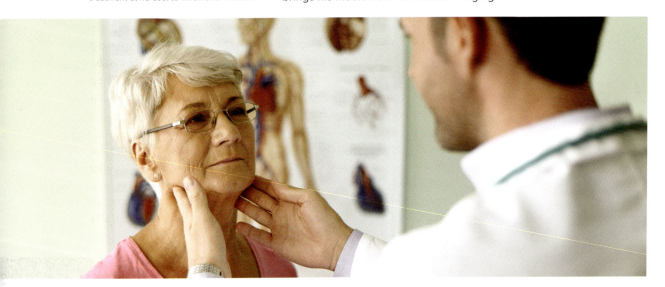

In the first place are those who know they are sick and who are desperately looking for help. They have been suffering from the ravages of the illness and have tried all kinds of remedies, none of which has worked. Having given up hope, they feel sure they are going to die. When the doctor diagnoses the problem and offers medicine for its cure, they leap at the opportunity. They are grateful to him for his hard work and his willingness to treat them, and they readily give themselves into his care, staying as close to him as possible.

In the second place are those who have caught the dread disease, but are not yet aware of it. Either the symptoms are not yet bad enough to worry them, or they have misdiagnosed their problem. But when the doctor arrives and explains what they are really suffering from and how serious the disease is, they accept his diagnosis and eagerly begin their treatment, again with gratitude.

In the third place are people who, like those in the second group, are unknowingly infected by the disease. But the members of this group think that they are healthy and in no need of curing. When the doctor explains to them that they are very sick and that they need treatment to avoid dying, they refuse to accept his diagnosis. They are angry at him for bringing the matter up at all, and they tell him to go elsewhere with his troubling news and his medicines.

Jesus encountered all three types. Those tax collectors and sinners who rejoiced to meet him and were ready to repent were in the first group. They ran to Jesus as the only one who could help them in their dire need. Sick as they were, they found hope and life in being near him, because they knew he had come to heal them. Among the second group were some of the Apostles, notably Peter and Paul. Peter was busily catching fish, and Paul was tracking down Christians to throw them in jail, when they encountered Jesus and his message. They stopped what they were doing, changed direction, and embraced the treatment of the divine physician, becoming his special aides in getting the medicine to all who needed it. In the third group were the Pharisees and scribes spoken of in the reading from the Gospel of Luke. They would not admit that they were ill, and they resented Jesus for insisting that they needed treatment.

It is clear from these three responses to the message of Jesus that the Good News is only experienced as good if first the difficult news is fully understood. Those who are sick are happy to hear of a way to get well. Those who are in denial about their sickness do not want to hear about its cure and avoid everyone who brings it up. We often encounter this attitude of denial today.

Jesus calling the tax collector, Zacchaeus, who rejoiced to meet him and was ready to repent.

What coach wants his players never to improve their technique or to learn better team play?

Love Desires Change

In recent years, it has become common for people to say that if you really love someone, you will not want them to change. The lyrics of many popular songs include something along those lines. As an expression of affection and an affirmation of the goodness of another person, saying that we do not want someone to change is a charming sentiment. But if it becomes a principle of thought and life, it gets us into trouble. The truth is exactly the opposite. The more we love someone, the more we want that person to change. Of course, we do not want those we love to change into entirely different people, but we do want them to continue to learn, to grow, to become better, all of which involve change. What mother wants her beloved five-year old never to change, never to learn how to read, or gain a skill, or mature as a person? What coach wants his players never to improve their technique or to learn better team play? What lovers do not hope to see the one they love growing in happiness and goodness? The only people whose change we do not desire are those we simply do not care about.

The truth that love desires change has something to do with our incomplete state. We are still on the way to our full humanity, and we all need to keep learning, growing, and maturing. But this truth extends even further. We desire change in those we love, not only because they are not yet in their final form, like a child who has not yet grown up. We desire change in one another because we know that we are deeply flawed; because there is a darkness working in us; because we are afflicted by a serious moral disease. We want to see our loved ones freed from the ravages of that sickness. It would be odd to go to a doctor for relief from a splitting migraine, only to have him tell us that he would prefer not to do anything about it because he likes us just as we are. We are happy to find that our doctors like us, but we do not want them to like our diseases.

So it is with God: he loves us with a strength and steadiness that infinitely surpasses the deepest love we can have for another person. But just because of that strong love, he hates the diseases that ravage and destroy us. This is why God is so opposed to sin. It is for the same reason that a doctor is so opposed to the cancer eating away at the life of his patient. So it makes sense that the first recorded word out of the mouth of Jesus, who came among us with burning love in his heart, was "Repent!" (Mt 4:17), which simply means, "Change!" Jesus is that doctor who has come looking for us with a cure for our disease, but he can only administer the cure to those who are willing to receive his treatment.

Sin is an offense against reason, truth, and right conscience; it is failure in genuine love for God and neighbor caused by a perverse attachment to certain goods. It wounds the nature of man and injures human solidarity.

Catechism of the Catholic Church, 1849

This understanding of love helps to explain the father's response to his prodigal son in Jesus' parable. The son knew that he had sinned, and he thought his father would be counting his sins and keeping a tally. He expected to find his father angry with him for squandering his inheritance and betraying his family. But he had not yet understood the nature of genuine love. His father had grieved over his son's profligate behavior, not because his pride was insulted, but because he knew that it was destroying someone he loved. He had been eagerly hoping and waiting for the moment when a change might happen. When his son turned away from what was killing him—when he repented—and began to make his way back home, his father was overjoyed and ran to welcome him. "I tell you," said Jesus, "there is joy before the angels of God over one sinner who repents" (Lk 15:10).

from **St. John Paul II,** *Dives in Misericordia (Rich in Mercy)* [1980]

In the teaching of Christ, this image [of a merciful God] inherited from the Old Testament becomes at the same time simpler and more profound. This is perhaps most evident in the parable of the prodigal son....That son... in a certain sense is the man of every period, beginning with the one who was the first to lose the inheritance of grace and original justice....

The analogy turns clearly towards man's interior. The inheritance that the son had received from his father was a quantity of material goods, but more important than these goods was his dignity as a son in his father's house. The situation in which he found himself when he lost the material goods should have made him aware of the loss of that dignity....He measures himself by the standard of the goods that he has lost, that he no longer "possesses," while the hired servants of his father's house "possess" them. These words express above all his attitude to material goods; nevertheless under their surface is concealed the tragedy of lost dignity, the awareness of squandered sonship.

It is at this point that he makes the decision: "I will arise and go to my father, and I will say to him, 'Father, I have sinned against heaven and before you; I am no longer worthy to be called your son. Treat me as one of your hired servants.'" These are words that reveal more deeply the essential problem. Through the complex material situation in which the prodigal son found himself because of his folly, because of sin, the sense of lost dignity had matured. When he decides to return to his father's house, to ask his father to be received—no longer by virtue of his right as a son, but as an employee—at first sight

he seems to be acting by reason of the hunger and poverty that he had fallen into; this motive, however, is permeated by an awareness of a deeper loss: to be a hired servant in his own father's house is certainly a great humiliation and source of shame.

Nevertheless, the prodigal son is ready to undergo that humiliation and shame. He realizes that he no longer has any right except to be an employee in his father's house. His decision is taken in full consciousness of what he has deserved and of what he can still have a right to in accordance with the norms of justice. Precisely this reasoning demonstrates that, at the center of the prodigal son's consciousness, the sense of lost dignity is emerging, the sense of that dignity that springs from the relationship of the son with the father....

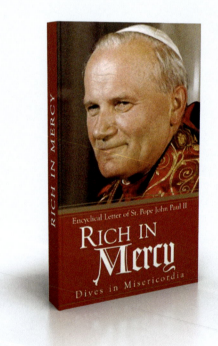

This picture of the prodigal son's state of mind enables us to understand exactly what the mercy of God consists in. There is no doubt that in this simple but penetrating analogy the figure of the father reveals to us God as Father. The conduct of the father in the parable and his whole behavior, which manifests his internal attitude, enables us to rediscover the individual threads of the Old Testament vision of mercy in a synthesis which is totally new, full of simplicity and depth. The father of the prodigal son is faithful to his fatherhood, faithful to the love that he had always lavished on his son. This fidelity is expressed in the parable not only by his immediate readiness to welcome him home when he returns after having squandered his inheritance; it is expressed even more fully by that joy, that merrymaking for the squanderer after his return, merrymaking which is so generous that it provokes the opposition and hatred of the elder brother, who had never gone far away from his father and had never abandoned the home.

The father's fidelity to himself…is at the same time expressed in a manner particularly charged with affection. We read, in fact, that when the father saw the prodigal son returning home "he had compassion, ran to meet him, threw his arms around his neck and kissed him." He certainly does this under the influence of a deep affection, and this also explains his generosity towards his son, that generosity which so angers the elder son. Nevertheless, the causes of this emotion are to be sought at a deeper level. Notice, the father is aware that a fundamental good has been saved: the good of his son's humanity. Although the son has squandered the inheritance, nevertheless his humanity is saved. Indeed, it has

been, in a way, found again. The father's words to the elder son reveal this: "It was fitting to make merry and be glad, for this your brother was dead and is alive; he was lost and is found." … The father's fidelity to himself is totally concentrated upon the humanity of the lost son, upon his dignity. This explains above all his joyous emotion at the moment of the son's return home.…

The parable of the prodigal son expresses in a simple but profound way the reality of conversion. Conversion is the most concrete expression of the working of love and of the presence of mercy in the human world. The true and proper meaning of mercy does not consist only in looking, however penetratingly and compassionately, at moral, physical or material evil: mercy is manifested in its true and proper aspect when it restores to value, promotes and draws good from all the forms of evil existing in the world and in man. Understood in this way, mercy constitutes the fundamental content of the messianic message of Christ and the constitutive power of his mission.

The Speck and the Log

In light of God's astonishing offer of mercy, it would seem that the healing and renewing of the human race should be a fairly straightforward process. Yet we know that many people reject the Gospel today and have rejected it in the past. To return to the analogy of the divine physician, if there really were an epidemic—such as Ebola—raging through the population and a competent physician arrived with medicines to treat it, only very foolish people would refuse medical help. We may know of situations where someone was seriously ill and refused to admit it, but cases like that are rare.

Yet in this much more important matter of the health of our souls, a matter upon which the whole of our future depends, many have been reluctant to receive the diagnosis Jesus gives and have avoided taking his medicine. That reluctance has never been more widespread than it is today. While there are philosophies and cultural trends that can help to explain why our age has had a special difficulty in admitting the disease of sin, the real problem goes deeper. So many of us avoid Jesus and his remedies because the main symptom of the moral disease that afflicts us is precisely this refusal to admit the problem; we are unwilling to recognize that we are sinners in need of mercy and help. And the more deeply we have been infected by the disease, the more furious our denial will be. We suffer from a peculiar kind of moral blindness that makes it difficult for us to see straight. The name given by Scripture and tradition to describe this state of denial is pride. Our tendency to pride is a kind of bad moral eyesight. To the degree that we are afflicted by it, we will not rightly see ourselves, others around us, and God. Humility, pride's opposite, is the quality that restores our true sight. Once we have gained a measure of true sight with God's help, we are on the road to recovery.

There is one vice of which no man in the world is free; which everyone in the world loathes when he sees it in someone else; and of which hardly any people, except Christians, ever imagine that they are guilty themselves. I have heard people admit that they are bad-tempered, or that they cannot keep their heads about girls or drink, or even that they are cowards. I do not think I have ever heard anyone who was not a Christian accuse himself of this vice. And at the same time I have very seldom met anyone, who was not a Christian, who showed the slightest mercy to it in others. There is no fault which makes a man more unpopular, and no fault which we are more unconscious of in ourselves. And the more we have it ourselves, the more we dislike it in others. The vice I am talking of is Pride or Self-Conceit.

C. S. Lewis, *Mere Christianity* (1952)

It was no accident that Jesus so often healed people of blindness. In addition to the immediate blessing of giving them their sight back, Jesus was making a deeper point about a different kind of blindness he was helping people to overcome. When Jesus healed a man who had been blind from birth, and he was attacked by some Pharisees for doing the deed on the Sabbath, he made this broader point of his mission clear: "'For judgment I came into this world, that those who do not see may see, and that those who see may become blind.' Some of the Pharisees near him heard this, and they said to him, 'Are we also blind?' Jesus said to them, 'If you were blind, you would have no guilt; but now that you say, "We see," your guilt remains'" (Jn 9:39–41). In their pride, the Pharisees were blinded to their own sinful state, a blindness deeper and more debilitating than the mere absence of physical sight. As a result, they could not be healed of their guilt.

El Greco, Christ Healing the Blind, *c. 1570, Oil on canvas, The Met, New York, NY, USA.*

The great teachers of Christian spirituality tell us that the beginning of spiritual growth is self-knowledge. In saying this, they were not recommending that we undergo a detailed examination of our psychological and temperamental state. Whatever the value of such an internal map might be, they were speaking about something else. They were addressing the blindness of pride. God is a lover of truth, and he deals with us on the basis of what is real. Like a good doctor or, for that matter, a good friend, he will not let us hide from the truth when to do so harms us and hurts others. If we obstinately cling to the illusions that pride has woven around us, we will have a hard time seeing God, and we will avoid or even resent his care for us. We will also have a hard time helping anyone else.

Jesus once drove this point home with a bit of humorous exaggeration. In speaking to his disciples about making moral judgments, he said to them. "Why do you see the speck that is in your brother's eye, but do not notice the log that is in your own eye? Or how can you say to your brother, 'Let me take the speck out of your eye,' when there is the log in your own eye? You hypocrite, first take the log out of your own eye, and then you will see clearly to take the speck out of your brother's eye" (Mt 7:3–5). We all know how annoying it is to have something in our eye and what a relief it can be when someone helps us to remove it. Using that common experience, Jesus then extends the image to the point of caricature. No one can actually have a log in his eye; the thing is impossible. But we get the idea. Even a speck can make the eye bleary and the vision blurry, but a log? If such a thing could be, the result would be total blindness. It is clear from the context that Jesus is not speaking only to those few people who are obvious hypocrites and who have "logs" in their eyes, unlike the rest of us who are pretty clear-sighted. He means the teaching to apply to everyone. Every one of us suffers from serious blindness about our true moral state. All of us are caught by the illusion of pride. All of us need to have a log removed from our eyes—to be healed of our blindness—if we are to get to the truth about ourselves and to be of help to our brothers and sisters.

If we obstinately cling to the illusions that pride has woven around us, we will have a hard time seeing God, and we will avoid or even resent his care for us.

The first business of the Mass is for all present to acknowledge their sinfulness and their need for the mercy of God.

God's loving insistence on dealing with us truthfully has a vivid expression in the order of the Mass. Mass always begins with what we call the Penitential Act. As soon as the opening procession and hymn are concluded and the sign of the cross is made, the first business of the Mass is for all present to acknowledge their sinfulness and their need for the mercy of God. The *Confiteor* puts the matter strongly: "I confess that I have greatly sinned… through my most grievous fault… Lord, have mercy." We can sometimes miss the point of the rite and be a little confused by it. We can think of it as a kind of mini-sacrament of reconciliation where we ask forgiveness for any sins we have committed since the last time we went to confession. But that will not do: even if we walked right out of the confessional into Mass, we would still be expected to pray the prayer. Maybe then the point is to feel bad in God's presence? To beat ourselves up by remembering all the bad things we have done? But that also seems strange: does not God forgive our past sins and forget them? Why do we keep dragging them out again? And surely God does not simply want us to feel bad when we spend time with him. The Penitential Act at the beginning of the Mass has a different significance. We are coming before the God of truth, and we are dealing with him in the clarity of truth. No good relationship can be founded on falsehood, lies, or illusions. This is true even between humans, but it is overwhelmingly true in relating to God. Our acknowledgement of our sinfulness is a simple expression of reality. It is a way of clearing out any prideful illusions that can so easily crop up and blind us regarding our true state. We can then be ready for God's healing work.

When a group of recovering addicts or alcoholics gather for support, the first thing said by anyone who speaks is: "I am an addict." This essential practice is not meant to humiliate the participants or as a confession of having fallen back into drug or alcohol use since the last meeting. It is a way of keeping hold of a key truth that is essential to their recovery, but that can easily get lost. If they remember and keep before them the truth that they are recovering addicts, they have a good possibility of continued freedom. If they forget that truth, they are likely to fall back into bondage. So with us: we are all recovering sinners who are liable to forget our true state. With the Penitential Act at Mass we remember a key truth that often eludes us: without Christ and the medicine he brings we are lost and dying like the prodigal son. Having once placed our time with God on a true footing, we are then ready for the remedy Christ brings to us through his Word and in his Body and Blood.

As we continue our examination of the faith, the parable of the prodigal son can help us keep two essential truths before our eyes. The first truth is that, like the prodigal, we are members of a race that is sick from sin and is in desperate need of help. The second truth is that we have a Father in heaven who is rich in mercy and has gone to extraordinary lengths to bring us the very help we need. In light of these two truths, we can also learn from this parable the road each person needs to travel if the misery of prideful living in a far country is to be transformed into the freedom and joy of living in our true home.

In our next chapter, we will examine first-hand the far country in which many of us are living, the strangeness of which we must first apprehend before we can turn towards the light and say, "I will arise, and go to my Father."

We have a Father in heaven who is rich in mercy and has gone to extraordinary lengths to bring us the very help we need.

Review Questions

1. Does the parable of the prodigal son apply universally? Can you think of literary characters, historical figures, or members of your extended family to whom this story applies in whole or in part?

2. Why is forgiveness such a wonderful gift? Can you think of an episode in your life in which you were forgiven by a parent, sibling, relative, friend, coach, or teacher for something you had done wrong? With that recollection in mind, how would you describe what forgiveness does and why it is so good?

3. What is the "difficult news" of the Gospel and why do people have a hard time accepting it?

4. Why does God hate sin? How does the Church's definition of sin (see CCC 1849) help us to answer this question?

5. Why do you think that people are so often inclined to deny the reality of sin? Is it not, as Chesterton quipped, "the only part of Christian theology which can really be proved"? If so, what is so difficult about admitting that such-and-such a deed or omission is a sin?

6. How is the Penitential Rite at the beginning of Mass suited to preparing us to worship God?

Put Out Into the Deep

The selection from St. John Paul II's encyclical *Dives in Misericordia* teaches us that the parable of the prodigal son is, at its deepest level, an interior drama about human dignity. As that dignity is founded both upon our nature as intelligent and free beings and upon our creaturely relation to God—our being his sons and daughters—we suggest that you reflect on the Catechism's beautiful discussion of conscience in the context of this chapter. See *Catechism of the Catholic Church*, 1776–1802.

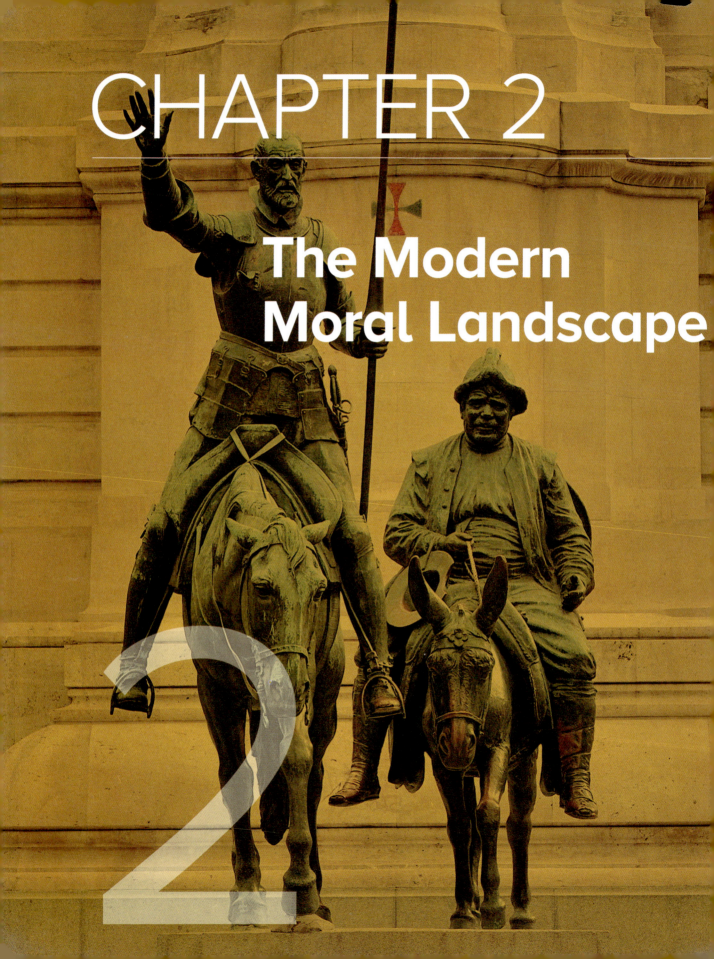

CHAPTER 2

The Modern Moral Landscape

2

At that moment they caught sight of some thirty or forty windmills, which stand on that plain, and as soon as Don Quixote saw them he said to his squire: 'Fortune is guiding our affairs better than we could have wished. Look over there, friend Sancho Panza, where more than thirty monstrous giants appear. I intend to do battle with them and take all their lives. With their spoils we will begin to get rich, for this is a fair war, and it is a great service to God to wipe such a wicked brood from the face of the earth.'

'What giants?' asked Sancho Panza.

'Those you see there,' replied his master, 'with their long arms. Some giants have them about six miles long.'

'Take care, your worship,' said Sancho; 'those things over there are not giants but windmills, and what seem to be their arms are the sails, which are whirled round in the wind and make the millstone turn.'

'It is quite clear,' replied Don Quixote, 'that you are not experienced in this matter of adventures. They are giants, and if you are afraid, go away and say your prayers, whilst I advance and engage them in fierce and unequal battle.'

Those who have read Cervantes' masterpiece *Don Quixote* will know who got the worst of it in this battle with the "giants." An overheated, "quixotic" imagination spurred the down-and-out Spanish nobleman to think he was acting heroically, when in fact he was tilting at windmills and failing to see reality clearly. Eventually, he will be healed of the ills of his imagination and able to see things as they are. For the moment, however, he is a stranger to the world and to himself. Today there are many people—men and women, young and old—who, like Don Quixote, are unable to see the world accurately. They may not mistake windmills for giants, but they do have difficulty distinguishing the real from the imaginary.

One truth about reality often missed or denied today is that we can reliably know what the good consists in and what will make us happy. Early in volume 1 of *Why Believe?*, we discussed our lives as quests for the Ultimate Good, the good found by living the truth in love. And in chapter 7, we saw that the person who claims that there is no reliable knowledge of the good has staked out a self-defeating position. Here we will do something different; we will actually visit the "far country" we talked about in the last chapter, the mental world inhabited by today's prodigal sons and daughters. By examining the moral landscape of our age, we will become better able to judge the merits of the various truth-claims we encounter from our classmates, co-workers, and perhaps even friends and family.

The Culture of Relativism

For a map of the contemporary moral landscape, we turn to the wide-ranging work of sociologist Christian Smith, who, with his colleagues, studied the religious and moral attitudes of a random sampling of 18- to 28-year-olds from across the country. They summarized their findings under six headings: moral individualism, moral relativism, moral sources, moral compromises, happiness and instinct, and moral dilemmas. A few words about each will help to provide a lens through which we can see that the relativism characterizing today's culture is not the truth about the world, but instead a product of the imagination.

Six out of ten people Smith and his team interviewed indicated their belief that "morality is a personal choice, entirely a matter of individual decision" and that "moral rights and wrongs are essentially matters of individual opinion." These moral individualists are not all moral relativists; some of them have strongly-held moral views, but they believe that no one should judge anyone else on moral matters. Some

may, for instance, think abortion is wrong but be unwilling to support legal restrictions upon the practice. They would say that all are equally entitled to their own personal opinions about what is good and bad, right and wrong. The respondents to the survey applied this restriction on judging both to themselves and to others. People should not allow themselves to be judged by anyone else. "It's personal," they typically said. "It's up to the individual. Who am I to say?" And naturally it follows that people should not be allowed to force their views on others.

Not everyone who expresses views Smith and his team describe as moral individualism are also moral relativists, but the two stances are closely related. Moral relativists, as Smith understands them, are those who claim that there are no real standards of right and wrong, that morality changes from time to time and place to place, that different cultures believe and teach very different things about good and bad, right and wrong, and that morality therefore is nothing more than subjective personal opinion or cultural consensus at any given point in time. What relativists "take to be morality," Smith reports, "has no real objective, natural, or universal basis outside of people's heads. Morality is purely a social construction. Even things like slavery or rape, on this view (when it is held consistently) could not be called 'objectively wrong.' There is simply 'what people thought at the time' or 'what that person thought was right,' because even if slavery or rape is 'wrong to me,' it might not be 'wrong to them.'"

Smith and his colleagues found that, whatever view of morality their respondents held, very few could give any answer to questions such as: Where does morality come from? What is morality's basis? What is the source of morality? What are the grounds or basis for moral truths or moral judgments? Fully one in three of those they interviewed, for example, replied that they "had no idea about the basis of morality"; "*they simply did not know what makes anything morally right or wrong*" (emphasis in the original). "Tellingly," Smith and his team found, "some of these stumped interviewees could not even understand our questions on this point." When pressed, interviewees were unsure, but offered answers ranging from "it would be right" if things were "way better" than before and wrong if they were "way worse," to "it would be wrong" if it "hurts other people," "it depends on what other people would think about you," and "it's karma."

How do we address moral dilemmas where there is a real conflict between moral values or moral imperatives?

Unsure of why things should be considered right or wrong and not usually willing to be judged by others for their moral choices, many of Smith's respondents admitted they would be willing to compromise their own moral rules if they thought they could gain an advantage by doing so. Fully one in three of those interviewed admitted that they might do something they considered morally wrong if they knew they could get away with it. The reasons given for their willingness to "compromise" reflected their conviction that "it's a dog-eat-dog world," "everybody does it; it's just the way the world is." Thus, because everyone lies, cheats, and steals, people have to take what they can get if they want to succeed.

When asked how they would make moral choices in situations of uncertainty, 39 percent of emerging adults said they would decide based on "doing what would make me feel happy." When pressed, many teens and young adults admitted that they made such decisions based on a kind of instinct. They would "just know." People should simply "go with their intuition" or "go with their gut." If doing something is wrong, they expected to "feel badly" about it. Many respondents did not think making moral decisions was terribly difficult. They assumed it was mostly a matter of "using your common sense."

What then about moral dilemmas where there is a real conflict between moral values or moral imperatives, for instance, between saving the life of an unborn child or the life of the mother, or between one's concern for the environment and the call to permit off-shore drilling for oil in order to wean the United States from dependence on foreign oil and reduce the price of fuel for the benefit of the poor? Among those surveyed by Smith and his team, 33 percent simply could not think of any moral dilemmas that they had personally confronted. They replied, "I really don't know, 'cause I've never had to make a decision about what's right and what's wrong," and "Nothing really is coming to mind. I haven't had too many really huge moral dilemmas that I've had to navigate through in my lifetime." Others mistook moral dilemmas for practical decisions they were required to make: whether to buy a second cat litter box, whether to rent an apartment, whether to park in a certain spot and risk getting a fine, and whether to wear certain clothes.

In mistaking simple practical decisions for serious moral decisions, in their lack of any account of what might make an act "moral," and in their stated willingness to compromise their own values and principles if a benefit would be achieved, many emerging adults manifested a lack of clarity about what the term "moral" means. They had not been taught much about it, had not given the topic much thought, and did not seem comfortable talking about their judgments. They knew many people had moral beliefs that led them to consider certain things right and others wrong, but they did not know on what basis such decisions could be made other than by gut instinct, and they did not think it was right to question another person's judgments or to have their own judgments challenged.

Freedom makes man a moral subject. When he acts deliberately, man is, so to speak, the father of his acts. Human acts, that is, acts that are freely chosen in consequence of a judgment of conscience, can be morally evaluated. They are either good or evil.

A morally good act requires the goodness of its object, of its end, and of its circumstances together.

Catechism of the Catholic Church, 1749, 1760

We should not, then, be surprised that the Ten Commandments have come under fire in recent years. For people who embrace moral relativism, ancient precepts such as "honor your father and mother" and "you shall not bear false witness against your neighbor" (Ex 20:12, 16) represent giants to attack. The removal of plaques and signs bearing the Ten Commandments in public buildings has been defended on the grounds that such displays violate the first amendment to the U. S. Constitution. Arguably, the underlying objection to these displays is that the mere presence of the Ten Commandments imposes a specific set of moral values on others.

The question we must ask now is whether Smith's findings provide an accurate picture of the cultural context in which we are living? Granted, Smith's account will not fit every community and certainly not every family. Does it, however, describe the general attitude of what may be called the dominant culture in America? An affirmative answer seems hard to avoid. Today the Christian understanding of right and wrong, good and evil, is widely misunderstood and opposed without ever being taken seriously.

Elements of Truth in an Inadequate View

Before we continue, let us acknowledge that there are some good reasons why so many people have embraced moral relativism. They are not ignorant, nor are they merely wrong. Rather, they are in possession of the kind of partial truths we discussed in chapter 7 of the last volume. We will respond to them by once again drawing upon the wisdom and the practice of classical philosophy. It is especially the example of Aristotle's character as a philosopher that we now need. He was not content to show why his opponent was wrong; he also sought to show how a reasonable person could draw such an erroneous conclusion. In the spirit of Aristotle's respectful engagement with rival philosophers, let us consider the elements of truth in these otherwise problematic views.

Consider, for example, the moral individualism embraced by so many today. It allows for a strong sense of moral responsibility—that morality, whatever it is, is based on personal choice—and so contains a partial truth. If you ask yourself, "Who is responsible for making decisions?" the answer is: "You are." You cannot simply duck that responsibility and put it on someone else. You are the one who must do the choosing, and you are the one who must sort through all the confusing theories and approaches to ethics clamoring for your attention in order to arrive at a responsible judgment.

The people who question us, especially about the presuppositions we rarely think much about and which may have become invisible to us, often do us the greatest service.

Moral individualism, however, leads us into trouble if we think that each of us must decide apart from anyone else, that we must decide without seeking anyone else's wisdom or being open to any serious critique of our judgments. The presidents of major corporations are responsible for their judgments, but they would be foolish not to seek out all the best information and advice. We, too, profit from keeping company with people who test our thoughts by taking a contrary position and showing where our thinking may be in error. It is precisely the people who question us, especially about the presuppositions we rarely think much about and which may have become invisible to us, who often do us the greatest service.

And yet, do we generally view our questioners this way? Consider, if you were doing something morally wrong—presuming for the moment that you believed there was at least *something* that was morally wrong, whether it was prejudice against minorities, cruelty to people who are misunderstood, or the emotional wounding of a friend—would you want someone to tell you? Most people do not like to be told they are doing something wrong. Others hedge their reply. "It depends on who it is, and how they tell me," they say. "It would need to be a good friend, someone who really cares about me." Could this good friend come right out and tell you that you are doing something wrong? No, they admit; the person would have to do it "gently," "without seeming to be judgmental" or "not just to tear me down."

These responses are understandable, but might we be creating a list of requirements which is not only difficult, but perhaps even impossible to meet? "You can tell me I'm wrong," one is tempted to tell a friend, "but only if you are the perfect person who tells me in the perfect way with the right tone in your voice and look on your face when I am in the mood to hear you." In this case, the moral responsibility lies with your friend to tell you in the right way, not on you to be sure you listen to things you need to hear if you are really going to be responsible for your decisions and make the kind of choices that will make you the person you want to become. Because make no mistake: what is at issue in such matters is becoming the kind of person you want to become. We make decisions, and those decisions make us. Who are you becoming with the choices you make?

Freedom is the power, rooted in reason and will, to act or not to act, to do this or that, and so to perform deliberate actions on one's own responsibility. By free will one shapes one's own life. Human freedom is a force for growth and maturity in truth and goodness; it attains its perfection when directed toward God, our beatitude.

Catechism of the Catholic Church, 1731

A consistent moral individualist should affirm those who believe premarital sex to be morally wrong. But this is not what typically happens. Young people encouraging their peers to engage in premarital sex do not usually see themselves as trying to impose their moral values on others, even though they are. If a young woman values her education and future potential and is convinced that premarital sexual activity threatens those possibilities, and so has decided to refrain from the activity, attempting to convince her that she should engage in this behavior would be an attempt to impose other values on her. The claims of "openness" and "tolerance" tend to be discarded when the value someone is expressing is a belief in the good of chastity. A person under assault in this way might justly reply: "Are you saying I shouldn't be allowed to live the life I want if I choose to wait for marriage? Are you trying to impose your values of so-called sexual liberation on me?"

Moral individualism, however, does have the element of truth which we have noted: we are personally responsible for our choices. But it should be immediately noted that we are also responsible for searching out the best information and advice from others. People who disagree with us can help us to clarify our own views or to correct them when needed. If we refuse to engage with people who hold alternative views, we do not really show them respect or openness. When we refuse to engage the views of others or allow our own views to be critiqued, we communicate—even if unintentionally—a dismissive attitude toward others. "Let's agree to disagree" can be another way of saying, "It is not worth the trouble to try to sort through our differences." Agreeing not to talk about an issue is not the same as fostering dialogue.

As for moral relativism, experience of the changeableness of other people may tempt some to embrace the perspective. After all, people do not always review the arguments for and against a position first and only afterwards make up their minds about what to do. Often, they make up their minds first and then look for arguments to support their chosen position. Indeed, many people have not given much thought to why they think certain things are right or wrong and admit that they rely on their gut instinct. This phenomenon would seem to justify those who come to believe that moral arguments are no more than a means that allow people to get what they want.

Those people who think that moral decisions are merely a matter of common sense often judge people who disagree with them to be ignorant or stupid, the kind of people whose reasons for having different moral convictions are not worth trying to understand. They are unable to see common sense or are making bad faith arguments that are a cover for their greed, their prejudices, or their ill will. The odd result is that, while plenty of people say that we should not judge other people, there is plenty of judging going on. Now it is important to make a distinction here: while it is true that we should not judge other people's souls, since we can never really know what is going on in their

If a young woman values her education and future potential and is convinced that premarital sexual activity threatens those possibilities, and so has decided to refrain from the activity, attempting to convince her that she should engage in this behavior would be an attempt to impose other values on her.

While plenty of people say that we should not judge other people, there is plenty of judging going on.

heart of hearts, we must judge their actions. Rape is wrong, keeping slaves is wrong, mugging old ladies is wrong, murdering millions of innocent Jews is wrong. Modern moral relativism causes many young people to refuse to judge actions, but the same people are often more than willing to judge the motives of their opponents: "They're racist;" "They're haters;" "They're greedy;" "They don't care about anyone but themselves." How is it that we are not supposed to judge actions we can see, but then allow ourselves to judge the hearts we cannot see?

What seems to be happening—and this may seem counter-intuitive at first—is that the morally relativistic and individualistic perspectives the culture has inculcated in youth with the goal of making them tolerant has resulted in its own brand of intolerance. Instead of learning to discuss moral judgments openly, many refuse to engage in moral arguments at all. As a result, we are often enough defenseless and timid when we need to stand up for our own moral judgments if they go against the opinion of the mob and intolerant of other people's moral judgments when they disagree with us. Students who believe, as many today do, that "arguments can prove anything" (and thus nothing) and who have lost confidence in reason's ability to arrive at truth, will often be left assuming that those on the other side of an issue have no good reasons for what they say, hence they can only hold the positions they hold because they have ill will or are "bad people." It is by this odd, circuitous route that an ostensibly non-judgmental culture becomes a decidedly judgmental one, and often not in a healthy way where such judgments are thoroughly examined and critically considered.

Confusion and disagreement in moral matters, however, do not prove that there are no better or worse ways of thinking about these problems. Students often come up with different answers in calculus, but that does not mean that there is no right answer. The balance of this book will explore that right answer, the Christian view of the human person and of human happiness.

People sometimes claim support for their moral relativism based on the notion that cultures disagree about what is right and wrong. But there is a great deal of agreement about basic moral principles; injunctions such as "do not kill," "do not steal," and "do unto others as you would want them to do unto you" are common among cultures throughout the world. Where societies differ is in the application of those general principles to specific instances. Some cultures bury the bodies of dead people, others burn them. Both agree, however, that respect should be shown to the dead. Where they do not coincide is in how that respect is to be shown. If we find a culture that does not show respect for the dead and dying or does not show respect for innocent women and children, the common wisdom of cultures throughout the world suggests that something is wrong.

Moral Compromises and the Destruction of My "Self"

The most disturbing revelation from Smith's study is how often people who do not have any secure basis for their judgments report that they would be willing to compromise their own principles when they think they might be able to get away with it. When asked about their life goals, about what they would want someone to be able to say honestly about them after their death, young people often respond along the lines of: "I want people to be able to say that he was a good friend who loved his family," "that she cared about people and tried to make their lives better," "that he was honest and straightforward, not prejudiced, and could be relied on, especially when things got tough." For understandable reasons, we do not hear people say: "I want to be known as a creep who cheated old ladies out of their pensions, lied to everyone he knew, betrayed his friends constantly, and cared about no one but himself." Most of us do not set out to be this way, but as we all know, there are people who achieve it. What happens? Somewhere along the way, they get side-tracked. They set out to become one kind of person, and they end up becoming another.

Literary and cinematic examples of this kind of tragedy abound. In the popular television series *Breaking Bad*, the character Walter White set out to be a good man, and even when he started to manufacture meth, he did it thinking he was providing for his family. But as the seasons passed and his moral compromises built one upon another, his descent into villainy became a free-fall from which he could not extract himself.

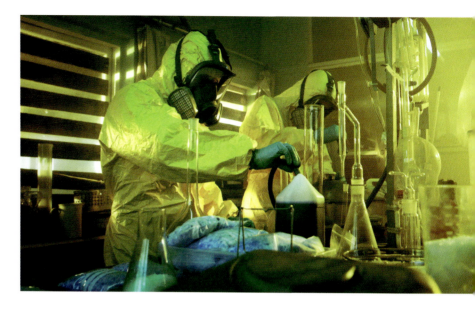

Walter White set out to be a good man, and even when he started to manufacture meth, he did it thinking he was providing for his family.

In the Harry Potter saga, Peter Pettigrew was originally one of James and Lily Potter's friends. But as the years went by, Pettigrew fell more and more under the influence of Voldemort, probably with small infidelities at first, which eventually caused him to admit to himself that he had become a double-agent. And so when James and Lily Potter were forced into hiding with their son, it was their "friend" Peter who betrayed them and brought about their deaths.

Perhaps the most well-known character who sets out to be good and ends up serving the forces of evil is Anakin Skywalker, the powerful young Jedi who was, at first, a great hero and defender of the powerless, but who in time became one of the most iconic villains of movie history, Darth Vader. Anakin is said to have been seduced to the Dark Side by his desire to gain enough power to keep bad things from happening to those he loved. And yet, once he had obtained the power he sought, he used it to kill a group of Jedi children and then even threatened the lives of his best friend and the woman he claimed to love. Eventually his rejection of the goodness he swore to uphold led to his downfall and disfigurement. No one else defeated Anakin. He destroyed himself, and Darth Vader rose from the ashes.

When people say they might compromise their own values, they are saying: "Although I want to be an honest person, I might choose not to be." But when you make a choice, your choice makes you. If you choose to lie, cheat, or steal, you can no longer say about yourself (nor can anyone else who knows you say honestly about you): he was an honest person; she was a person who could be depended upon. When you compromise your values, you become a person you did not want to be. Indeed, you may have turned yourself precisely into the kind of person that, in your earlier years, you would have hated. And that can

If we keep ourselves in the dark, we might be able to tolerate the disjunction between who I want to be and who I have turned out to be, at least for a while. In the end, however, only the reliable contact with the same reality that other people inhabit will secure for us the happy life we desire.

be tragic. It is not necessarily a tragedy from which a person cannot recover, but the choices you make do make you. When you compromise your own values, you cease to be the person you say you want to be.

Many of us are reluctant to search very deeply into the question "Who am I?" for fear of what we may find. If we keep ourselves in the dark, we might be able to tolerate the disjunction between who I want to be and who I have turned out to be, at least for a while. In the end, however, only the reliable contact with the same reality that other people inhabit will secure for us the happy life we desire. Only the truth, that is, can set us free and direct our steps so that we become the kind of person we admire and want to be. The good news is that this is just what God wants for us: a happy end. Part of Don Quixote's happy end was his re-orientation to a proper understanding of things as they are: "My judgment is now clear and free from the misty shadows of ignorance...I know my folly now...Now, by God's mercy, I have learnt from my own bitter experience." The lesson of Don Quixote, and of good literature generally, is that reality is our most trustworthy teacher. Christians believe that God's Word testifies accurately to that reality. Over the next several chapters, we will examine that testimony with great care.

Review Questions

1. Sociologist Christian Smith suggests that many emerging adults espouse a view he describes as "moral individualism." What is moral individualism and how does it differ from moral relativism? Evaluate the arguments that people use to defend their moral individualism and moral relativism.

2. Moral individualism and moral relativism are problematic moral theories from a philosophical point of view. But what elements of truth might there be in these otherwise problematic views? Where do they fall short?

3. How and why has the culture of moral relativism generated the apparently ironic effect of making people less tolerant of moral views they do not themselves hold?

4. Although there is confusion and disagreement in moral matters, this alone does not prove that there are no better or worse ways of thinking about these problems. Explain.

5. People sometimes claim support for moral relativism based on the argument that cultures differ about what is right and wrong. Is this argument decisive? Explain.

6. According to Christian Smith's study, many young adults admit they might compromise their own values if they thought they could get away with it and it would benefit them. What is the contradiction at the heart of this way of thinking?

7. Many people are reluctant to search very deeply into the question "Who am I?" for fear of what they may find. Who are you? Who do you want to be? Is there a disconnection between who you say you want to be and who you are? If so, why?

Put Out Into the Deep

For an engaging discussion of moral relativism and how to counter it with good arguments, see Edward Sri, *Who Am I to Judge? Responding to Relativism with Love and Logic* (Ignatius Press & Augustine Institute, 2016). Some of the short videos associated with the *Why Believe?* curriculum have been taken from Dr. Sri's video series *Who Am I to Judge?*, which was produced by Augustine Institute Studios.

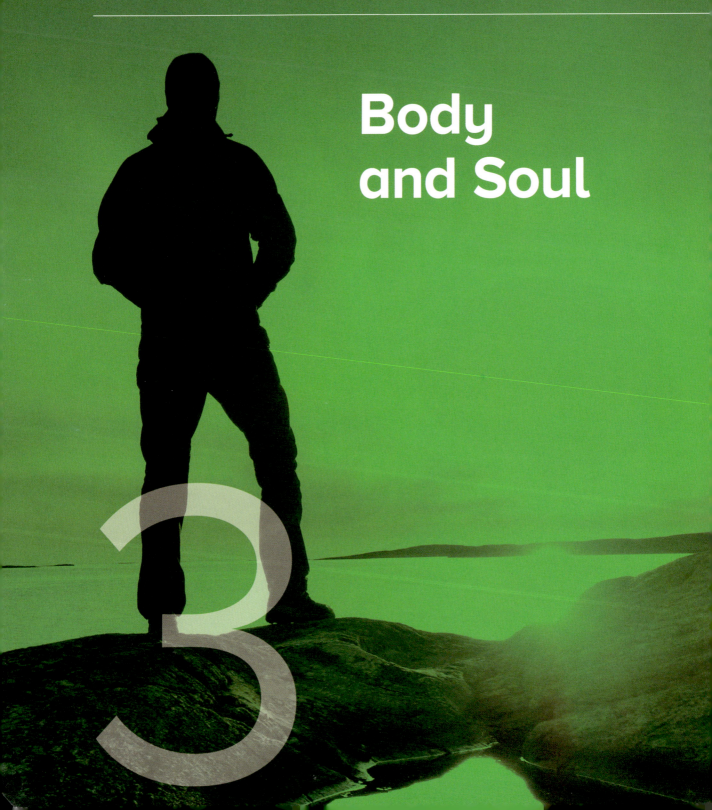

CHAPTER 3

Body and Soul

The Christian response to relativism should now be clear: it offers an imaginary account of human life. And it should also be evident that this imaginary story is dangerous. We can fool ourselves into thinking that good and evil are nothing but names and that conscience, as Shakespeare's Richard III claimed, "is but a word that cowards use, devised at first to keep the strong in awe." In the end, however, reality will assert itself. When it does, we may discover that we do not like the person we have become. It is, then, the narrative approach to life that we first began to discuss at the beginning of volume 1 of *Why Believe?* that enables us to see through the imaginary world of the modern moral landscape and perceive reality as it is. The narrative approach also teaches us that we all face the same antagonist, death. "The first absolutely certain truth of our life, beyond the fact that we exist," as St. John Paul II affirmed, "is the inevitability of our death" (*Fides et Ratio*, 26). The context within which the stories of our moral lives unfold is determined by our bodily birth, life, and death. In this chapter, we will consider that context directly and find that it serves as an anchor for our understanding of the human good.

The great philosophers have always urged men and women to ponder the subject of death so that we may better understand life. One of Plato's most celebrated dialogues, *Phaedo*, records the last conversation of Socrates. The subject of the dialogue is the immortality of the soul, and it offers several ingenious arguments in support of that truth. But the dialogue's climactic moment is when Socrates drinks the fatal hemlock

and dies. This is the climactic moment because his acceptance of death proves beyond doubt that Socrates was a man of his word. Socrates had declined the opportunity to flee Athens and to prolong his life and its pleasures, citing his duty to the city that had given birth to him and formed him by its laws. In his final speech and by his noble death, Socrates once again taught what he had so often taught before: the true good for man is an interior one, a good of the soul.

Christians, of course, affirm the same truth and hold it very dearly. Jesus repeatedly testified to the reality of life after death and insisted that, within the context of our earthly journey, the interior lives of our souls are more important than the bodily goods of strength, beauty, and health, and far more important than our possessions. "I tell you," he said emphatically to his disciples, "do not be anxious about your life, what you shall eat, nor about your body, what you shall put on. For life is more than food, and the body more than clothing" (Lk 12:22–23). The word here translated as "life" is, in the original Greek, the word "soul." The soul, then, is more than food and greater than any material thing. Even apart from the Lord's direct affirmation of this truth, we would still know it to be part of divine revelation, for only in light of it can we make sense of the moral teachings of Christ, St. Paul, and the other apostles. It is the intellect, that mysterious immaterial power of seizing upon the universal natures of things and making them parts of our mental world, that sets us apart from the beasts, provides for our freedom, and illuminates the world with the light of the good. And our will, that is, our ability to choose what we have judged to be good, is our intellect's complement. Who we are, most essentially, is determined by what we choose, and what we choose by what we have understood.

The Christian View of the Human Person

Given the centrality of this truth about the soul and its immaterial powers of intellect and will to the Christian view of the world, it is not surprising that over the centuries some Christians have lost sight of the importance of the body. We will consider an example of this mistake in the words of a contemporary of ours, television journalist Bill Moyers (born 1934):

> I suppose I've always been interested in the relation of mind and body, growing up as I did in a culture that separated them distinctly. In science class we studied the material world, which we expected would someday be understood and predicted down to the last molecule. In philosophy, we studied models of reality based on the rational mind that took no notice of conditions such as male and female, sick and well, rich and poor. And then in church, we learned that we would someday take off this body as we might a suit of clothes and live as disembodied souls.

Moyers's description of his childhood beliefs is perhaps less strange to us than it ought to be. It is, indeed, a common enough perspective to hold that the Christian faith is absolutely distinct from natural science and its object, material reality. There is, however, a significant problem with the point of view as expressed here: Christians do not believe that we will "take off this body as we might a suit of clothes and live as disembodied souls." If Moyers had taken the Apostle's Creed as his standard of Christian belief, he would have understood that the faith includes a claim about the resurrection of the body. It is a teaching that goes back to the earliest days of the Church. We find it repeatedly in the letters of St. Paul (for example, 1 Cor 15:52), and it clearly distinguished Christianity from other ancient religions, most of which would have found the notion of a bodily resurrection absurd. Indeed, the Catholic faith insists that God created us body and soul, that Christ became incarnate in a real human body, that he is the Word made flesh, and that the just will ultimately enjoy the resurrection not only of their souls, but of their souls together with their bodies.

But what does any of this have to do with our beliefs about right and wrong, with ethics?

When Bishop Robert Barron of Los Angeles was asked to give a presentation to all the high-school teachers, staff, and administrators in the Archdiocese of Los Angeles on the topic of morality, he answered this question. He chose not to address any of the controversial subjects of the day, even though he is no stranger to intellectual sparring. What he spoke about instead was the Christian view of the human person, or Christian anthropology, "a fancy way," as he put it, "of saying the articulation of what play we're in and what role we've been given in that production." In other words, we must know what kind of being we are in order to know what will make us happy.

The truth about the human person was also a topic at the center of St. John Paul II's pontificate. In their common insistence on the importance of understanding human nature, both Bishop Barron and John Paul II in their own ways echoed a long tradition of Christian humanism which influenced several important documents of the Second Vatican Council (1962–1965). One of those documents that then-Bishop Karol Wojtyla (the future John Paul II) had a major hand in writing was the *Pastoral Constitution on the Church in the Modern World* (*Gaudium et Spes*), a document to which he would often return in his later work. In *Gaudium et Spes*, the Council fathers observed that many of the problems facing the modern world—including death from famine, lack of education and access to adequate health care, the ravages of political oppression, the increasingly destructive character of war, and the damage done to the environment by industrial production—persist because of failure to understand and respect the nature and dignity of the human person. What the Church has to offer the modern world, they said, is the truth about the human person, a truth revealed especially in and through Jesus Christ, and a truth which, once understood and accepted, changes hearts.

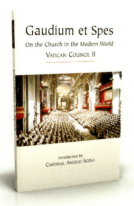

Several important documents echoing a long tradition of Christian humanism, including Gaudium et Spes, *came out of the Second Vatican Council.*

The average Christian today does not turn to the Church's moral teaching expecting to find a distinctive view of the human person. What we may expect to find is a discussion of actions permitted and not permitted, what we are obliged to do and what is forbidden. These topics are by no means unimportant, but to understand why the Church teaches what she does about human choices, it is necessary to understand how those teachings are founded on a view of the human person. The negative prohibitions of the Church are all based on a positive conception of human dignity. When people hear only the negative without understanding the positive, they think the Church is trying to destroy their freedom. What the Church is really trying to do is to facilitate our true flourishing. To see this, however, we have to appreciate the Christian view of the human person.

That view is a biblical one. In the creation accounts of the Book of Genesis, we find two key elements, both of which are important to keep in mind when we think about human nature. From Genesis 1, we learn that God made all of creation in six days and on the sixth day made the animals that live upon dry land, including man; but man alone he created "in the image of God" (Gen 1:27). Man is an animal, but an animal with a divine element: an ability to mirror God to others. According to Genesis 2, human beings were made from the dust of the earth, into which God breathed his own spirit. The imagery deployed in the two accounts is different, but the underlying teaching about the human person is the same. The first lesson in that teaching is that we are material beings, animals not entirely unlike the other animals that are warm-blooded and feed their young with milk from the mother's body, what biologists calls mammals.

The human person, created in the image of God, is a being at once corporeal and spiritual. The biblical account expresses this reality in symbolic language when it affirms that "then the Lord God formed man of dust from the ground, and breathed into his nostrils the breath of life; and man became a living being" (Gen 2:7). Man, whole and entire, is therefore willed by God.

Catechism of the Catholic Church, 362

There is, however, a crucial second lesson. Although we are material beings and indeed animals, we have something other bodily creatures do not. In chapter 5 of the previous volume, we learned that our ability to grasp universal concepts separates us from all other animals and indicates that our souls have an immaterial power, the intellect. We are conscious and self-aware; we think, understand, and plan; we speak to others, gather evidence, and make judgments. We create art and appreciate beauty. We look at the world and ask "Why?" No other bodily creature does these things. And yet what we learn about the world comes to us first through our senses, without which we would have nothing to think about. We are not merely a body, a fleshy machine. Nor are we a mind trapped in a body. Each of us is a unique and harmonious union of body and soul, flesh and spirit, designed by God to be a living, breathing knower of truth and lover of the good.

We are conscious and self-aware; we look at the world and ask "Why?" No other bodily creature does these things.

Being Treated as a Person

Throughout history, the Church's teaching about human nature has been opposed by rival accounts. Some have insisted that human beings are nothing but atoms and molecules. "Man is what he eats," said Ludwig Feuerbach (1804–72), and he meant it literally. Others have denied that our bodies are integral to our being and claimed that the only really human part of us is our mind or spirit. The famous dictum of René Descartes (1596–1650) reminds us of that perspective: "I think, therefore I am." The body, on this latter view, is merely a shell that could be replaced or a tool to be manipulated for the pleasures it affords. The Church has labored throughout the centuries to oppose both misconceptions.

Those who deny the body's goodness may style themselves as spiritual and ignore the Church's teachings about the Incarnation and the resurrection of the body. Perhaps they follow instead the so-called spiritualism of certain Eastern traditions, where the elite few are said to ascend to a higher plane by ascetic practices meant to free them from the body. Calming one's body and clearing one's mind of the constant noise of everyday life can indeed be a good way to prepare for prayer. Yet it should not be mistaken for prayer itself, which is not merely a quieting of one's spirit or even an ascent of one's mind, but is a dialogue with the loving God, who, though infinitely beyond our ability to grasp, deigns to "speak to men as friends" (*Dei Verbum*, 2; and see Ex 33:11 and Jn 15:14–15). Nor can a view that denigrates the body make sense of our everyday experience of charity. Even something as simple as holding a door for a person whose hands are full is a good deed done with our bodies and for the bodily comfort and convenience of another. Yet it is also a deed understood and chosen as good because it recognizes the dignity of the person being helped. It hardly needs to be said that caring for the sick, injured, and disabled is a bodily work in every way but also deeply, even supremely, good.

A table is made up of atoms and molecules. So is your mother. Is there then no fundamental difference between the table and your mother?

In opposing radical materialists, the Church has never denied that we are material, organic beings. The question is whether that is all we are. A table is made up of atoms and molecules. So is your mother. Is there then no fundamental difference between the table and your mother? Even organically, there are important differences. Yet in addition to these, is there not another difference? Yes, your mother is a person. When we go to the doctor's office, we do not want her to probe and poke us as if she were a mechanic fixing a car. We have no problem if the auto mechanic throws open the hood and starts tinkering with the engine. But we would resent being treated this way during a physical exam. We want to be treated as a person, not as an object. We insist that the physician have all the relevant knowledge about the biological and chemical aspects of the human organism. But since each of us has an intellect and will, we expect her to communicate that knowledge to us in ways that we can understand so that we can make good choices about our health. We have emotions—fear, grief, anxiety, joy, and hopes for the future—and so expect her to have what we call a "bedside manner." Above all, we want to be treated with dignity and respect, and a good physician must show that respect across a broad spectrum: she must respect the patient's body, emotions, intellect, freedom, and spiritual yearnings.

In the thirteenth century, German emperor Frederick II wanted to know what language children would speak if they were raised without hearing any words at all. To find out, he sponsored a terrible experiment. He took several newborn children from their parents and gave them to nurses who were not only forbidden to talk to them but were not even allowed to hold them. The babies, of course, did not learn how to speak. In fact, the horror was that they all died before reaching the age at which they could have learned. What the experiment showed, then, was that sympathetic physical touch is a primal need, as necessary for human flourishing as food, clothing, and shelter. There is plenty of additional evidence in support of this conclusion. For instance, massages not only produce measurable benefits in the circulatory systems of nursing home patients; they help in the battle against anxiety, depression, and senility. Treating people with dignity involves more than merely speaking to them politely or respecting their freedom; it includes recognizing the contribution that their bodies make to their flourishing.

The unity of soul and body is so profound that one has to consider the soul to be the "form" of the body: that is, it is because of its spiritual soul that the body made of matter becomes a living, human body; spirit and matter, in man, are not two natures united, but rather their union forms a single nature.

Catechism of the Catholic Church, 365

The way we relate to one another as male and female is an especially illuminating sign of the unity of body and soul. Should a woman say, "I don't want to be loved just for my body," she plainly is not looking for someone to respond, "I love you, but hate your body." It is hard to imagine anyone ever saying something like that. What she means is that she does not want to be treated as an object. The mistake we sometimes make is not that we find bodies beautiful, but that we stop at the body alone rather than seeing the body as part of the whole person with talents, hopes, and plans—in short, with dignity. What if a woman received a beautiful diamond engagement ring from her fiancé as a symbol of his love and then, after showing it off for a while, said to herself: "I have the ring; why do I need the guy?" When the ring stops being a sign of love and becomes instead a monument to vanity, you stop owning the ring and the ring starts owning you. When the body of the person you love is no longer a sign of the whole person and becomes instead a monument to your ego, the only person you are in a relationship with is yourself. Only by appreciating the unity of body and soul can we properly understand human sexuality or indeed the human condition at all.

Only by appreciating the unity of body and soul can we properly understand human sexuality or indeed the human condition at all.

A Sacramental View

Catholics are called upon to take a view of material things that may be called incarnational or sacramental. This is the view expressed by the apostle John at the beginning of his first epistle: "That which was from the beginning, which we have heard, which we have seen with our eyes, which we have looked at and touched with our hands, concerning the word of life" (1 Jn 1:1). In other words, as he said later in the same letter, in Christ, the love of God has been made manifest to us (see 1 Jn 4:9). Christ is fully and completely the embodiment and instrument of God's love, and because a sacrament is an efficacious sign of God's grace or presence, then Christ may be thought of as the universal sacrament. The seven sacraments of the Church are extensions of Christ's embodied grace and love; they are "powers that come forth from the Body of Christ" (CCC 1116). To see the world sacramentally is to consider material things as potential embodiments and instruments of God's love and as being so many extensions of his entry into the material world through the Incarnation.

Can we become instruments of God's love? Ought we to lift up the material things of the world to God the way the priest lifts up the bread and wine at Mass and say, "Lord, make these gifts you have given us into instruments of your love for the world." Yes. We should offer ourselves and all God's gifts up to him so as to be transformed by his grace. The bread and wine at Mass are not unimportant—we cannot substitute cake and fruit juice, and we do not merely imagine bread and wine in our minds—but we do not consume the bread and wine for physical nourishment. The consecrated bread and wine communicate to us God's real presence, as real today as when he told Thomas to put his hand in his side. When we receive holy communion, we receive the special grace of union with Christ through the eating of his body and blood. At the same time, we recognize that the sacrament is a sign, that it signifies or points to something beyond itself: Christ's love for us, a love so great that he laid down his life in order to redeem us.

Signs of love are important. It would be laughable, but not altogether a happy thing, for a man to think that since the card and the flowers are signs of his love, he can forego them and simply say to his wife: "But you know I love you." It is a mistake to claim that because love is spiritual it does not therefore require material expression. Indeed, you will have to embody your love in all sorts of gifts and actions over the course of your life: going to piano concerts you may not want to attend; staying up with a spouse or children when illness comes; sending small messages to loved

We are physical beings who need to feel the physical water of cleansing and hear the words of absolution, saying: "Your sins are forgiven."

ones throughout the year, week, or day, as appropriate; remembering important dates and anniversaries in the lives of family members and friends. And this relationship between the sign and what it signifies is, of course, reciprocal. It would be tragic if someone were to kiss another person romantically, as if saying the words "I love you," when it was not true. People sometimes fool themselves into thinking, "I can do one thing with my body, while intending something else with my thoughts and feelings." This is a form of lying—if not with one's words, then with one's body, because the sign has been emptied of its meaning.

People sometimes ask whether God needs a priest to forgive sins or water to make us members of his Church. No, God does not need these things. We do. We are physical beings who need to feel the physical water of cleansing and hear the words of absolution, saying: "Your sins are forgiven." We are embodied creatures, and thus the body is not insignificant; nor, however, is the spirit. As Aquinas's doctrine about the necessity of the sacraments makes clear (see insert on page 48), human well-being requires that our interior and bodily lives be united in an integral and harmonious whole.

We learn through our senses, and so God engages our senses in teaching us about his love. We see this in the story of the Frenchman who, when asked what he did in the hours he spent sitting in front of the tabernacle in a quiet church, replied, "I look at him, and he looks at me." And here is St. Augustine on the same theme: "I am mindful of my ransom. I eat it, I drink it, I dispense it to others, and as a poor man I long to be filled with it among those who are fed and feasted."

St. Thomas Aquinas on the Necessity of the Sacraments

Sacraments are necessary for man's salvation for three reasons. The first is taken from the condition of human nature which is such that it must be led by material and sensible things to spiritual and intelligible things. Now, it belongs to Divine providence to provide for each one according as its condition requires. Divine wisdom, therefore, fittingly provides man with means of salvation in the shape of material and sensible signs that are called sacraments.

The second reason is taken from the state of man who in sinning subjected himself by his affections to material things. Now the healing remedy should be given to a man so as to reach the part affected by disease. Consequently, it was fitting that God should provide man with a spiritual medicine by means of certain material signs; for if man were offered spiritual things without a veil, his mind being taken up with the material world would be unable to apply itself to them.

The third reason is taken from the fact that man is prone to direct his activity chiefly towards material things. Lest, therefore, it should be too hard for man to be drawn away entirely from bodily actions, bodily exercise was offered to him in the sacraments, by which he might be trained to avoid superstitious practices, consisting in the worship of demons, and all manner of harmful action, consisting in sinful deeds.

It follows, therefore, that through the institution of the sacraments man, consistently with his nature, is instructed through sensible things; he is humbled, through confessing that he is subject to material things, seeing that he receives assistance through them.

The Resurrection of the Body

We have talked about the body in light of creation, the Incarnation, the sacraments, and the eucharist. Christianity is a fleshy religion. It is well, then, that we should finish where we began—with the resurrection of the body. As we saw, Bill Moyers propagated his misunderstanding of Christian teaching, saying that "in church, we learned that we would someday take off this body as we might a suit of clothes and live as disembodied souls." But if our bodies are temporary suits of clothes to be exchanged for an eternal incorporeal existence, then we might well ask whether, as some have thought, the body is a kind of prison. Is it possible really to entertain such an idea? Without a body, there would be no smells and tastes; no feeling of the crisp, cold air in the fall; no feeling of the warm sun on our skin; no feeling of the wind on our faces

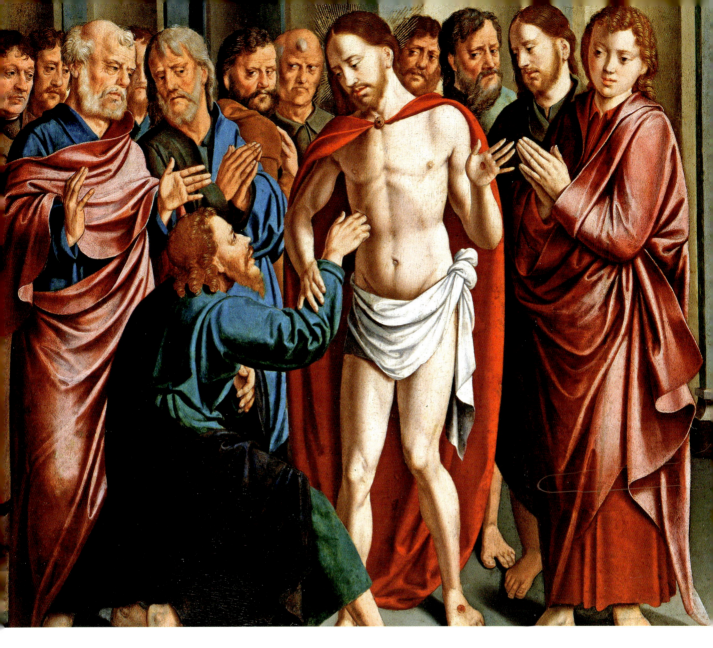

when we run down a hill. Without a body, we would have none of these things. Are these experiences things we must leave behind? The Christian belief in a bodily resurrection suggests that we do not.

The resurrection appearances showed the first Christians that the Risen Christ is the same person they knew as Jesus of Nazareth. His risen body retained the marks of the nails and the lance. The disciples recognized him by means of familiar gestures. He called Mary Magdalene by name. He broke bread with them. He sent the disciples out to catch fish. Think about how the story could have been told. An angelic figure could have appeared to the disciples and said, "I am *the Christ* who existed within the man Jesus. With his death, I am set free. He is gone, but I now live truly as you will soon be set free from your bodies to live." This is the way many gnostic cults throughout history have told the story. If this were the truth about the resurrection, what would it reveal to us about our lives? Would it not tell us that our current life, with all its experiences and relationships, is something to be shed, like a useless worn out coat? Would it not suggest that this life is empty and meaningless, something we should get beyond?

And what might such a story suggest about the afterlife? A common image portrays our destiny as a drop of water returning to the ocean. It is perhaps a peaceful image, but it is problematic. When the drop returns to the ocean, its identity is lost. An afterlife in which we lose our personal identity is not really something to hope for. What gives Christians hope that the loss of personal identity will not be their fate after death? First, the doctrine of the Blessed Trinity. God's perfect unity does not destroy the diversity of Persons, and the diversity of Persons does not destroy God's perfect unity. The promise implicit in the doctrine is that we can be united to God and not lose our personhood. Like the Risen Christ, we will still be the person we have been and still in some way be united with those we have loved. And what does Christ's glorified body tell us? It tells us that the eternal life we are offered does not result in our obliteration or negation, but in our transformation and glorification. All that is sinful in us, all that keeps us from loving God and loving others the way the Son loves the Father, must die. But what is left, as wheat separated from the chaff, is our true self, including our body. We do not lose those connections with our loved ones or even with the places we love. Those connections are deepened. The Risen Christ prepares us for the "new heaven" and the "new earth" (Rev 21:1) promised in the Book of Revelation. The Christian hope for salvation is not an escape from our bodily condition and from the material universe. On the contrary, the Christian faith includes the belief that our bodies will be redeemed and will find a home. He is risen! The Good News, as St. Paul tells us, is that Jesus Christ is "the first fruits of those who have fallen asleep" (1 Cor 15:20), a fruit which nourishes us and the world even now.

Review Questions

1. Explain why it was reasonable for Bishop Robert Barron to teach about human anthropology when he had been asked to speak on morality at a meeting of high-school teachers, staff, and administrators.

2. What are the two key elements of the human person that we find in the creation accounts of the Book of Genesis? How can understanding the truth of these accounts help us to resolve two false views of the human person?

3. Are we souls trapped in a body? What are the consequences of answering one way or the other?

4. What are the implications for our daily lives of the Church's sacramental view of creation and of the human body?

5. What message does Jesus deliver about our life in this world by means of his resurrection appearances before his ascension into heaven?

Put Out Into the Deep

For a thorough introductory exposition of the Church's view of the human person through the eyes of St. Thomas Aquinas, see Steven J. Jensen, *The Human Person* (Catholic University Press, 2018).

CHAPTER 4

Emotion
and Reason

4

Why would anyone watch a movie more than once? We know the plot, the ending, the characters, the dialogue. We even know every melodic theme in the soundtrack. After multiple viewings, there is almost nothing about the story that can surprise us. So why do we watch a movie twice, three times, perhaps five times or more?

The answer is that we want to feel a certain way again. Repeated viewings of a movie are not about figuring out who did it (if the movie is a mystery) or if the hero or heroine will get away to safety (a thriller) or whether the romantic leads will declare their love for one another (a romance). We know these things already but want to experience again that feeling of intrigue or suspense or romantic passion. We human beings cherish emotional experience. If possible, we want to experience emotions such as intrigue, suspense, and romantic passion in our real lives. It is because real life does not often deliver emotional experience in a heightened way that we go looking for that intensity where we can find it more readily: at the movie theater.

One thing we can learn from the movies is that emotional experience can be dangerous. Sometimes an emotion like romantic passion can sweep us into the arms of the love of our lives, but at other times it can deceive us into thinking a relationship is good for us that really is not. All romantic comedies worthy of the name testify to this truth. They show us someone learning not how to reject or suppress romantic passion, but how to feel it in the right way, for the right person, at the right time.

To learn how to experience emotion rightly is to learn how to bring emotion under the rule of reason. Men and women have been engaged in that difficult task since the beginning of recorded history. One famous approach to the problem is found in a story told by Socrates. The tale, found in Plato's dialogue *Phaedrus*, purports to be a way of understanding the human soul by likening it to a chariot with two horses. The chariot is directed by a person but pulled forward by the horses, one of which is noble and obedient, the other base and unruly.

> *When the charioteer beholds the vision of love, and has his whole soul warmed through sense, and is full of the prickings and ticklings of desire, the obedient steed, then as always under the government of shame, refrains from leaping on the beloved, but the other, heedless of the pricks and of the blows of the whip, plunges and runs away, giving all manner of trouble to his companion and the charioteer, whom he forces to approach the beloved and to remember the joys of love. They at first indignantly oppose him and will not be urged on to do terrible and unlawful deeds, but at last, when he persists in plaguing them, they yield and agree to do as he bids them.*
>
> *And now they are at the spot and behold the flashing beauty of the beloved, which when the charioteer sees, his memory is carried to the true beauty, whom he beholds in company with Modesty like an image placed upon a holy pedestal. He sees her, but he is afraid and falls backwards in adoration, and by his fall is compelled to pull back the reins with such violence as to bring both the steeds on their haunches, the one willing and unresisting, the unruly one very unwilling. And when they have gone back a little, the one is overcome with shame and wonder, and his whole soul is bathed in perspiration; the other, when the pain is over which the bridle and the fall had given him, having with difficulty taken breath, is full of wrath*

and reproaches, which he heaps upon the charioteer and his fellow-steed, for want of courage and manhood, declaring that they have been false to their agreement and guilty of desertion. Again they refuse, and again he urges them on, and will scarce yield to their prayer that he would wait until another time. When the appointed hour comes, they make as if they had forgotten, and he reminds them, fighting and neighing and dragging them on, until at length he, on the same thoughts intent, forces them to draw near again. And when they are near, he stoops his head and puts up his tail, and takes the bit in his teeth and pulls shamelessly. Then the charioteer is worse off than ever; he falls back like a racer at the barrier, and with a still more violent wrench drags the bit out of the teeth of the wild steed and covers his abusive tongue and jaws with blood and forces his legs and haunches to the ground and punishes him sorely.

And when this has happened several times and the villain has ceased from his wanton way, he is tamed and humbled and follows the will of the charioteer, and when he sees the beautiful one he is ready to die of fear. And from that time forward the soul of the lover follows the beloved in modesty and holy fear.

In this passage, Socrates presents an allegory of the relationship between the emotions and reason. He imagines reason as a charioteer attempting to guide two powerful horses. The horses stand in for two sets of emotions. The noble horse stands for passions such as shame

Socrates imagined reason as a charioteer attempting to guide two powerful horses.

which are guided by a keen sense of honor and dishonor, while the base horse represents passions such as sexual desire which gratify the wants and needs of the body. The allegory tells of a situation in which sexual attraction occurs. The base horse wants to bolt toward the pleasure; the noble horse chooses to refrain from an act judged to be shameful. The charioteer, meanwhile, has the job of keeping the horses running in tandem, but the unruliness of the base horse finally overcomes both him and the noble horse, and they are dragged along toward pleasure. But before anything actually happens, the charioteer is reminded of "true beauty"—that is, of what reason knows to be the nature of true love—and pulls back hard on the reins. The base horse resents being denied sexual pleasure, while the noble horse is overcome with shame for having been led by ignoble desire.

It may seem that the lesson of the allegory is that reason is good and that emotions are bad. Yet this interpretation would be too simplistic. While the allegory does show us that emotions need to be guided by reason, it also testifies that we cannot do without the emotions, which are, after all, what propel the chariot forward. Indeed, as we shall see, the emotions provide us with crucial information about the world and play an important role in the moral life.

Emotions provide us with crucial information about the world and play an important role in the moral life.

A Response to Rationalism

As we saw in the last chapter, the preeminent nobility of intellect and will has led some people to think of human beings as though we were minds that can put on and take off a body as if it were an overcoat. This view of the human person can be traced back to the ancient world, but the modern thinker most often associated with the idea is the seventeenth-century philosopher Descartes. Several years ago, neurobiologist Antonio Damasio responded to this point of view with his book *Descartes' Error: Emotion, Reason, and the Human Brain*. Much like Bill Moyers, Damasio grew up in a culture that presumed a separation of mind and body. Damasio's complaint was that Descartes had conceived of the processes of the body in terms of clockwork mechanics and suggested that thought sufficed to identify the human being. When Descartes posited his famous *cogito ergo sum*—"I think, therefore I am"—he identified himself as a "thinking thing," as distinguished from his non-thinking, material body, which he called an "extended thing" and described in strictly mechanical terms.

Descartes was a precursor to the Enlightenment and a proponent of what is called rationalism. Because the emotions have a powerful bodily component (sweat, cold clammy palms, distracted jitters, anxious stomach), devotees of rationalism insisted that our thinking be kept separate and protected from the corrupting influences of our feelings. Just as Moyers grew up being told that the soul and the body were completely separate, so Damasio grew up being told that "emotions and reason did not mix any more than oil and water."

During his research, however, Damasio encountered a patient with all the "instruments usually considered necessary and sufficient for rational behavior"—the requisite knowledge, attention, memory, and linguistic skills, as well as the ability to perform calculations and tackle problems in abstract logic. At same time, there was one significant defect in him: a marked inability to experience emotions due to a severe brain lesion. This inability did not merely make him "cold." His condition was much worse than that. "His practical reason was so impaired," reports Damasio, "that it produced, in the wanderings of daily life, a succession of mistakes," creating "a perpetual violation of what would be considered socially appropriate and personally advantageous" behavior. Damasio concluded that "reason may not be as pure as most of us think it is or wish it were," and "emotions and feelings may not be intruders in the bastion of reason," but should instead be seen as "enmeshed in its networks, for worse and for better."

Our emotions, or feelings, can cause havoc in the processes of reasoning under certain circumstances.

Psychological studies have repeatedly validated what we all know from our experience: that our emotions, or feelings, can indeed, as Damasio put it, "cause havoc in the processes of reasoning under certain circumstances." And yet the absence of emotion or feeling is no less

St. Peter cutting off the ear of Malchus in an attempt to prevent the arrest of Jesus. Our emotional condition shapes our ability to make practical, moral decisions about how we ought to behave and treat others.

damaging. We cannot make decisions based on our emotions alone, but they are nevertheless "indispensable for rationality." We have a certain feeling as though something is touching our leg, and we jump back instinctively. We walk down the street in a certain neighborhood and the hairs on the back of our head start to tingle, telling us something is not quite right. A mother will often have a sense that her child is hurt or upset without being able to describe how she knows. These are signals we should not ignore or discount simply because they are pre-rational.

Our senses and emotions give us important cues about the world. Fear is the proper response to danger. Anger is the proper response to injustice. Sympathy is the proper response to suffering. Wonder is the proper response to mystery and beauty. Indeed, studies have repeatedly shown that something must be lit up by our emotions in order for us to want to learn about it. We must first find something interesting or compelling—we first must care about it—before we will commit it to memory or begin to reflect on it and ask about its causes. And our emotional condition shapes our ability to make practical, moral decisions about how we ought to behave and treat others. Can we really treat someone with respect if we have no feeling for the difference between respect and contempt, or even respect and a curt dismissal? Experience suggests that we cannot.

Aquinas on the Passions

Many of these studies confirm the wisdom of the Fathers and Doctors of the Church. Descartes envisioned human beings as thinking things whose intellectual faculty was only accidentally connected to the senses and sense appetites, but the Catholic tradition has not agreed with him. We will again consider the work of one of the most prominent figures in that tradition: St. Thomas Aquinas. In his *Summa Theologiae*, Aquinas devoted a long section to what he called the passions. The word *passio* in Latin, from which we get our English word "passion," was used by Aquinas in the same way we use the word "emotion." Both terms suggest something that happens to us; we are passive and moved, sometimes not even knowing why. We say that we "fall" in love. Someone might even say, "I did not want to fall in love, but I did." We say, "I was paralyzed with fear" or "grief overcame me." All these expressions suggest that there is a passive dimension to our emotional responses. A man may not want to get angry, but he does. He feels the rage building inside of him. A woman may not have expected to feel paralyzing anxiety in front of the crowd, but there it is, that horrible feeling in the pit of her stomach she cannot seem to control.

Did Aquinas think that the passions and the desires that they elicit in our bodily appetites are evil? Did he think at least some of them, such as anger and the desire to rectify a wrong, are evil? No. In themselves, the passions are neither evil nor good, nor are the appetites that are the seats of our desires. One person feels fear in closed spaces, another looking down from a tall building, a third when she gets on an airplane. Feeling fear is not a moral fault. What matters from the perspective of good and evil—from the perspective of your freedom—is what you do or choose not to do when you feel fear or anger or joy or any of the other passions. And from the perspective of your character, that is, your disposition to act in this way or in that, what matters is whether your appetites are apt to be in accord with your reasonable choices or whether you have allowed them to become unruly by failing to rein them in appropriately.

Consider for a moment a basketball player who takes a hard foul. He is likely to experience the emotion of anger, complete with clenching fist and jaw, pressure in the heart, and perhaps a sharp intake of breath. This is a natural response to physical assault. Our initial evaluation of the response will be to say that it was good insofar as it shows his senses are working. But we will not make a moral evaluation—a judgment about the player's will and character—until his response to the assault is complete. Will he dwell on the offense and let the anger build? Or will he bridle his anger appropriately? One way of dealing

When there is a hard foul or a bad call in basketball, you will often hear coaches tell their players: "Keep your head in the game!" You need to control your anger and not let your anger control you.

with anger of this sort is to let it motivate you to play harder. Another way to react, however, is to strike back. Once you reward the player who fouled you by fouling him even harder, he is likely to revenge himself on you. And on and on it goes. When there is a hard foul or a bad call in basketball, you will often hear coaches tell their players: "Keep your head in the game!" You need to control your anger and not let your anger control you if you want your team to win.

How about joy? Joy seems to be a good emotion. But what if you were to show joy at someone else's suffering? And what if your expression of joy at your victory demeans your opponent? Excessive celebration was once generally considered unsportsmanlike and with good reason. Joy may seem to be an inherently good emotion, while anger seems as though it would be an inherently bad one. But there are proper times and manners of expressing each and ways in which either can go wrong.

Aquinas's settled doctrine is that the passions of the soul "in so far as they are contrary to the order of reason, incline us to sin; but insofar as they are controlled by reason, they pertain to virtue." We will have more to say about the virtues later, but note that, for the Catholic tradition, the virtues involve our ability to discipline and direct the passions and the appetites to which they are connected, not to stifle them. When we are seeking the right thing and our choices are well-ordered, our passions help us to achieve the good end.

Sorting Out Emotions

To be sure, the passions can obscure our judgment or blind us to the truth. We say of someone that he "fell into a blind rage." Some passions can diminish the praiseworthiness of an act. It is always a good thing to do an act of charity, but it is better to do it from generosity than from pity. When a person perceives a right course of action, this act of understanding can motivate the will and inspire the passions. One can be filled with zeal to try to right an injustice. There can be great joy in a job well done or in the appreciation of beauty. If the emotional response of compassion at the suffering of another moves you to self-sacrifice on behalf of that person, then your emotions have made a real contribution to a noble deed.

Sometimes our feelings and emotions are clear, sometimes confused. You want to help, but you are terrified. You say you love this young man, but the prospect of marriage is paralyzing. Part of you wants to get the new job in the faraway city, but part of you is not so sure. Sometimes our emotional responses to a given set of circumstances are irreducibly complex. This is one reason why the emotions cannot be our sole guide when we are seeking to make prudent decisions. They can give us important information, but they cannot be trusted to be always clear and consistent.

In can happen that young Christian men and women who have dated for a while face the question of whether they should get engaged to be married. There are two mistakes that they ought to avoid. The first mistake would be to heed nothing but their emotions. The problem is that their emotions can change; their feeling of being in love will not last forever. Time, fidelity, good will, and God's grace can transform that feeling into a mutual regard that is even sweeter and more reliable. For that to happen, however, the relationship must have a firm foundation in something more solid than feelings. The second mistake would be to ignore the emotions completely. Sometimes Christian men and women convince themselves that they should marry the person they have been dating because "he is a good man" or "she is a good woman" even though they lack any real delight in the other's company. So too, good Christian men and women sometimes choose a line of work because it is a noble thing to do, even though they find no joy in it. Being a teacher is a noble thing to do, but not if one dreads being in charge of a classroom or finds working with students unbearably frustrating.

The emotions warn us and motivate us but cannot be allowed to tell us how to make up our minds. This is the job of reason, which draws upon the data from our emotions, among other things. There are some feelings we need to set aside because they are irrational. St. Francis of Assisi is said to have had a special distaste for lepers. He forced himself to conquer that feeling by kissing a leper. That courageous deed proved to be perhaps the single greatest turning point in his life and hence a significant moment in the life of the Church as well.

If the emotional response of compassion at the suffering of another moves you to self-sacrifice on behalf of that person, then your emotions have made a real contribution to a noble deed.

Sometimes people judge something to be wrong because they "feel" it is wrong but cannot say why they think so. They may be basing their judgment on irrational prejudice alone. If so, then the feeling needs to be ignored in favor of rational judgment. Nevertheless, we do not want to discount instinctual feelings altogether. Sometimes a feeling of revulsion can be an important help to reason. There are plenty of people who react to some forms of biotechnological experimentation by saying they "just feel it is wrong" without being able to give a reasoned account of their disapproval. That may be a healthy instinct when the technology is changing so quickly that we seem to need new arguments every day, arguments so varied and complex that few can master them. And, to be sure, evil ought to inspire revulsion.

The protestors in Birmingham who demonstrated against allowing black students into the white-only schools were very angry. Just because one has strong emotions does not mean that one's cause is just.

How do we know which feelings we should discount and which we ought to listen to? Ultimately, feelings and emotions must be assessed and guided by reason. And by reason we mean all the various ways of perceiving reality, including ways based on truths we hold by faith in God. You may feel as though you want to kill your evil next-door neighbor. Remember: "Thou shalt not kill." There are many versions of the song lyric which asks: "How can this be wrong when it feels so right?" It can. We are fallen creatures living in a fallen world. As a result, our emotions have become untethered from our reason, and our reason has in some cases been blinded by our pride. It is better to be guided by the wisdom of the Church, which has the benefit of God's grace and divine revelation, than to have our emotions manipulated by advertisers and the writers of dramas. They know how to pull those emotional strings, and we need to be on our guard against them.

If we are to be able to resist being manipulated by imagery, our emotions must be teachable, and they are, but sometimes we are required to be very demanding teachers. Indeed, strong emotions have the potential to lead us far astray. If you look at the film footage of the protestors in Birmingham who demonstrated against allowing black students into the white-only schools, you will see that many of them were very angry. Terrorists who plant bombs are also very angry. Just because one has strong emotions does not mean that one's cause is just. It is possible to feel strongly about something and still be wrong. Hence our emotions and appetites need to be guided by reason and by what reason tells us about what is good. The stronger the emotion, the more careful we should be that it not lead us astray. It is not wrong to be passionate—in fact, in can be a very good thing to be passionate—but it is wrong to be passionate about the wrong things. Great passion in defense of evil does not make the evil any better; it usually makes it worse.

There are many passages in scripture that tell us that our dedication to God should be with mind and body, spirit and flesh. St. Paul says that the "first fruits of the Spirit" is the "redemption of our bodies" (Rom 8:23). Our bodies are often at war with our minds. But this disorder is not what God intended. We are meant to be whole and unified in God's service. Just as my intellect and will should apprehend and love the reality of things as God has created them and should not try to bend reality into what I think I want it to be, so too my passions and appetites should be purified by the truth I understand and the good that moves me. The moral law should be written not only in our minds, but also in our hearts, and then inscribed finally in our bodies by the virtues aided by grace and the sacraments.

Disciplining the Passions

We must begin in small ways. One does not expect to finish a marathon in the first week of training or to be able to throw a 90-mph fastball on one's first-ever pitch. We begin by disciplining simple desires for simple things. During Lent, we may want the delicious piece of chocolate cake we see in a shop window, but we say "no," not because chocolate cake is evil, but because we know we must learn to discipline our desire for it. I can either eat or not eat the cake. I have control over myself; the cake does not have control over me. The same can be said if the object of our desire is a beautiful new BMW, a great pair of shoes, an expensive bike, or an especially attractive person of the opposite sex. Are you in control of yourself, or are your desires for these things in control of you, causing you to do things you know to be wrong or foolish?

We discipline our passions, such as love, desire, and joy, and their opposites, hatred, dislike, and sorrow, by means of the virtues of temperance and fortitude. These virtues discipline our passions and appetites to produce the right balance between too much and too little. Temperance is the virtue that disciplines our appetite for the pleasures of touch and taste. You can want a certain kind of coffee drink too much, just as you can love your car too much. Would you be willing to split your coffee with a friend? Do you spend more time caring for what you drink than you do caring about your friends? Does gossip that damages a person's reputation and damages relationships cause you very little grief while a barista's mistake sends you into fits of rage? Maybe it is time to reassess what is truly important. Perhaps it is time to start disciplining your emotions and caring less about your coffee.

During Lent, we may want the delicious piece of chocolate cake we see in a shop window but we say "no." Are you in control of yourself, or are your desires for these things in control of you?

Sometimes, what we want is not a simple good like a coffee, but something difficult to obtain, like victory in the World Series or running a mile in under five minutes or solving a complex math problem. The passions having to do with obtaining difficult goods are hope, when we think we can obtain it, or its opposite, despair, when we think we cannot. When we perceive something as evil, as dangerous, hence as something to be avoided, we have the passion of fear. But if we are moved by a passion to attempt something difficult in spite of the danger, we call this passion daring. Fortitude is the virtue we need to discipline these passions. As with temperance, fortitude disciplines our passions and appetites to produce the right balance between too much and too little. Too much fear causes cowardice. Too little fear produces foolish daring. A foolish and excessive hope can bring crushing disappointment. Too little hope breeds despair. Fortitude allows you to quiet your fears and dismiss your despair enough to act, without prompting in you false hopes or causing you to do foolish things beyond your abilities.

The Christian perspective on Socrates' allegory of the chariot is to affirm that the charioteer needs two horses, that is, the full complement of the passions, but that he must wield the reins with wisdom and vigor. The virtues are what yoke the passions together and bring the appetites they stimulate or suppress under the firm guidance of reason. In an earlier part of the myth, Socrates tells Phaedrus that the gods have chariots pulled by winged horses that carry them heavenward. Christians, too, believe that we can have a share in that upward ascent. As Christ is risen, so he carries all of us upward by means of the gift of his Spirit. When we are animated by the gift of God's grace and become like Christ to others, then our emotions can take wing and fly, drawing us up to heaven. No one is more dead inside than the man blown about by his passions, lost in fleeting pleasures and despair. And no one is more alive and passionate than the saint.

Review Questions

1. Summarize the allegory of the chariot from Plato's *Phaedrus* and explain what it teaches about the emotions.

2. What, according to Antonio Damasio, was Descartes's error? How does the approach to the human person Descartes initiated relate to the question of the passions? How might the Church's teaching on the unity of soul and body illuminate this question?

3. What does Aquinas teach about the passions? Are the passions evil? How can the passions become evil? Can the passions increase the goodness or badness of an act?

4. How do we know which feelings we should discount and which are telling us something we ought to listen to? Is this analysis difficult or easy?

5. How do we discipline the appetites that our passions affect? Can you think of an example in which you successfully gained self-mastery in some way? What general lesson did you learn from that experience?

6. How do temperance and fortitude act upon us? Why are these two qualities called virtues? Why would you like others to think you self-controlled and brave (and, of course, truly to be so)?

7. Given the prominence of marketing strategies based upon enflaming the passions, is the virtue of temperance subversive of our dominant culture today? Be prepared to defend your answer with concrete examples and principled arguments.

Put Out Into the Deep

A good way to take the next step in thinking about the emotions or passions would be to gather a group of your friends and classmates together to discuss the novel or play you are currently reading in your literature class from the perspective you have encountered in this chapter. Every work of literature dramatizes the emotional responses of its characters; good works of literature do so with insight, and great ones with the wisdom that comes from understanding how rightly-ordered emotions contribute to and are part of our flourishing as rational beings. Jane Austen's novels are especially worthwhile in this respect.

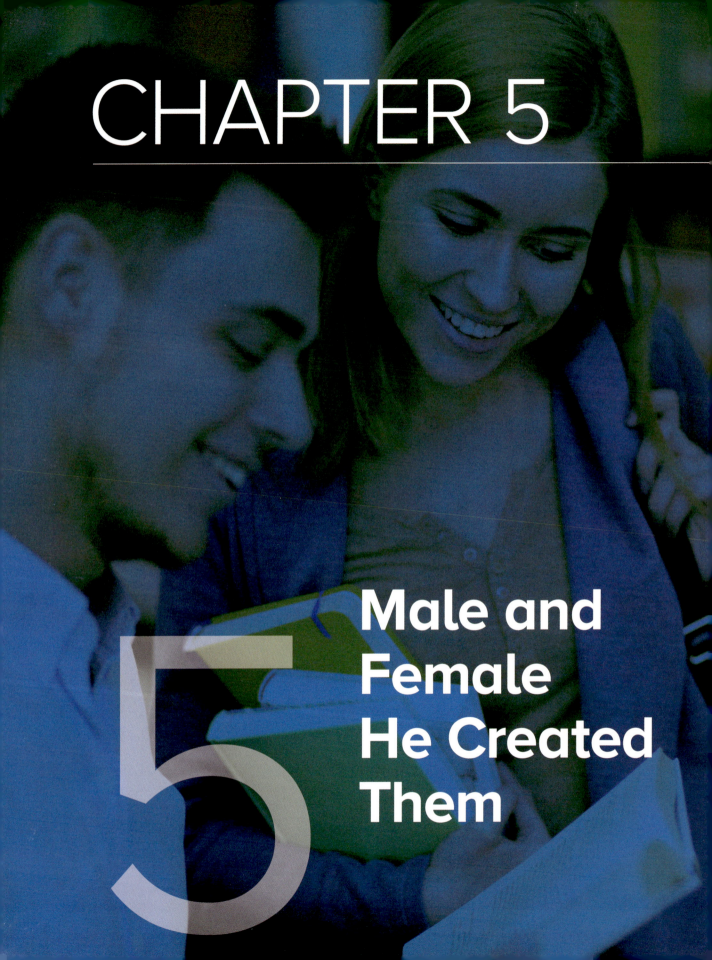

CHAPTER 5

5

Male and Female He Created Them

Can robots have sex? They could presumably be designed with the requisite parts. Is not sex, after all, just a certain placement of parts in relation to one another? Some people think so. If it involves something more, what is it?

Why would anyone design robots to have sex if the robots have no chance at all of reproduction? Why would anyone waste the time, the money, and the resources to design that function (if we can call it that) into a robot? It would seem that the only possible reason for doing so would be to give some kind of vicarious pleasure to humans. To call what these robots would be doing a sexual act could only be metaphorical, like the way we talk about the "male" and "female" ends of the plugs on an extension cord. Theirs would be only a simulation of a sexual act, not an organic union ordered to the procreation of new life.

Yet the coupling of two robots would be what some people think human sex is: two bodies in contact with each other in a certain way. If that is how we think of sex, then the obvious question is: Why would it ever be wrong to have sex? What is it about that configuration of human bodies which makes it morally significant? One reply would be to point out that human bodies have a nature which requires they be treated in certain ways. We all know what it is like to have our personal space too closely encroached upon or to be mistakenly touched in a way that makes us uncomfortable. Our various parts are not all the same; they are bearers of meaning just as our bodies as wholes are. It is not the same to say, "Your car needs a new carburetor," as it is to say to someone, "There is something wrong with the shape of your nose." A nose is part of the human whole in a different way than a carburetor is part of a car.

Sexuality without limits is advocated and glamorized by the news media, entertainers, many politicians, and most of the leaders of our educational institutions.

The Way We Think Now

Let us say there are two people who, having deep feelings for one another, engage in an act which in other circumstances can lead to the procreation of children, but in this case cannot because of their contraceptive measures. Why does the deliberate exclusion of this one, single dimension of the act—the possibility of having children—make the act something that is morally problematic according to the Catholic Church? How is this situation different, many people ask, from the same sort of act between a married couple who have sex during times of infertility, when that dimension of the act (the possibility of having children) is similarly absent?

The Church faces a severe test in maintaining its fidelity to Jesus and his teaching that human sexuality finds its proper and good home in the life-long marriage of a man and a woman. Sexuality without limits is advocated and glamorized by the news media, entertainers, many politicians, and most of the leaders of our educational institutions. And there are many corporations dedicated to making billions by detaching men and women—and especially boys and girls—from the boundaries that families and wisdom traditions have imparted, so that they can subsequently detach them from their money as they pursue products and services that promise to make them more attractive. Yet even if these passions are being stirred up by clever marketing, young people feel them as their own. Indeed, one of the most diabolically clever parts of the marketing program directed at youth is to sell them things precisely as means to their freedom and self-expression. If you want to be free, you must get away from the limits your parents and church impose on you. Create your own identity (so the story goes, with palpable irony) by buying what we are selling.

In today's culture, most of those who ask about the Church's teaching are not usually looking for moral guidance and wisdom. They usually want to know how anyone could possibly think the kind of things Catholics think—not about the Trinity or the Incarnation or the Sacraments (people are supposed to be allowed to believe in anything they want, whether it is zombies, crystals, or UFOs), but about moral questions, such as abortion, contraception, and same-sex marriage.

People want what they want. Why should they not have it?

This perspective, however, is not a good starting point for thinking about morality and not the way the Church thinks about human sexuality. The Church prefers to think about an individual act in the context of a whole human life and about our whole human life, in turn, in the context of our obligations both to God and to neighbor. From this perspective, an individual act is not adequately characterized by its immediate physical component.

There is a school of moral thinking that says: "A man takes a knife and cuts a woman's flesh; he could be a murderer or a surgeon saving her life. The act is the same in either case." The correct reply is straightforward. The physical act of taking a knife and cutting flesh may be the same, but the human act is not the same at all. And no one really mistakes the one for the other. We do not usually describe a murder or a surgery as merely the physical act of taking a knife and cutting. We also consider what the person is doing, why the person is doing it, and the relevant circumstances of the act. In the case of the medical operation, what the surgeon is doing is removing a woman's gall bladder. This is fine if removing her gall bladder is to save her life or improve her health. This is not fine if the doctor merely wants to see what happens when he takes out a gall bladder or if he means to sell it to someone else for money. If the circumstances are such that, given her blood pressure, an operation to remove this woman's gall bladder will kill her, again the procedure is not fine. In the case of the murderer, what he is doing is killing an innocent woman. It does not matter whether his intentions seem good ("I am saving her from a life of sin") or whether the circumstances are such that killing this one woman will help doctors cure cancer. Killing an innocent woman is always wrong.

But having sex is not always wrong, not at all. The Church is clear on this point. Indeed, a common criticism of Catholics is that they do not abstain from sex more. All those babies! Can't those Catholics control themselves? Very few groups have insisted that sex is always wrong. The question we tend to ask today is whether sex between consenting adults or teens is ever wrong.

Natural and Healthy Eating

One way of approaching this question is to ask about whether another entirely natural and healthy human activity—eating—is ever wrong. Like sex, no one would say that eating is intrinsically wrong. Like sex, eating is a good, healthy, and, broadly speaking, necessary part of human life. We must eat to live, but we do not necessarily have to eat right now. Similarly, humans must procreate to survive as a species, but it is not necessary for any particular couple to have sex right now. Eating is not intrinsically wrong. Does that mean it is always right?

We all recognize there are ways of eating that can be harmful. Bulimia, anorexia, over-eating, under-eating, and eating without sufficient nutrition are ways of eating that can be harmful to our health. Eating alone with no joy, never joining together to talk with others during a meal, is a way of eating that can be harmful emotionally. Notice that it would be impossible to respond adequately even to the worst of these problems if the question were asked in this way: "I want to eat this large piece of chocolate cake right now. Why should I not be allowed to do so?" Providing a necessary and sufficient set of reasons when the question is posed in this way would be difficult. The questioner wants a set of categorical reasons why it is always and everywhere wrong to eat *this* piece of chocolate cake when in fact it is not always and everywhere wrong to eat a piece of chocolate cake. And yet it may be wrong for you to eat *this* piece of chocolate cake if you are hypoglycemic or have a sugar addiction, just as it is not intrinsically wrong to drink a glass of wine but may be wrong for an alcoholic to do so.

From this line of reasoning, it does not follow that all moral principles are relative. It simply means that we should not expect all moral rules to take the form of exceptionless prohibitions such as "innocent persons are not to be killed." Individual acts have contexts, and those contexts are important. The Church teaches us to think about an individual act in the context of thinking about a whole human life and the complete flourishing of the human person, body and soul.

To eat only for pleasure while excluding nourishment would be detrimental. But to eat only for nourishment while excluding the pleasures of taste and the benefits of camaraderie would also be harmful.

Consider, for example, the following two cases. You meet a person with bulimia who says: "I love to eat and eat and eat, so tell me why it is wrong if, when I eat, I merely cut out this one dimension of eating, actually keeping the food in my stomach? Why does the lack of that one, single dimension of eating render the act morally objectionable? After all, I am realizing the other goods of eating, such as pleasure and communion with others. Nourishing my body is the only thing lacking. Why does the lack of that one thing make eating immoral?" Now let us say you meet another person who tells you: "I am really, really hungry and want nourishment, but I just cannot bring myself to eat anything. The thought of food disgusts me. So what would be wrong with just putting a tube in my body to dispense nutrients directly into my stomach? If the good of nutrition is the primary, essential goal of eating, and if I am realizing the good of nutrition, why should the lack of pleasure and/or companionship with others render my act disordered and therefore morally objectionable?"

Notice, first, that you and these two questioners would all be using the same word, eating, but not with the same understanding of its full meaning. For Person #1, eating is only something involving the physical ingesting of food which results in pleasure. For Person #2, eating is nourishment, but the physical act of taking food in through the mouth has become loathsome. If you are convinced that eating has both physical and relational dimensions, corresponding to the twofold nature of the human person as both body and soul—that eating, therefore, should both nourish the body and facilitate the communal dimension of the human person—then you may wonder whether what these two people do should be called eating at all. To eat only for pleasure while excluding nourishment would be detrimental. But to eat only for nourishment while excluding the pleasures of taste and the benefits of camaraderie would also be harmful.

What is Sex?

Now let us return to the question of sex. Like eating, sex can be a perfectly good, healthy, and indeed necessary part of human existence. For one thing, without it, there would be no more human life to replace us after we die. And yet the questions we should be asking are: (A) Is every act of sex healthy, leading to full human flourishing? And if the answer to (A) is "No," then: (B) Are there ways of engaging in sex which are healthier (both physically and emotionally) and more likely to lead to human flourishing than others? We all know there are. Rampant loveless sexual activity with multiple anonymous partners would be one example of behavior threatening to damage you physically and make you miserable emotionally. Are there others?

Let us consider two situations that are analogous to the ones we examined above with regard to eating: the first was the bulimic, who loves the pleasure of eating, but who has cut out the good of nutrition; the other was the person who wanted the good of nutrition, but who found physically taking in food loathsome. Both wanted to know why their actions, though lacking only one dimension of eating, should be considered wrong. We can imagine two similar cases when it comes to sex: on the one hand, a person who wants the pleasure of sex, but wants nothing to do with the procreative dimension of the act, and on the other, a person who might want the good of procreation, but who finds the thought of joining bodily with a member of the opposite sex loathsome.

As in the case of eating, we have people who are using the same word—in this case, sex—but who have very different ideas of what that word means. From the Church's point of view, describing what many people today think sex is would be like describing what the bulimic does as eating. The physical act of putting food into the mouth, chewing, and swallowing has taken place, but to do all that while cutting off the possibility of nutrition seems not only unhealthy but also to shun the act's purpose. The chewing, swallowing, and all the rest only make sense as part of a series of acts directed toward nutrition. Nourishment is not the only thing that can be accomplished by eating—camaraderie is another—but without that for which the act is being done, we are hard pressed to call it eating. To eat and vomit repeatedly is not really eating. That is merely chewing and swallowing. Taking a rock and changing its location so that, instead of sitting on the ground, it is now sitting in your stomach is not what we mean by eating. We would say, "he swallowed a rock," not "he ate a rock." The difference between swallowing and eating is that swallowing merely changes the location of an item, whereas eating involves digesting and nourishing.

To engage in some form of genital stimulation— without any possibility of procreation is, from the Church's point of view, a bit like chewing and swallowing while cutting off any possibility of nourishment.

So too, from the Church's point of view, to be engaged in the act of genital stimulation is not what is meant by "sex" (or to be more precise, what the Church means by "the conjugal act"). To engage in some form of genital stimulation—whether by oneself or with another person having the same or opposite sort of genitalia or with several others with any of the various combinations of the same and/or opposites—without any possibility of procreation is, from the Church's point of view, a bit like chewing and swallowing while cutting off any possibility of nourishment. And as in the case of the bulimic and eating, it is precisely the natural consequences of the act that are found terrifying and thought necessary to be avoided at all costs. It is not that a dysfunction of the body must be cured. It is precisely the proper functioning of the body that must be by-passed or destroyed. To the bulimic, the goal would be the possibility of taking in food while bypassing the digestive system entirely. So too for the sexual bulimic, the great desire is to be able to engage in an act which by its nature involves placing semen (seed) into an area where female ova (eggs) are produced, and yet bypass the reproductive system entirely.

The first person, the non-eating eater, is asking: cannot I just turn off my digestive system entirely while I am eating? If this person is asked: "Why not just refrain from eating?" or "Why not develop healthier, more natural eating habits in accord with the natural cycles of your body?" the only possible answer would be: "Because I want to keep doing it this way! Because I love eating!" To which one might respond: "I do not think you do love it. I think you hate it. What you love is an unhealthy simulation of real eating. When you eat, you are dominated by fear. You are terrified that your body will actually absorb the food you are taking in. So you go to great lengths to make sure that the natural, healthy outcome of the act you are engaged in does not actually occur."

Nourishment is not the only thing that can be accomplished by eating—camaraderie is another—but without that for which the act is being done, we are hard pressed to call it eating.

So too with the person engaged in bulimic sex. If this person is asked: "Why not refrain from having sex during the fertile periods?" or "Why not develop healthier, more natural sexual habits, in accord with the natural cycles of your body?" the only possible answer would be: "Because I want to keep doing it this way! Because I want sex!" To which one might respond: "It does not seem that you do want sex. What you want is a simulation of the conjugal act: it looks like it; the body parts are stimulated in a similar way; but it is not actual conjugal union. When you have what you call sex, you are dominated by fear. You are terrified that your bodies will actually do the thing your bodies are designed to do: procreate. So you go to great lengths to make sure that the natural, healthy outcome of the act you are engaged in does not actually occur."

What the Church notices about sex, which many people seem to want to forget, is what sex is and what the intrinsic end of the act is. The sexual act (properly understood) involves the deposit of seed in potentially fertile soil.

Fertility is Not a Disease

What would be healthy conjugal sexuality? Or to put this another way, how do we include sex in a healthy manner in our lives in a way analogous to the way we include eating in a healthy manner in our lives? There are all sorts of ways of missing the mark when it comes to eating (too much food, too little food, the wrong kind of food, eating alone all the time, eating on the run, never enjoying food and drink, being enslaved to food and drink), so too there are all sorts of ways of missing the mark when it comes to sex. Is there a right and healthy way to include sex in a whole, complete human life?

As we saw in chapter 3, the Church holds that matter is good and that the body is good, indeed "very good" (Gen 1:31). The Church has always held that pleasure is the healthy response to a certain kind of bodily stimulus and that desire is good when it moves us toward what is in accord with our flourishing, that is, in accord with the love of God and neighbor rightly understood. The Church, then, is not opposed to pleasure in sex any more than in eating. What the Church notices about sex, which many people seem to want to forget, is what sex is and what the intrinsic end of the act is. The sexual act (properly understood) involves the deposit of seed in potentially fertile soil. The man and woman having sex may not want the natural consequence of that mixing to bring about a new life, but they should not really be surprised if it does. If you take sunflower seeds and spread them all over your garden, should you be shocked to find sunflowers sprouting up after a few weeks? What did you expect? And why were you out spreading sunflower seeds around in the first place? Just to get rid of them? But if you dump them in a place where they can grow, do not be surprised if they do. This is simple biology. There is nothing scandalous in this. There is nothing especially religious in this. It is the reality of the world. No one is punishing you. You planted seeds, and they grew.

The Church, nevertheless, in urging men to the observance of the precepts of the natural law, which it interprets by its constant doctrine, teaches that each and every marital act must of necessity retain its intrinsic relationship to the procreation of human life. This particular doctrine, often expounded by the magisterium of the Church, is based on the inseparable connection, established by God, which man on his own initiative may not break, between the unitive significance and the procreative significance which are both inherent to the marriage act. The reason is that the fundamental nature of the marriage act, while uniting husband and wife in the closest intimacy, also renders them capable of generating new life—and this as a result of laws written into the actual nature of man and of woman. And if each of these essential qualities, the unitive and the procreative, is preserved, the use of marriage fully retains its sense of true mutual love and its ordination to the supreme responsibility of parenthood to which man is called. We believe that our contemporaries are particularly capable of seeing that this teaching is in harmony with human reason.

St. Paul VI, *Humanae Vitae*, 11–12 (1968)

A Miracle or a Tragedy?

So, try as you might to avoid it, it is possible in every true sexual act for a new life to be created. Couples should ask themselves whether they are ready for a new life to be created as the fruit of their act. If not, then they ought not to be engaged in the act. Because there are few things more tragic than a young woman saying to a young man, "We have accomplished the most miraculous thing two human beings can do. Together we have created an entirely new life, a new human being," and the young man saying in reply: "Oh, dear God, no!" The horror that such a couple might consider taking the innocent human life in the womb by aborting the child is now plainly in view. There are other foolish replies: "How did this happen?" Is he really unclear how it happened? Then there is: "Why didn't you take care of this?" as though such things are primarily a woman's fault and she is somehow to blame for something they did together. New life is a miracle. It is tragic to turn it into a curse.

One thing to think about when it comes to sex is how to avoid turning it into a potential curse, something which can lead to significant burdens and hardships. How do you do that? One way would be only to have sex with someone with whom you would be willing to raise a child. Otherwise your sexual act is always going to be accompanied by fear—fear that the natural, healthy consequence of the act might actually come about. This is like throwing a baseball up in the air in your house and swinging your bat at it, knowing that if you actually hit it, it will probably knock over a lamp, break a window, or damage a wall. Is your mother being unreasonable if she says, "Don't do that"? Is the Church being unreasonable if she says about potentially tragic sexual couplings: "Don't do that"? You might get away without severe damage a couple of times, but you are risking an awful lot. If something breaks, should you really look around and say, "Why me?"

How do you know that this person is someone with whom you should be willing to raise a child? Well, how long would you be a parent to that child? One answer is: 18 years. The better answer is: the rest of your life. There is never a time in that child's life when you will not be his or her parent. Is it so ridiculous, then, for the Church to advise young people that healthy conjugal sex happens between a man and a woman who are committed to one another for life? Or is it more ridiculous to say: "Well, it is a gamble—an especially big one, given the possible consequence of pregnancy—but you should just take it anyway for the few minutes of pleasure you get"?

There is never a time in a child's life when you will not be his or her parent.

Sex is an absolutely natural, healthy thing, and the desire for sex and sexual pleasure can be an absolutely good thing. Not everyone believes that, but Christians do. These are gifts from God. The tragedy comes when we misuse God's gifts and turn what should be a joyful miracle into a life-altering tragedy, something that should be a total, mutual self-gift of partners into a fearful mixing of two frightened young adults who have no idea what they are doing other than what the culture—and their hormones—tell them they are supposed to do when they are young and in high school.

Perhaps it is time for young people to stop doing what a toxic culture has told them they are supposed to do and start doing the sort of things the wise sages of every time and culture have advocated. Every Buddhist monk, every Confucian sage, every Hindu rishi, every ancient Greek poet and philosopher, the proponents of pretty much every wisdom tradition in the world—they have all recognized that the human desire for sex can be a divine force for good or a demonic force driving people to rob, lie, kill, and betray friends and countries. You can either order that powerful force in constructive ways or let it consume you and create chaos all around you.

What *Kind* of Relationship?

Now we can return to our opening question: "So let us say there are two people who love one another and engage in an act that in other circumstances can lead to children, but in this case cannot. Why does the planned absence of this one, single dimension of the act—the possibility of having children—make it something morally unacceptable to the Catholic Church?" As we have seen, there is already a problem with the notion of "sex" here. Lacking that one dimension makes it not exactly "sex" as the Church understands it, but rather a simulation of the conjugal act. The act in question would be analogous to what the two robots engage in: there is some sort of placing of certain parts next to or in or around other parts, which may result in physical pleasure, but there is no possibility at all of procreation. What they are having is sex-unrelated-to-procreation or sex-divorced-from-procreation, while what the Catholic Church recommends—and what God ordained by creating us male and female—is sex-open-to-the-possibility-of-procreation in a committed-for-life relationship.

The problem has nothing to do with the quantity or depth of the love involved. The two people may love each other a great deal. But the love must be of a certain kind. We love all sorts of things and many different people: fellow students, brothers, sisters, friends, parents, neighbors. There are obligations we have to each of these individuals.

Sometimes we are dutiful in fulfilling those commitments, sometimes less so. But either way, one's commitment to a spouse is different in kind from one's commitments to any of these others, not merely different in degree. The difference is the commitment to having and raising a family. And one is definitely not committed to anyone else—and certainly not to any institution—in that way. So, when someone begins a question by saying: "So let's say there are two people who love one another and are committed to one another the way you and your wife are committed to one another," the question is whether this person is mistaking passionate intensity in a relationship *not* devoted to having and raising a family with those same dispositions in a relationship that *is* devoted to having and raising a family. Those two are different, not merely in degree, but in kind.

One's commitment to a spouse is different in kind from one's commitments to any of these others, not merely different in degree. The difference is the commitment to having and raising a family.

At this point, many today would raise the question of same-sex marriage and argue that within the context of a life-long relationship dedicated to the raising of children, sexual relations between persons of the same sex are morally equivalent to the conjugal sexuality of husband and wife. In the next chapter, we will address this question from the point of view of the family. Here we will restrict our treatment of this highly controversial topic to the point of view of the chastity to which God calls every human being. The biblical witness is plain: all offenses against chastity are serious sins (see, for instance, Leviticus 18 in its entirety and Matthew 5:27–32). With respect to homosexual activity, the witness of the animal world confirms and supports human experience: the complementarity of male and female is life-giving, promotes the good of the species, and is the norm with respect to which sexuality may be rightly valued. The Church applies this norm to all her members and calls persons who experience same-sex attraction to a life of chastity, all the while recognizing the special difficulties and crosses that they bear and insisting that they be treated with compassion and respect (see CCC 2358–59). As part of her confession that nature's teaching is rooted in the Creator's wisdom, the Church is further obliged to testify that homosexual activity cannot bring authentic and lasting happiness to those who engage in it (see Rom 1:18–32).

What is the difference between a couple having "sex-entirely-and-purposefully-divorced-from-procreation" and "sex-open-to-procreation" done during the infertile period? The difference is not simply based on a couple's ultimate long-term intention. There are undoubtedly plenty of couples who intend eventually to have children, but who are now engaging in "sex-entirely-and-purposefully-divorced-from-procreation." What distinguishes the first couple from the second in the mind of the Church is that the first couple is treating fertility as a kind of disease that needs to be treated. And both the man and the woman are motivated to treat the entirely natural consequences of their act as a dysfunction precisely because of their fear of the natural consequences.

If the couple that is having sex only during the infertile periods is also motivated by fear of the natural consequences—as may sometimes happen—then they too are in the wrong place. This is not a true openness to new life. This does not mean that they must always in every act intend to have children. But they must always be open to the possibility. "Sex," "love-making," on the understanding of the Church, is supposed to be a free act of total self-giving.

To ask your wife to "take care of" her fertility is like asking her to change a fundamental part of her identity before you will accept her. The same is true if the wife asks the husband to "fix" his fertility. This is not how the Church understands love. In the Church's view, there is no need for a spouse to "get fixed" before you accept him or her.

Another way of approaching this question is to ask, "What do you want to be able to say to your children?"

> (A) "We took every human precaution possible to prevent your coming into this world, but you somehow squirmed through anyway, so when we found out, we just made the best of a bad situation, and here you are."

> *or*

> (B) "Granted, we were not intending you at the time you were conceived, but there was never a time when we were not open to new life, and so when we found out you existed, we were overjoyed—nervous, yes, but still really joyous. We never had sex with fear because we never feared the possibility of you."

What do you want to be able to say with honesty? Which would you prefer to be true?

Not an Unrealizable Ideal

Most people would prefer to unite both dimensions of the conjugal act, just as they would prefer to have happy, committed marriages. But they often do not think they can. One of the challenges the Church faces when she shares her positive view of human flourishing is that it can seem overly idealistic. "Sure, that is the *ideal*," people will say, "but who can reach that standard? Not us fallen human beings." The problem with us human beings, however, is not that we want too much, but that we settle for too little. God has put into our hearts a desire for an infinite good, and we settle for potato chips, television, and cheap, loveless sex-as-pleasure-seeking instead of sex-as-selfless-act-of-love. The Church's view of human relationships directed toward the goal of human flourishing is not an unrealizable ideal. It is not simple, that is true. It is not our default mode. But then again, real authentic freedom is not our default mode. We tend to be too quick to sell out to the crowd and to our lower impulses. To live open to life takes effort and discipline. And it requires hope. But it is not impossible, and it contains a tremendous promise of happiness.

Review Questions

1. What sort of problems and questions are raised by the prospect of robots being designed for sexual activity?

2. We have repeatedly stressed that the Church considers individual human actions within a variety of contexts, including that of the human life considered as a narrative whole but also within the context of communities. What contexts must we think about to understand human sexuality? Be prepared to explain your answers.

3. What can we learn about human sexuality by considering it in light of human eating?

4. The perspective of the Church—most famously expressed in St. Paul VI's encyclical *Humanae Vitae*—is that the unitive and procreative qualities of human sexuality are not to be separated from each other. Can you explain and defend this point of view? What are some of the rival points of view about human sexuality? What are their implicit presuppositions?

5. How do the discussions of friendship and truth from volume 1 of *Why Believe?* help to shed light on the proper context of human sexuality in the lifelong marriage of a man and a woman?

Put Out Into the Deep

There is a broad and deep literature on these questions, with many fine contributions from scholars and pastoral counselors such as Dr. Janet Smith, Fr. John Harvey, O.S.F.S., and, of course, St. John Paul II. As a next step and an introduction to that literature, we recommend Edward Sri's *Men, Women, and the Mystery of Love: Practical Insights from John Paul II's Love and Responsibility*, 2nd edition (Servant, 2015).

CHAPTER 6

Honor Your Father and Mother

6

And Jesus went away from there and withdrew to the district of Tyre and Sidon. And behold, a Canaanite woman from that region came out and cried, "Have mercy on me, O Lord, Son of David; my daughter is severely possessed by a demon." But he did not answer her a word. And his disciples came and begged him, saying, "Send her away, for she is crying after us." He answered, "I was sent only to the lost sheep of the house of Israel." But she came and knelt before him, saying, "Lord, help me." And he answered, "It is not fair to take the children's bread and throw it to the dogs." She said, "Yes, Lord, yet even the dogs eat the crumbs that fall from their master's table." Then Jesus answered her, "O woman, great is your faith! Let it be done for you as you desire." And her daughter was healed instantly (Mt 15:21–28).

The encounter between Jesus and the Canaanite woman is one of the more arresting passages in the Gospels. Jesus tests the woman to see whether she is willing to witness to the faith that he knows to be within her. The drama of the words and reactions is stark. The woman is plainly in agony. The disciples display impatience and a lack of compassion. Jesus himself is not only stern—saying that he has come only for the Chosen People—but would seem to have purposely insulted the woman. There are so many difficult and fascinating aspects to the passage that upon a first or even a second reading we may miss that it is about motherhood. Yes, motherhood. The faith of the Canaanite woman is a mother's faith, elicited by her love for her daughter. "Have mercy on *me*," she says, and, kneeling before Jesus, "help *me*." The daughter was being tormented by a demon, but it is the mother who is in agony. She asks not for help for her daughter, but for herself. Should her daughter be healed—and she was—then she, the mother, will experience God's mercy. Yes, Jesus tested the Canaanite woman, but he did so for our benefit, so that she would fully display for us the depths of a mother's love for her child and provide the Lord with the occasion to bless that love.

In the first chapter of this volume, we saw in the parable of the prodigal son a beautiful and instructive image of fatherhood. Here, with the story of the Canaanite woman, we have an image of motherhood. These are only two of the many passages of Sacred Scripture in which God teaches us about some of the most significant traits of human character through the examples of mothers and fathers. And he has, of course, revealed himself to us as Father through the words of his Son, who was born of a woman and raised by a human father. If we are to understand the Christian faith, we must understand the human family, a task which poses evident challenges in the present climate of opinion.

Communion and Complementarity

The Book of Genesis tells us that "God created man in his own image, in the image of God he created him; male and female he created them" (Gen 1:27). The next verse adds the words of mission: "And God blessed them. And God said to them, 'Be fruitful and multiply'" (Gen 1:28). At the very beginning of revelation, then, we are presented the good news that God did not create us to be alone, but instead to be united in life-giving bonds of creative communion— that is, in families.

We are given a similar message using different imagery in Genesis 2, where after forming man from the dust of the earth and breathing into him his own Spirit, God took a rib from the side of the man and formed the woman. The ancient Jews understood this to mean that Eve had sprung forth from the source of Adam's life and love. "This at last is bone of my bones, and flesh of my flesh" (Gen 2:23), Adam says, as if to imply: "She and I are one, while being two." And when he and she unite with each other bodily and God bestows upon them the blessing of a child, together they can look upon the newborn and say, "This at last is bone of my bones, and flesh of my flesh." Spouses have many things that delight them: a house, some nice dishes, common friends, perhaps

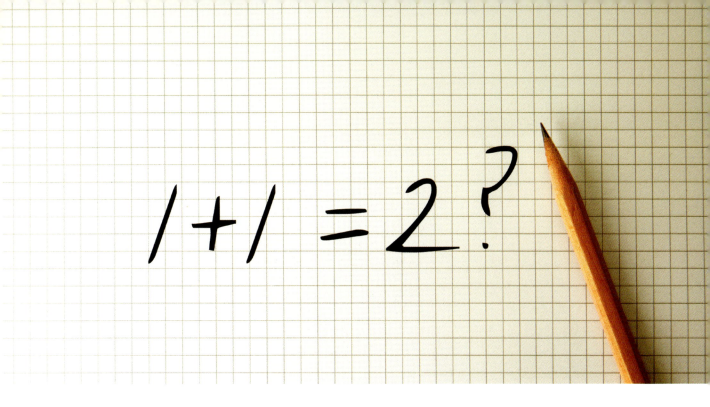

St. John Paul II often said that marriage is founded on "the primordial unity and complementarity of man and woman. The two spouses complement and complete each other so that the whole is greater than the sum of the parts.

even a friendly dog. But none of these is flesh of their flesh. Adam's amazement upon seeing his wife is reenacted every time a mother and father look upon the face of their newborn child, the embodiment of their love. When the love between father and mother becomes a person, we could point to the child and think, "There goes the love of John and Mary, walking down the street!"

The account in Genesis 2 finishes with this statement: "Therefore a man leaves his father and his mother and clings to his wife, and they become one flesh" (Gen 2:24). Jesus recited this passage to the Pharisees when they asked him about marriage (see Mt 19:5, Mk 10:7), and St. Paul also recalled it (see 1 Cor 6:16, Eph 5:31). What does it mean to say that the two "become one flesh"? It suggests, as St. John Paul II often said that marriage is founded on "the primordial unity and complementarity of man and woman." The two spouses complement and complete each other so that the whole is greater than the sum of the parts.

There are different kinds of unity. A pile of bricks has a certain unity, a less ordered and less permanent one than the kind of unity the bricks have when they are joined together in a wall. A button in a button-hole and tongue-and-groove joints have a more impressive kind of unity. Each part can exist without the other, but each was made for the other, and it is not possible to say what either is without some reference to the other. Together they accomplish what neither could accomplish alone. This is the kind of unity meant to exist between a father and a mother in the family. Only this unity is not merely physical; it is also emotional and spiritual. It is a unity of mutual love and care, or, at any rate, that is both what we all want and what God intended it to be.

After the Fall

To consider the Fall through the lens of the family is instructive and sobering. Because Adam and Eve wanted to decide for themselves what is good and evil rather than to discover and heed the reality of good and evil in the world as God created it, they alienated themselves from God and from each other. When God asked Adam whether he had eaten of the fruit of the forbidden tree, Adam blamed the woman. Eve, in her turn, blamed the serpent. Rather than becoming "gods" to rival the one God, they became the kind of unimpressive people who cannot even take responsibility for their own choices. And instead of bringing them closer together, their sin gave rise to recrimination and strife. Their passions and appetites became disordered, so they hid their bodies from each other, and, tragically, their mutual attraction was now able to be used as a means of domination (see Gen 3:16). Thus began the "war between the sexes," which neither side can ever win because every so-called victory merely worsens the loneliness. And children? Adam and Eve's eldest son killed his brother in a fit of jealousy, to the great shock and unspeakable horror of his parents.

We know all too well that these first manifestations of original sin repeat themselves daily in our society. Seduction, rape, adultery, divorce, domestic violence: many and bitter are the tragedies that play out in what God meant to be the privileged home of love, the relationship between man and woman. And the tragedy extends further. In his *Letter to Families* (1994), St. John Paul II asked, "Are children really a gift for

Because Adam and Eve wanted to decide for themselves what is good and evil rather than to discover and heed the reality of good and evil in the world as God created it, they alienated themselves from God and from each other.

their parents? A gift for society?" He answered in a provocative mode: "Apparently nothing seems to indicate this. The birth of a child means more work, new financial burdens and further inconveniences." And we all know that faced with that burden, millions of mothers and fathers since the legalization of abortion in 1973 have made the terrible and very wrong decision to kill their child. Indeed, as St. Mother Teresa declared in her Nobel Lecture (1979), "the greatest destroyer of peace today is abortion…because if a mother can kill her own child—what is left for me to kill you and you kill me—there is nothing between." Original sin began in a family, and its most harrowing manifestations today remain in that context.

Love is Demanding

As we saw in chapter 10 of the first volume of *Why Believe?*, Jesus presented himself as a prophet calling the People of God back to their Father and the true meaning of his Law. When the Pharisees challenged him, asking why his teaching about marriage was more demanding than Moses', he replied categorically, "For your hardness of heart Moses allowed you to divorce your wives, but from the beginning it was not so" (Mt 19:8). Jesus taught that marriage was for life. Whatever else we may want to say about this teaching, we must admit that it was consistent with the rest of his message. "Greater love has no man than this," he declared, "that a man lay down his life for his friends" (Jn 15:13). He then proceeded to do it. The Lord does not ask of spouses more than he was willing to give himself.

We need to be honest: love is demanding. Consider the Bible passage many couples choose to have read on their wedding day, the famous passage about love from St. Paul's first letter to the Corinthians:

> *Love is patient and kind; love is not jealous or boastful; it is not arrogant or rude. Love does not insist on its own way; it is not irritable or resentful; it does not rejoice at wrong, but rejoices in the right. Love bears all things, believes all things, hopes all things, endures all things* (1 Cor 13:4–7).

Any love which is "patient" and "kind," which "does not insist on its own way," and "endures all things" is a demanding love. But this is what makes loving relationships worthwhile: they challenge us to be better than we thought we could be. Love is not merely a warm feeling inside; it is a soul-expanding encounter. It is not chiefly about how you feel; it is about your care for the other person and how willing you are to be selflessly committed to him or her.

We must have the same perspective if we are to understand what it means to be a parent. If there is any relationship that most dramatically mirrors the self-emptying gift of Christ for his people, it is the love of parents for their children. How much would you have to pay someone to change dirty diapers and hold babies even when they throw up? And yet, out of deep and abiding (though imperfect) love, parents routinely perform selfless and often unpleasant tasks for their children. And then parents must spend years vigilantly protecting their children from harming themselves, whether it is by sticking their fingers in electrical sockets, pulling the ears of an ill-tempered dog, or, some years later, insisting they can drive after drinking too much. Few things teach more about the self-sacrifice of Christ than being a parent. Hence few things will make you more like Christ and require more of the grace of the Holy Spirit than becoming a parent. And few things will teach you more about God and the love he has for us!

Precisely because love is demanding, it can change us if we let it, if we dedicate ourselves to serving those we love. Yet this transformation can only come about if we give up our false ideas of freedom as freedom from all constraint and the freedom to do whatever we wish. Real freedom of the sort that allows us to love the way parents—when they are living up to the ideal—love their children requires an interior discipline. It is true: in a committed, loving relationship—in a family—we cannot simply give in to every passion and inclination that comes upon us. Loving others means putting the needs of others first. And this does not come easily or naturally.

If there is any relationship that most dramatically mirrors the self-emptying gift of Christ for his people, it is the love of parents for their children.

Along with the illusion that we can get the benefits of community without commitment, another lie our culture spreads is that something exists called "free love." This illusion is particularly dangerous, said St. John Paul II, "because it is usually suggested as a way of following one's 'real' feelings, but it is in fact destructive of love." To speak of "free love" is like insisting there is "free eating" or "free health." Who says, "I am going to consume this chocolate cake because I have to follow my 'real' feelings?" Who says, "I have to sit on this couch all day instead of exercising because I have to be true to the 'real' me?" If we love and care for ourselves, we will not follow these feelings, which can be very powerful. Instead, we make a judgment about what is best for us as whole and complete persons. However we may feel at the moment, what we really want is to be healthy and well. So we put certain strong desires aside and focus on those things which are in accord with what is really best for us. Should we not do the same when we love others?

Actions have consequences. And when we fail to act, there are other consequences. Physical health does not come without self-discipline, nor do healthy relationships. They require time, care, and attention. Without these, one's proclamation of love is but an empty sound one makes to keep the other person pleased or to keep benefits coming in one's direction. St. John Paul II exposed the contemporary practice of temporary marriage or marriage-with-divorce-at-will for what it is: an exploitation of human weakness that supplies "a certain veneer of respectability" to a situation in which "not all of the consequences are taken into consideration, especially when the ones who end up paying are, apart from the other spouse, the children, deprived of a father or mother and condemned to be in fact orphans of living parents."

Along with the illusion that we can get the benefits of community without commitment, another lie our culture spreads is that something exists called "free love."

"Orphans of living parents:" the phrase is terrifying. But what else can we call children of divorce deprived of a father or mother and who cannot be entirely sure of the dedicated care of either? The family, the communion of persons that is supposed to provide stability and loving care, becomes just another zone of conflict and uncertainty. A sober assessment of these modern challenges confirms the claim that love is demanding. Love can be hard. If selflessness were easy, everyone would be doing it. It does not come without sacrifice. But then, nothing worthwhile is achieved without discipline and the willingness to sacrifice.

Grandparents

In many cases, modern society has made marriage harder than it needs to be. We too often abandon couples precisely when they most need our help. In healthy societies, fathers, mothers, and children are embedded in a supportive social context that makes their sacrifices less burdensome and more meaningful. This support is not only an investment in child care or baby-sitting; it is also the help and encouragement to pass on wisdom and to establish good character.

The Church has long held that the family is, as St. John Paul II affirmed, "the first and basic expression of man's social nature." The family is not only an expression of our social nature, it is how young people are socialized. It provides their first lessons in how to live in community. But if these lessons are to be effective, the family—although at its core the communion between the parents and their children—must radiate outward to embrace the extended family, including aunts, uncles, nieces, nephews, and grandparents. By means of these interactions, the communion of the family becomes a communion of generations.

Young people can learn from their grandparents how to respect and live with older people. They can learn that aging is not a disease but instead the natural course of human development. And, contrary to what the media often portrays, they can learn that older people have a full life and wisdom that would be invaluable if received and acted upon. Rather than this healthy symbiosis between the generations, we are often left with the odd situation whereby we have too many elderly people left alone with no one to talk to except other elderly people, and, at the same time in other places, young people left alone with no one to talk to except other young people. Encouraged by the wisdom and teachings of the Church, we should find ways to bring those two groups together more often so that they might learn from each other.

We tend to think that families are just there, like the hair on your head. This is a consequence of the facile notion that love should be easy, natural, and not particularly demanding. Recall the friendships of pleasure and utility we discussed in volume 1. Someone who values his family only for what he can get out of it has instrumentalized his most fundamental relationships. Are we satisfied having only the kind of friend who likes us because of the fun or help we provide? The kind of friend who only returns our call when we have left a voicemail proposing to entertain him or her? Friendships and marriages can be mutually beneficial, but here is the paradox: only if both parties enter in selflessly and not for what they can get out of it. Good, solid friendships are built on trust that your friend will be there for you when you need him. The relationships between the members of a family are not the same as those between friends, although family members often will be friends, but the relationships in a family must be built on the same kind of trust.

Honor

The traditional way of stressing the importance of a foundation of trust is expressed in the 4th Commandment, "Honor your father and mother." This commandment is intended to help cement the interior unity and solidarity of the family. "In order to bring out the communion between generations," St. John Paul II explained,

> *the divine Legislator could find no more appropriate word than this:* "Honor" (Ex 20:12). Here we meet another way of expressing what the family is. This formulation does not exalt the family in some 'artificial' way, but emphasizes its subjectivity and the rights flowing from it. The family is a community of particularly intense interpersonal relationships: between spouses, between parents and children, between generations.

Honor is the outward show of respect that we give to a person in light of his or her relationship to us and to the community. All rise when the President of the United States walks into the room. Priests we call "Father" and nuns we call "Sister" or "Mother." By the gestures and words, we recognize the responsibility that these persons have taken within our community and toward us, and, however inadequately, we repay them for that gift.

We might have thought the commandment should read, "Love your father and mother." According to the Christian tradition, all seven commandments on "the second tablet" of the two that Moses brought down from Mt. Sinai deal with loving our neighbor as ourselves. This includes the commandment to "honor your father and mother." So there is a close connection here, as the Pope points out, between honor and love:

> The fourth commandment is closely linked to the commandment of love. The bond between "honor" and "love" is a deep one. Honor, at its very center, is connected with the virtue of justice, but the latter, for its part, cannot be explained fully without reference to love: the love of God and of one's neighbor. And who is more of a neighbor than one's own family members, parents and children? Honor is essentially an attitude of unselfishness. It could be said that it is a sincere gift of person to person, and in that sense honor converges with love.

An example of the attitude of unselfishness that the Holy Father commended here is the venerable custom of standing when an older person comes into a room in which one is sitting—by standing we stop whatever it is we were doing and signify that our attention is owed to the person who has just entered. It is a small repayment for the burdens that our elder has carried for us over the course of a long life.

It is the note of honor being something owed that we particularly need to consider if we are to understand how honor differs from love. We love our friends; we love our brothers and sisters. But the love we owe our parents is a different sort. Our friends are not responsible for us, for our care and upbringing. Our parents are. Honor should be seen as a two-way street because it makes demands on both parties. The children you babysit should honor you because you are honoring them, not only with your time and concern, but also because you are directing them for their benefit and good, not your own. But you must show them that this is what you intend by the way you act toward them. If by your actions you show that you are not responsible and do not really care, then you cannot expect them to honor you because you have not made yourself worthy of their honor. So too, as St. John Paul II taught, parents must "act in such a way that your life will merit the honor (and the love) of your children."

We might ask what it means for parents to merit the honor of their sons and daughters today. To merit the honor of their children, parents must treat their children according to what they deserve, as St. John Paul II put it, "simply because they are alive, because they are who they are," that is, as human persons who depend upon their parents for their every need. Because the lives of children are so fragile, it is imperative that we approach the duties of parents towards them from the point of view of what the children need and deserve, not from the point of view of what the adult or adults may happen to want.

The Church's teaching on this point is unswerving: children deserve both a mother and a father who live together and care for them as a faithful married couple. The principle or foundation of that teaching lies in the complementarity of the sexes and the truth that, as we read in the *Catechism*, "Being man or being woman is a reality which is good and willed by God" (CCC 369). By extension, we can affirm that being a father or being a mother is a reality which is good and willed by God. To say that children do not need mothers and the uniquely feminine contribution to their care that mothers offer is to undervalue women. To say that children do not need fathers and the uniquely masculine contribution to their care that fathers offer is to undervalue men. Either failure is a falling short with respect to the standard that both common human experience and the Word of God offer to us as normative. It is because of the complementarity of man and woman, therefore, that the Church holds that a same-sex relationship is not the moral equivalent of the marriage of a man and a woman.

It is worth remembering the old proverb that says, "The best way to love your children is to love their father or mother." "Honoring" fathers and mothers is not merely good advice for children; it is good advice for fathers and mothers. They pledged in their marriage vows to "love"

Children deserve both a mother and a father who live together and care for them as a faithful married couple.

The family is the social foundation of any just civilization, especially if it is to be a civilization of love.

and "honor" each other. The Church teaches that most of us get our first lessons on how to become unselfish, how to have true friendships, and how to live in community in the family. This will only happen, however, if all the members of the family—mothers, fathers, and children—are willing to put in the time to devote themselves to one another: men honoring their wives as mothers; women honoring their husbands as fathers; children honoring their parents, both father and mother; and parents meriting the honor of their children.

This kind of love is not easy. Love, as St. John Paul II admitted, "is not a utopia," rather "it is given to mankind as a task to be carried out with the help of divine grace." If we wonder why love seems so lacking in the world today, we might begin with the problems of families. But if we trace the lack of love to families, we will have to trace it back to its true source—in ourselves and our own refusal to love and honor each other. The family is the social foundation of any just civilization, especially if it is to be a civilization of love.

The Wedding at Cana

There is no way of getting around the fact that this sort of mutual, selfless love makes great demands upon mothers and fathers. But we know from his compassion to the Canaanite woman that Jesus viewed a parent's love for a child as something sacred and universal, a quality of soul worthy to be honored with a miracle of healing in spite of the objection of his disciples. We also know that Jesus blesses the mutual commitment of spouses to one another, a life-long commitment made at their wedding day, in spite of their uncertainty about the future and even perhaps their uncertainty about each other. There is no true love

without the possibility of disappointment. And so, to men and women considering marriage, St. John Paul II gave a stirring call to courage: "Do not be afraid of the risks!"

> *Everywhere the Good Shepherd is with us. Even as he was at Cana in Galilee, the Bridegroom in the midst of the bride and groom as they entrusted themselves to each other for their whole life, so the Good Shepherd is also with us today as the reason for our hope, the source of strength for our hearts.*

The Pope's reference here, of course, is to the occasion of Jesus' first miracle at the wedding feast at Cana (Jn 2) when the wine ran out. The feast was headed for an abrupt end. To prolong the festivity and save the hosts from embarrassment, Jesus turned six jars worth of water into the finest wine. As in the case of the Canaanite mother, so also at Cana, Jesus worked a miracle of compassion and generosity for the sake of the good of family life. Truly, our Good Shepherd loves families.

For most of us, marriage is not only the foundation of social life; it is not only the seed of future generations; it is the means of our salvation. We learn the faith first in our families. We learn first to love in our families. And we learn first what it means to sacrifice selflessly for others in our families. For Catholics, marriage is not merely an institution, like a partnership or legal corporation; it is a sacrament, an instrument or embodiment by which God imparts his grace and life to us. You eat the eucharistic bread, and Christ is present transforming you. You go to confession, and Christ is present there too, forgiving your sins and helping you to transform your life. You enter freely into a marriage and unite yourself "in one flesh" with your spouse, as Adam and Eve were originally "one flesh," and you need not be afraid: God will transform you as surely as he does in any of his other sacraments. You do your part, and God will do his.

Review Questions

1. The miracle of healing that Jesus performed at the plea of the Canaanite woman was a marvelous affirmation of his love and respect for mothers. Can you think of analogous episodes from your life that shed light on the love of mothers for their children? What general lessons could you share with the class that those experiences illuminate?

2. The Book of Genesis tells of both the creation of the first family and the damage caused by original sin. Do you see contemporary relevance to that story? Is that story in some sense the story of the human race in all ages, even in cases when families are intact and parents and children live in comparative harmony and peace?

3. A popular proverb suggests that "it takes a village to raise a child." Does the Catholic way of looking at the family support such a notion in whole or in part?

4. What does the commandment to "honor" your father and mother require, and how does that commandment challenge our contemporary culture?

5. St. John Paul II recognized that marriage can be challenging. What are some of the ways in which the Christian faith gives us hope that we will be able to meet this challenge?

Put Out Into the Deep

The passages from St. John Paul II reproduced in this chapter are quotations from his *Letter to Families* (1994), which is one of the most accessible and moving documents of his pontificate. In addition to commending this letter—really a small book—to your attention, we would encourage you to read one of his shorter documents, also offered from the depths of his heart, his *Letter to the Elderly* (1999).

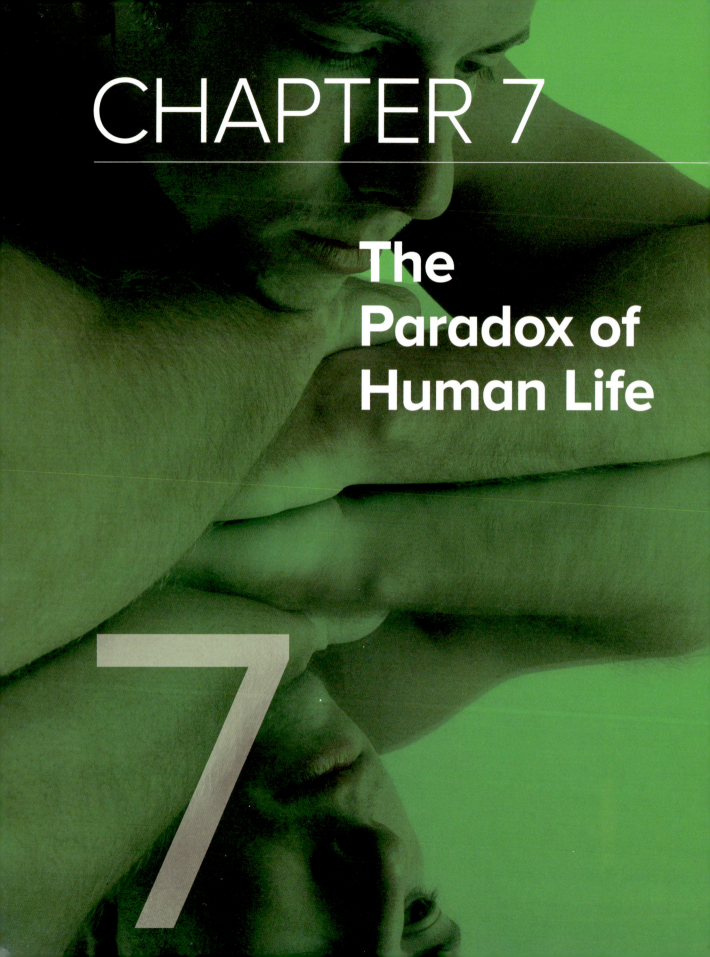

CHAPTER 7

The Paradox of Human Life

7

And the Lord sent Nathan to David. He came to him, and said to him, "There were two men in a certain city, the one rich and the other poor. The rich man had very many flocks and herds; but the poor man had nothing but one little ewe lamb, which he had bought. And he brought it up, and it grew up with him and with his children; it used to eat of his morsel, and drink from his cup, and lie in his bosom, and it was like a daughter to him. Now there came a traveler to the rich man, and he was unwilling to take one of his own flock or herd to prepare for the wayfarer who had come to him, but he took the poor man's lamb, and prepared it for the man who had come to him." Then David's anger was greatly kindled against the man; and he said to Nathan, "As the Lord lives, the man who has done this deserves to die; and he shall restore the lamb fourfold, because he did this thing, and because he had no pity." Nathan said to David, "You are the man" (2 Sam 12:1–7).

This interchange between the prophet Nathan and King David is one of high drama. David—chosen by God, anointed by Samuel, victorious over Goliath, successor to the throne of Saul—was guilty of a terrible crime. In a monstrous abuse of kingly power, he sent for Bathsheba, committed adultery with her, and then, with cruel calculation, sent her husband Uriah the Hittite to his death (see 2 Sam 11). And now the prophet of God risked his life by bravely confronting the sinner, drawing forth an expression of righteous anger and then turning the tables on him: "You are the man."

As the Russian novelist Alexander Solzhenitsyn (1918–2008) observed, the line dividing good and evil passes through "the heart of every human being." Nathan made David look within himself. When he did, David saw and deplored the evil he had done and so became the man he was meant to be, a man after God's own heart (see 1 Sam 13:14). He did not kill the prophet or make excuses; rather, he acknowledged his sin and spoke his famous act of contrition:

> Have mercy on me, O God,
>   according to your merciful love;
> according to your abundant mercy blot out my transgressions.
> Wash me thoroughly from my iniquity,
>   and cleanse me from my sin!
> For I know my transgressions,
>   and my sin is ever before me.
> Against you, you only, have I sinned,
>   and done that which is evil in your sight,
> So that you are justified in your sentence
>   and blameless in your judgment (Ps 51:1–4).

It would have been better had David not committed these heinous crimes. Yet he responded rightly when shown the evil of his ways. He recognized his sin, confessed it, and began his penance. David's fall and repentance is a precious testimony to the fundamental paradox in every human life: we choose what we think will make us happy, but we often choose the wrong thing. Because of the wound of original sin, we sometimes act irrationally and so become, as St. Augustine put it, a puzzle—or paradox—to ourselves.

No one sets out to be miserable. And yet many of us end up that way. Moreover, we disagree in our judgments about what can make us happy. As we have discussed in volume 1, some think wealth will make them happy, others fame, power, pleasure, romantic love, or authenticity. None of these things is necessarily bad or evil, but none can satisfy our desire for true, lasting happiness. The paradox of human life is that, although we choose what we do because we think it will make us happy, not everything we choose actually does. We often make mistakes; we fail to hit the mark. Indeed, the Greek word the New Testament authors used for "sin," *hamartia*, originally meant "to miss the mark." We are made for happiness, and although God has provided all that we need to be happy—at least, to be happy with the happiness of mortal beings on our earthly pilgrimage—we continue to choose things that diminish our happiness.

When we sin, we choose what is contrary to our flourishing and destructive of our happiness. Worse yet, the more we sin, the less we understand our own choices. And the more society is dominated by sin, the more powerful is its negative influence on its members and the more difficult it is to be good. Indeed, sometimes societies will turn against the virtuous and punish them precisely for being virtuous—for defending the innocent, for standing up against injustice, or even for worshipping God.

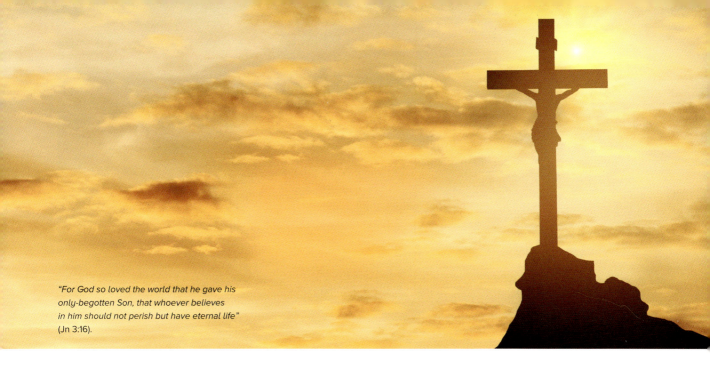

"For God so loved the world that he gave his only-begotten Son, that whoever believes in him should not perish but have eternal life" (Jn 3:16).

What is a Good God to Do?

When we turn away from God, the source of life and goodness, we bring upon ourselves darkness and unhappiness. What is God to do? Should he leave us in our sin? Will he just look on from a distance while we destroy each other and the world he created? No. God loves us, and he will never cease working to save us, to gather us to the home he has prepared for us. The Christian faith teaches that God became man so that man could be reconciled with God: "For God so loved the world that he gave his only-begotten Son, that whoever believes in him should not perish but have eternal life" (Jn 3:16). Christians are united in the faith that it is through Christ's death and resurrection that the reign of sin and death is conquered. What we need to examine now is how we participate in that saving act, how we cooperate with God so that we are changed and become the wise, free, and loving people he intends us to be.

God's Plan of Salvation

The authors of the books of the Bible, inspired by the Holy Spirit, believed that God had entered into history to save his people. He did not create the world like a big clock, set it running, and then go off somewhere to sleep. No, the God who revealed himself in the Old and

"Lord, now let your servant depart in peace, according to your word; for my eyes have seen your salvation" (Luke 2:29–30).

New Testaments is the Lord of History, not merely a passive observer of it. As we have noted in volume 1, the word "Christ"—Greek for "anointed" and so the equivalent of the Hebrew "messiah"—signifies that the New Testament authors saw Jesus as the fulfillment of the Old Testament promises. Christ himself declared that he did not come "to abolish the law and the prophets . . . but to fulfill them" (Mt 5:17).

Salvation history is a story: God is carrying out his plan to help restore and elevate mankind to the communion with him and with each other that he had intended from the beginning. Considering the part of that story which is the decisive event of the Old Testament, the Exodus, can help us to understand more deeply what Christ meant when he said that he came to fulfill the Law and the prophets. In the Exodus event, God saved his Chosen People from their slavery, rescuing them from Egypt by mighty miracles. Then he led them to a mountain in the wilderness where he made a covenant with them and gave them his Law. After his people spent forty years of wandering in the wilderness, God brought them into a land where they could live and worship freely, without fear. We call this the "Passover" event because the angel of death "passed over" the Chosen People who had marked their doorposts and lintels with the blood of a lamb, and also because the Israelites "passed over" the Red Sea while God held the waters back and were able to "pass over" the wilderness and across the Jordan River into the Promised Land.

When Catholics celebrate the Easter Vigil, the one Old Testament reading which is always a part of the liturgy is from the Book of Exodus. The Passover is also remembered earlier in the same liturgy, when the ancient *Exsultet* hymn is sung and the faithful hear these words:

> *These, then, are the feasts of Passover,*
> *in which is slain the Lamb, the one true Lamb,*
> *whose Blood anoints the doorposts of believers.*
>
> *This is the night,*
> *when once you led our forebears, Israel's children,*
> *from slavery in Egypt*
> *and made them pass dry-shod through the Red Sea.*
>
> *This is the night*
> *that with a pillar of fire*
> *banished the darkness of sin.*
>
> *This is the night*
> *that even now, throughout the world,*
> *sets Christian believers apart from worldly vices*
> *and from the gloom of sin,*
> *leading them to grace*
> *and joining them to his holy ones.*
>
> *This is the night,*
> *when Christ broke the prison-bars of death*
> *and rose victorious from the underworld.*

Jan Van Eyck, Adoration of the Mystic Lamb, c. 1430–32, Oil on panel. St. Bavos Cathedral, Gent, Begium.

Note the Old Testament imagery: the blood of the lamb on the doorposts, the crossing of the Red Sea, the pillar of fire that protected the Chosen People from their enemies at night. Why does the Church commemorate the Exodus on the night of Christ's resurrection?

The Church through her liturgy wants to emphasize Christ's teaching that he is the fulfillment of the Law and the Prophets. The Passover of the Chosen People is a sign, a type, a foreshadowing, of Christ's Passover from death to life. As the Israelite people were rescued from their slavery in Egypt, so we are rescued from our slavery to sin. It is Christ's blood that saves us from the angel of death. His body is the bread that nourishes us for the journey. He is the Light in the wilderness, leading and protecting us. And it is in his body and blood that the New Covenant is ratified, as the Old Covenant was ratified in the blood of sacrificed animals. What did the Chosen People receive as a sign to ratify the covenant? God gave them his Law. It is the same for Christians, only we receive the New Law of the Gospel together with the grace of the Holy Spirit that enables us to keep it.

Christ is the Light in the wilderness, leading and protecting us.

God's Gift of the Law

We may sometimes think of the moral laws of the Church as burdensome and annoying. We ought to imagine what our lives would be like without them. We might not like abiding by the law ourselves, but we would usually prefer that other people abide by it when dealing with us. The writers of the Old Testament spoke of the Law as God's greatest gift to them and the sign of his love. Moses told the people to keep the statutes and rules the Lord God commanded, "for that will be your wisdom and your understanding in the sight of the peoples, who, when they hear all these statutes, will say, 'Surely this great nation is a wise and understanding people'" (Deut 4:6). In the Psalms, we find celebrations of the Law. Psalm 19 begins with eloquent praise of God's creation—"The heavens are telling the glory of God; and the firmament proclaims his handiwork" (Ps 19:1)—but then turns to this passionate praise of God's Law:

> The law of the LORD is perfect,
>> reviving the soul;
> The testimony of the LORD is sure,
>> making wise the simple;
> The precepts of the LORD are right,
>> rejoicing the heart.
> The commandment of the LORD is pure,
>> enlightening the eyes (Ps 19:7–8).

Understanding the Law from this perspective helps to correct the notion that the commandments are merely an expression of God's will—he commands, and we must obey, because he is God, and we owe him our obedience. Although it is true we owe God everything, it is also true that he has made us to be free—to come to know the good and love it freely. Thus, a better way of understanding the Law is to say that it is not only an expression of God's will but also of his wisdom that guides us to achieve our proper flourishing.

God has revealed moral laws for our benefit because we are so often blinded by sin and so may not learn or discover them on our own.

We can think of the Law as if it were an owner's manual of the sort that often comes along with a power tool, as if the designer were sending along a guide to ensure that it functions well. Such a manual might contain the top ten "do's" and "don'ts." Do make sure that you use your new tool for the purpose it is designed for. Don't use the tool without engaging its safety features. And so on. God's Law is similar. He is our Creator and the Creator of the entire universe. So, he sends along a manual to help us live in his creation wisely and well. Do make sure that you are pursuing your proper goal. ("Love God" and "Love your neighbor as yourself.") Don't murder the innocent. Don't take what isn't yours. Do respect families, starting with your own father and mother, and don't do things which will destroy families, such as committing adultery.

In the Catholic tradition, we say that these precepts are principles of the natural law because they relate to human nature and we would all know them by human reason if our wills had not been damaged by the Fall. Because they can be known by reflection on human experience, these basic commandments can be found in philosophical and wisdom traditions around the world. But God has also revealed them for our benefit because we are so often blinded by sin and so may not learn or discover them on our own. In this capacity, the Law serves as a teacher.

Rules such as "Do not kill," "Do not steal," "Do not commit adultery," and "Rest from all work on the Sabbath" do not help God, they help us. They make community possible. The actions they encourage or prohibit have much to do with protecting and fostering the dignity of each person. For example, the fact that we all need friends is why Aquinas, following the scriptures, took gossip—a way of bearing false witness—to be such a grave evil, while so many of us imagine it to be a minor fault. As Aquinas argued, none of us can live without friends, but gossip destroys friendship and, therefore, is a terrible misdeed. Is it merely an expression of God's will, then, that he forbids such things, as though he were commanding us to stand on our left foot for two minutes each day? Or are these commandments instead expressions of a deep wisdom about the world and about the respect we owe to each person?

The theme of the Law as a source of wisdom is one we find repeatedly throughout the scriptures. Another reading for the Easter Vigil taken from the book of the prophet Baruch contains this beautiful praise of the wisdom of the Law. "Hear the commandments of life, O Israel; give ear, and learn wisdom!" (Bar 3:9). The prophet then asks where wisdom can be found and who can teach it? His answer is: "He who prepared the earth for all time filled it with four-footed creatures; he who sends forth the light, and it goes, called it, and it obeyed him, in fear; the stars shone in their watches, and were glad; he called them, and they said, 'Here we are!'" (Bar 3:32–34). The reading concludes with this tantalizing comment: "Afterward she [Wisdom] appeared on earth and lived among men. She is the book of the commandments of God, the law that endures forever. All who hold her fast will live" (Bar 3:37–4:1).

According to the plain sense of the text, God's Law "appeared on earth and lived with mankind" as the embodiment of God's wisdom. Early Christian interpreters of scripture saw in this passage a foreshadowing of Christ's coming. In chapter 10 of volume 1, we examined this idea when we said that the Old Testament prefigured the coming of the Messiah, a "shadow" pointing toward the reality of his coming. The Mosaic Law, then, has two major functions. First, it is a tutor. It teaches us the fundamental principles of the natural law, of good and evil, which we could and should know by reason alone, but often do not, because we are blinded by pride. Second, the Law prepares us and points us forward toward Christ. As the Epistle to the Hebrews explains, the sacrificial laws of the Old Testament foreshadowed the perfect sacrifice of Christ. The Law thus represented a "shadow of the good things to come" (Heb 10:1), that is, a foreshadowing of the New Law of the Gospel and the grace of the Holy Spirit.

As the Epistle to the Hebrews explains, the sacrificial laws of the Old Testament foreshadowed the perfect sacrifice of Christ. The Law thus represented a "shadow of the good things to come" (Heb 10:1), that is, a foreshadowing of the New Law of the Gospel and the grace of the Holy Spirit.

The Law, Love, and Authentic Freedom

Love and law are two things we do not usually associate with one another, but we find them linked repeatedly in the Old and New Testaments. One way this relationship is expressed is to say that the two tablets of the Law that Moses brought down from the top of Mt. Sinai represent the two fundamental commandments Jesus presents as a summary of the Law and the prophets: "Love God" and "Love your neighbor as yourself." The "first tablet" commandments are those having to do more specifically with the love of God: treat nothing else as your "god" except God; do not take the name of the Lord in vain (as, for instance, by pairing God's name with a curse word); and keep holy the Sabbath day. The "second tablet" commandments are the ones having to do more specifically with the love of neighbor: honor your father and mother; do not kill; do not commit adultery; do not steal; do not bear false witness; and do not covet your neighbor's wife or your neighbor's possessions. In artistic depictions of Moses and the two tablets, there are often three commandments on one tablet and seven on the other, rather than five on one and five on the other. This arrangement signifies that at the heart of the commandments are the two great commandments to love God and love your neighbor as yourself.

In his encyclical *Veritatis Splendor* (*The Splendor of Truth*), St. John Paul II commented on the passage in Genesis 2:16–17, in which Adam and Eve are forbidden to eat of the tree of the knowledge of good and evil. Why is it so wrong for them to eat of this tree? Is not the knowledge of good and evil something beneficial to us? The Pope answered: "With this imagery, Revelation teaches that the power to decide what is good and what is evil does not belong to man, but to God alone." Our task is to discover the objective good and evil that is in the world and then to act accordingly, not to imagine that we determine good and evil ourselves.

The Law teaches us wisdom about the world and about ourselves; it teaches us how we should live if we are going to flourish in the creation God has given us as the kind of creatures God has made us to be. Lions are not given the commandment not to kill, nor are sharks. The beasts simply act in accord with their created nature without thought or reflection. As human beings, we have an extra gift which is also our task: we must choose. Birds and beavers do not ask themselves how they should live. If they are healthy, birds fly and beavers make dams. Humans must ask themselves, "Am I living a good life? Am I acting in a way that is truly humane?" "Humane," of course, is the adjectival form of the noun "human." We call bad acts inhuman and good acts humane, suggesting that we somehow know that to live fully as a human means living a certain way: living like Mother Teresa or St. Martin de Porres and not like systematic murderers such as Adolph Hitler, Josef Stalin, or Mao Zedong.

The man is certainly free, inasmuch as he can understand and accept God's commands. And he possesses an extremely far-reaching freedom, since he can eat 'of every tree of the garden.' But his freedom is not unlimited: it must halt before the 'tree of the knowledge of good and evil,' for it is called to accept the moral law given by God. In fact, human freedom finds its authentic and complete fulfilment precisely in the acceptance of that law. God, who alone is good, knows perfectly what is good for man, and by virtue of his very love proposes this good to man in the commandments.

St. John Paul II, *Veritatis Splendor*, 35.

Just as the Law reveals to us wisdom about how we ought to live in God's creation and as the creatures he made us to be, so also does it teach us what it means to be authentically free. The Chosen People saw it that way. God's Law was his gift, preparing them to be a free people living in the land he had promised. When they violated the Law, they subjected themselves to slavery, spiritual slavery at first, but eventually actual, literal slavery. Even though the Israelites had a powerful memory of having escaped slavery in Egypt, where they had been forced to work building Pharaoh's palaces, this memory did not keep wealthy and powerful men among them from subsequently enslaving workers to build their own palaces.

The prophets came, then, to warn the Chosen People about their injustices, about hardening their hearts against their neighbor, especially the poor and weakest among them, about enslaving others physically and themselves spiritually. Did the wealthy and powerful men of affairs really believe that the God who created everything and who knows us better than we know ourselves could be hoodwinked by mere external observances? In Psalm 50, we read: "What right have you to recite my statutes, or take my covenant on your lips? For you hate discipline, and you cast my words behind you" (Ps 50:16–17). To "follow" the Law in the sense of using the Law to enslave others; to "follow" it, not gratefully, but grudgingly; to "follow" it not out of love for God and neighbor, but merely out of fear of getting caught: none of these schemes can fool God. And none can bring about the true human flourishing God intended when he gave us the Law.

The prophets came, then, to warn the Chosen People about their injustices, about hardening their hearts against their neighbor, especially the poor and weakest among them, about enslaving others physically and themselves spiritually.

God sent them into exile so that there they might rediscover themselves and who they were meant to be by renewing their devotion to justice and God's Law.

The Chosen People thought, "We are God's people, so God will protect us." And that was true, but not in the way they had presumed. God was more interested in protecting them from staining their hands with innocent blood and from staining their souls with evil acts than he was protecting them from punishment at the hands of their enemies. So, after warning them through his prophets, God sent them into exile so that there they might rediscover themselves and who they were meant to be by renewing their devotion to justice and God's Law. In all of this, although God at times seemed far from them, he was always with them, exhorting them, teaching them, and helping them, even in exile, most often through the words of his faithful prophets.

Because we suffer similar temptations, it is important for us to remember the stories of the Old Testament. Like the Chosen People, we often want to "free" ourselves from the moral law, the law which protects the dignity and integrity of all God's creatures, in an attempt to make creation "ours." We want a freedom which is freedom from all constraint—the freedom to do whatever we want, no matter how it affects others—instead of a freedom for the good: our good and the good of all.

"God's law," as St. John Paul II affirmed, "does not reduce, much less do away with human freedom; rather, it protects and promotes that freedom." He contrasted this view with "some present-day cultural tendencies" which assert that there is an inherent conflict between freedom and law, that there is not true freedom unless one is untethered by any constraints or any notions of right or wrong. "These doctrines," warned the Pope, "would grant to individuals or social groups the right to determine what is good or evil. Human freedom would thus be able to 'create values' and would enjoy a primacy over truth, to the point that truth itself would be considered a creation of freedom. Freedom would thus lay claim to a moral autonomy which would actually amount to an absolute sovereignty." Absolute sovereignty might sound good when you are asserting it for yourself. But what is the reality when others are asserting it against you?

> Person #1: *Please stop playing your loud music at 4 a.m. I am trying to sleep.*

> Person #2: *Hey, I am free to do what I want! I am my own boss. I don't take orders from anybody!*

Oh? You don't take orders or accept wise counsel from anybody? We should be honest with ourselves. More often the truth is that we take orders and advice from those who are strongest, wealthiest, and most powerful. God's Law, by contrast, was given to protect the weak and powerless, so that we would learn to order our lives with and for them. Without a common respect for the moral law, what tends to happen is that a society that should be based on mutual discipline and respect becomes a battleground where might makes right.

We are truly free when we accept God's wisdom and love and become wise and loving like God—not like the gods of the pagans and of our imaginations, who dominate by raw power, but like the God who is provident, who cares for us, and who chose freely to sacrifice himself on a cross to make us free. We cannot have the freedom of God if we do not accept the responsibility to use our freedom as he has, showing selfless love and care for his people and for the world.

We cannot have the freedom of God if we do not accept the responsibility to use our freedom as he has, showing selfless love and care for his people and for the world.

The Need for Grace

Now if we were perfect, we would accept the information about our good gained by our intellects from our experience of the world or from God's law and then act accordingly. We are, however, fallen creatures, and one result of the Fall is that we lack the basic integrity we once enjoyed. Our intellects have been darkened, and our wills are now in rivalry with our intellects. The result is that our ability to judge the good and do it freely has been severely compromised—just as we saw in the case of David's sin against Bathsheba and Uriah.

Although God teaches the basic principles which should govern how we live if we are to flourish, it turns out that, even when we know the right thing to do, we do not always have the will to do it. St. Paul complains, "For I do not do the good I want, but the evil I do not want is what I do" (Rom 7:19). This is, once again, the great paradox of human life. It is not wrong for God to teach us by means of his Law. He has given us minds, and we should use them. It is right that we should try to understand as well as obey. But often the understanding of the intellect is not enough, especially if the action we are contemplating is dangerous or hard. How often have you said to yourself, "I know I should study," but found that this knowledge did not move you to actually study?

St. Paul suggested another example, with which many of us will sympathize. He knows that the Law says, "Do not covet." But does knowing this keep him (or us) from coveting? Sadly, no. Is the law sinful? No. But we are. St. Paul writes: "sin, finding opportunity in the commandment, wrought in me all kinds of covetousness." Hence "the very commandment which promised life proved to be death to me" (Rom 7:8–10). And so when we hear the law, because it is framed in view of the sort of person we want to become—virtuous, courageous, compassionate, and caring—rather than the person we are now—selfish, perhaps a bit cowardly, someone who gives up and sells out when the going gets tough—the moral law will often seem strange and alien to us, not a help but a burden. It can even prod us to greater sin. If you want people to do something, often the best way is to forbid them from doing it. If you say to your younger brother or sister, "I forbid you to pick up this baseball," you can be fairly sure that, whether they ever wanted to pick up that baseball before, they will most certainly want to pick it up now. Whether they do depends upon their respect for you, but the rule by itself can goad people on. This, however, is something happening in us; it is not the fault of the Law itself.

In Christ, God has saved us from our sin and given us the way to happiness and salvation. "I came that they may have life," Jesus said, "and have it abundantly" (Jn 10:10). The moral teachings of the Catholic faith are preeminently good, but by themselves they do not suffice, because even when we know the right thing to do, we often still cannot do it. God's law must be written not only on our minds, but also in our hearts—indeed, inscribed in our very bodies.

How is that "interior writing" to be achieved whereby we become one with the law of love? Along with giving us the gift of his law, God helps us to live what the law instructs by sending the gift of his Holy Spirit, by whom "God's love has been poured into our hearts" (Rom 5:5). The sort of discipline by which that charity of the heart, infused by the Spirit, radiates out to envelop us fully—mind, spirit, passions, and body—is achieved by developing the virtues: both the cardinal virtues (prudence, justice, fortitude, and temperance) and the theological virtues (faith, hope, and charity). It is for this reason that grace and the virtues must be the subjects of our next two chapters.

An Ancient Testimony to the Reality of Original Sin

Video meliora, proboque, deteriora sequor.

I see and approve the better; I follow the worse.

Ovid (43 B.C. to A.D. 17), *Metamorphoses*

Review Questions

1. What is the fundamental paradox of every human life? How have you seen this paradox play out—in general terms—in your own life and the lives of your friends and family members?

2. Would it be possible to retell the Gospel as the romantic adventure story of a divine suitor who has been spurned by his love? Can you think of movies or books that have in some way or another retold the Gospel in just that way? What lessons can we learn from trying to answer these questions?

3. What do you think about receiving the Ten Commandments as an expression of God's wisdom and love?

4. When does the Law become a burden? Answer with examples from literature and film.

5. What does it mean to write the New Law of the Gospel into our hearts, minds, and bodies? Can you give examples from the lives of the saints that illuminate this way of conceiving of the Christian faith?

Put Out Into the Deep

Shakespeare's *Hamlet* is a notoriously difficult play to interpret, and reasonable people can disagree about its meaning. It is, however, an eloquent and gripping drama. We suggest that you and your friends get together with a copy of Prince Hamlet's "To be or not to be" soliloquy and argue about its meaning. Whatever you decide, you will be confronting the paradox of human life.

CHAPTER 8

Law and Love

And as he was setting out on his journey, a man ran up and knelt before him, and asked him, "Good Teacher, what must I do to inherit eternal life?" And Jesus said to him, "Why do you call me good? No one is good but God alone. You know the commandments: 'Do not kill, Do not commit adultery, Do not steal, Do not bear false witness, Do not defraud, Honor your father and mother.'" And he said to him, "Teacher, all these I have observed from my youth." And Jesus looking upon him loved him, and said to him, "You lack one thing; go, sell what you have, and give to the poor, and you will have treasure in heaven; and come, follow me" (Mk 10:17–21).

The young man, as we know, did not accept Jesus' invitation because his love for his possessions was stronger than his love for God and neighbor. This sorrowful episode points to the greatest limitation of the Law: it is an external mover, not internal. People may observe the Law externally while remaining unmoved and uncaring in their hearts. The Law is good as a teacher. It can be a source of valuable wisdom. The Law is less effective at motivating our will or helping us to discipline our passions and appetites. The Law is written on our minds, not always on our hearts. Even when we know the right thing to do, we nevertheless may fail to do it.

The Law of Fear and the Law of Love

In order to appreciate how the limits of law can be addressed, let us return to an example from the last chapter. If you have a prized baseball, and you leave a note for your younger brothers and sisters which says, "Do not touch this, you little twerps, or I'll kill you!" they might obey you from fear or, goaded by your note into the very act you have forbidden, they might do it anyway, figuring you will not see or notice. But it is safe to say that your siblings would be more likely to comply with your wishes if you were to say to them in person: "Hey, guys, this baseball is very meaningful and important to me. It was signed by every member of the Cubs World Series team, and it was the last thing Grandpa gave me before he died. So, you can look at it, but please don't pick it up and throw it around like every other baseball, okay?" The personal touch makes all the difference. You have appealed not to their fear, but to their love for you and for your grandpa. And you have treated them with dignity by believing them capable of understanding the reason for the rule.

When we hear the words "Do not steal," what they signify needs to be written not only in our minds, but also in our hearts, especially if we are freely to choose what the Law requires. If you see a computer sitting on a desk, and no one is around, you might refrain from stealing it because you fear getting caught and punished. Or you might say to yourself: "I can't steal this computer because it belongs to someone else. People have all sorts of important things on their computers: papers they are writing, reports they have to give, pictures of their friends and family, important email messages they need to answer. If I lost my computer, it would be devastating to me. I would not want to do anything like that to anyone else." In the first case, the law for you is a law of fear. In the second, it is a law of love.

When you focus only on the computer, the commandment "Do not steal" becomes hazy and abstract. "Why should I not have this nice computer?" you may ask. When you start thinking more about what your theft would do to the person who owns the computer—she might lose all her family photos—then the real purpose of the Law comes into focus. It is only when we do things out of a deep respect for the dignity of others—out of love, rather than merely out of fear—that we can truly be said to do things freely. And to love God and our neighbor freely, treating God's creation, creatures, and our neighbor with the respect they deserve simply because they deserve it and not because we fear what might happen to us otherwise, is to live according to the Law as God intended and Christ modeled for us. His Spirit was entirely in accord with the Law and with the will of his Father.

You can follow the Law out of fear or our of love. God has given us the Law to perfect us in love. But we should be honest with ourselves: given our fallen state, we are more often motivated by fear than by love. Often enough we need the Law not merely to teach us, but to restrain us—to keep us from doing things contrary to the respect we owe others and the standards we must uphold if we are to become the people we say we want to be.

When you focus only on the computer, the commandment "Do not steal" becomes hazy and abstract. "Why should I not have this nice computer?" you may ask.

And so we are going to establish a school for the service of the Lord. In founding it we hope to introduce nothing harsh or burdensome. But if a certain strictness results from the dictates of equity for the amendment of vices or the preservation of charity, do not be at once dismayed and fly from the way of salvation, whose entrance cannot but be narrow (Mt 7:14). For as we advance in the religious life and in faith, our hearts expand and we run the way of God's commandments with unspeakable sweetness of love. Thus, never departing from his school, but persevering in the monastery according to his teaching until death, we may by patience share in the sufferings of Christ (1 Pet 4:13) and deserve to have a share also in his kingdom.

St. Benedict *(ca. 480—ca. 545), Rule,* prologue

And yet love is not something that can be commanded; it is something given and received freely. You can state honestly that love is needed— the love of God and neighbor—but it does not work to command someone, "Love me," or point to someone else and say, "Love that man sitting over there—right now!" St. John tells us that we love because God has loved us first (see 1 Jn 4:19). This is why the great Exodus came before the giving of the Law at Mt. Sinai. God did not say, "If you can obey these commandments, then I'll rescue you from Egypt." Instead, he rescued them first so that they would understand that the Law is the gift of a God whose steady intention is to love and care for them. So too, we noted in the previous chapter that Christ's sacrifice on the cross is the deepest expression of God's love for us. That sacrifice—together with the Law which God gave to his people and Christ confirmed—is not at odds with the loving act by which he created the world; it is rather a reaffirmation and glorification of it. Like the Chosen People, we can gratefully receive God's Law as an expression of his loving will to save us from our own ignorance and sinfulness, and so come to understand St. John's teaching that "perfect love casts out fear" (1 Jn 4:18).

Moral Development

What significance does this perspective have for our understanding of the moral life? Let us say for the moment that you resolve to make a concerted effort to become the kind of person you want to be in your most reflective moments. A first step would be say to yourself, "I cannot steal; I should not lie; I have to resist gossiping because it is a form of bearing false witness; and, I need to stop coveting."

Coveting? Yes. To want to possess as your own something that belongs to someone else is considered a problem in many societies. In some Asian cultures, if you look admiringly at someone's jacket or ring and praise it, he will take it off and give it to you to keep you from coveting it. You now are required to give him a gift of equal or greater value, but the lesson is: Do not covet! In other societies, to look covetously at someone's possessions is interpreted as "giving the evil eye." Your coveting is interpreted as a curse. You might not have thought "Do not covet" was a principle of the natural law applicable to all people, but a study of other cultures suggests it is.

So, you resolve to stop coveting the things which other people have and you lack. Fine so far. But you will likely find, as St. Paul did, that the rule which says "Don't covet" is not solving your problem. You are still coveting. Sometimes worse than before. Now what? One temptation will be to give in. "If I just release this pressure, then I will feel better." That is how we often fool ourselves. The idea is that we are something like a steam engine which builds up pressure, at which point the best thing to do is to let off some steam by opening the valves and letting it out. This was a popular image in the late nineteenth and early twentieth centuries when steam engines were common and people enjoyed comparing themselves to them. Each age has its preferred images, images which have benefits and drawbacks, and our age is no different. These images can be helpful, but they can also falsify a more complicated reality, as this one does.

The idea is that we are something like a steam engine which builds up pressure, at which point the best thing to do is to let off some steam by opening the valves and letting it out. These images can be helpful, but they can also falsify a more complicated reality.

The consequences of giving in to the temptation to sin go far beyond the effect of freeing ourselves from the pressure of temptation (if that in fact occurs). Both the wisdom of the ages and modern neuroscience tells us that when we give in, for instance, to viewing pornography, then what we have done is set up a new neural pathway, or reinforced an old one, which will make it more likely that we will engage in that activity in the future, not less. What we need to understand is that desires, like emotions, come in waves. Sometimes the crest of the wave is high, and it seems irresistible. But experience suggests that the wave will pass. Resistance is not futile.

But resistance is not enough. Living a life painfully resisting temptations is not what God has in mind for us. God does not want us to live like the charioteer in Plato's *Phaedrus*, exerting ourselves terribly from morning to night and alternately scourging our passions and giving them free rein. No, God wants us to be free and to choose the good with ease and joy. How is that to be achieved? If we check in again with advances in modern neural science, we learn of the value of developing habits. In basketball, you shoot foul shots over and over again until you can make them with ease. In soccer and hockey, goalies spend hours having the best players kick balls or shoot pucks at them until they have the skill they need to protect the goal. You or I might, with luck, block one shot on goal. But to be able to do it consistently, in all different circumstances, playing against really skilled strikers? That requires skill.

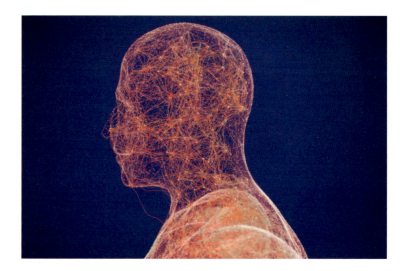

Modern neuroscience tells us that when we give in, what we have done is set up a new neural pathway, or reinforced an old one, which will make it more likely that we will engage in that activity in the future, not less.

Skills and Virtues

When someone has a skill, it often involves a remarkable fusion of the mental, emotional, and physical. A great soccer player knows the game and is in control of his emotions, being neither too nervous nor too relaxed, being able to keep him or herself at just that edge of emotional sharpness without losing composure. Great players often say about major sports events that a large part of the competition is mental and psychological. This can seem counter-intuitive at first because so much of what these players do is supremely physical. But a truly skilled player brings together all three in a unified whole.

Virtues are like these athletic skills but are even more powerfully integrated into our character. When someone has a virtue, she certainly must have the knowledge required to put it into practice, but she must also consistently act in accord with that virtue. Skills lack that requirement. I can be perfectly able to write in accord with the rules of grammar and simply be too lazy to do so—without undermining my possession of the skill. If, however, I am usually able to restrain myself in front of a large plate of cookies, but sometimes inexplicably eat uncontrollably to the point of making myself ill, then I do not yet have the virtue of temperance. Moral virtue is chiefly in the will. Skills, to the contrary, are chiefly in the intellect.

Virtues are similar to skills in the way that we gain them: through repeated practice. Some lucky people are naturally talented. But even naturally talented people need to practice. Great piano players practice scales for hours. Great writers write every day, whether or not they feel inspired, just as great potters sit at their potter's wheel throwing pot after pot, learning how to perfect their craft. Similarly, some people may seem to be naturally virtuous thanks to a sunny disposition. In truth, however, virtue is not innate. And those of us with sunny dispositions should be the first to admit that in the face of a severe test of character we must still choose to do the right thing.

How, then, do we become generous, honest, and compassionate? We start the way we started learning tennis, by hitting balls against a wall, or learning carpentry by hammering our first nail. We start small, with simple things, and then we continue to challenge ourselves to become better. As we discussed in chapter 2, it is rare that anyone would want to grow up to be a lying, cheating scoundrel. Many students want to grow up and act differently from the way they see many adults act. But we fool ourselves if we imagine, "I will cheat on this exam now and lie to my parents repeatedly, but when the critical moment comes and someone tries to bribe me when I am in a public office, I will remain honest and refuse the money." Wait a minute. You are saying that you will cheat on an exam when the stakes and rewards are relatively low, but will then be able to resist the temptation to cheat later in life when the stakes and rewards are very high? That would be like a mediocre player insisting, "I never practice, but I will certainly be great when the big game comes." It seems unlikely, to say the least. Those who cannot be trusted in small affairs can rarely be trusted in great ones.

Just like a great soccer player or artist, virtue will grow and develop and bear fruit the more you practice.

If you want to be a compassionate, caring person, you are going to have to act that way from now on.

If you want to be an honest person, there really is no shortcut: you are going to have to start acting like an honest person now. If you want to be a compassionate, caring person, you are going to have to act that way from now on. You may not yet be a compassionate, caring person any more than you are a great artist or great player when you imitate what the great artists or great players do. But you need to make a start. And with practice, the skill or the virtue will grow and develop and bear fruit. Instead of having to think every time you take a step dancing, the dancing becomes easier, then joyful. And when you have the skill, you can really be creative, knowing how to act in any difficult situation. Some actors are so skilled at their craft and so in tune with the play they are performing in that they can cover for other actors missing a line or even, in some cases, cover adequately for a technical glitch which causes the actors on stage to miss an entire scene. You may have met people who are so skilled at dealing with people that they seem to be able to handle any difficult social situation with kindness and grace. No one leaves his house feeling bad or unwelcome. Some people have natural talents in this area. But you should not mistake this and believe that everyone who is gracious was born that way. Most people had to learn. They had to watch others who were kind and gracious in this way, and they had to work at it themselves, making mistakes, and then learning from their mistakes.

So, you begin. You start with small things, simple things. Being honest with others. Never cheating a checkout clerk if you are given more change than you were owed. Seeking to see issues and conflicts from the other person's perspective. You know people who are living the kind of life you say you want to live. Watch what they do. Listen to what they say. Let their actions be a guide to your own. You will have to live your own life, and your challenges will never be quite the same as anyone else's, just as the championship game you play in will not be quite the same as the one LeBron James or Michael Jordan played in. But great players almost always have learned from watching other great players. So too you must learn from watching great people. That is why the Church gives us the saints.

At first, it will be hard. You will not always feel like you want to be honest or compassionate or selfless or just. You will probably feel like you want to throw it all aside and just do whatever you want. So, at first, we pretend that we are like the great men and women we admire, so that, in time, with practice, we actually become like them, but like them in our own way. Our ancestors had a clever saying that captured those first steps in becoming a better person: "hypocrisy is the compliment that vice pays to virtue." Our maxims today are shorter and more direct: "fake it 'til you make it."

Two Kinds of Virtues

Plato and the tradition of the virtues that follows him taught that there are four essential virtues: prudence, justice, courage, and temperance. These are the "cardinal" virtues from the Latin word for "hinge," because the various minor virtues "turn," or depend, upon them. In the Christian tradition, we add to these four virtues the three theological virtues of faith, hope, and charity. These are actually the most powerful virtues of all because they are the direct result of the gift of divine grace in the soul. Their presence in turn purifies and strengthens the soul in such a way that the otherwise natural virtues of temperance, courage, justice, and prudence are elevated and perfected as well. Let us now consider that dynamic, or power, of grace.

Above we mentioned that you might resolve to stop coveting but, having tried for a while, find that you are still failing. Many people who go to confession regularly find to their dismay that they are repeatedly confessing many of the same faults. If you find that this is the case, do not despair. Have hope. But on what basis can you hope? Experience has shown that you fail over and over. What makes you think it will be different in the future? What gives you hope? Is it faith in yourself?

People sometimes say, "You have to believe in yourself." This is not untrue, but it may not be entirely helpful since you are the one who has failed again and again, and you may not have much reason to believe in yourself. Can you have faith in other people? Can you have faith in the world? It is difficult to see how you can.

For Christians, hope comes from faith in God's power to transform us because this is what he said he came to do. Our hope is based on our faith in God's love and care. If properly understood, however, our faith in God is not contrary to believing in ourselves. God's grace does not replace nature; it perfects it. In human affairs, if your mother writes your essay, then you do not. If you write your essay, your mother does not. The two are mutually exclusive. But God's relationship with his creation is not like that. God can operate in and through you. This is what it means to be a member of the Body of Christ. The word here is not member as in member of a committee. The members of your body are your eyes, ears, arms, legs, hands, and feet. This is why St. Paul can say that, although there are many members in the Church, we are one body, the Body of Christ. Using a different metaphor, Christ says that he is the vine and we are the branches. His life flows through us; we are attached to him. That life is given by the Holy Spirit, who spreads charity abroad in our hearts.

For Christians, hope comes from faith in God's power to transform us because this is what he said he came to do.

Accepting Love

Have you ever noticed how much easier it is to do the things you know you should when you believe you are loved? Perhaps you have never experienced this yourself but have noticed it in friends. They seem so comfortable with themselves and others, and when you meet their family, you understand why. The loving environment they have supporting them enables them to live fully and with joy. Not everyone with a loving family is empowered, however. Some people have a hard time believing or accepting that they are loved. They imagine they are not worthy of love. But this is to make a crucial mistake. No one earns love. Love is always a free gift. A young man can be as nice as he can possibly be to a young woman, yet this will not make her love him. This can be tragic, but it is true. He cannot by his actions earn her love. He can, however, do certain acts which communicate his admiration for her so long as he does not expect that he will earn her love.

And so too with God. We do not earn God's love with our acts. Rather, we learn to act as we should because we know God loves us. But first we must believe in God's love. This is why faith precedes hope, and faith and hope precede love. But love is what drives the engine of the moral life.

Why not steal? Why not become a criminal? Why not sell drugs? Because these actions are bad? That is one answer, but it is insufficient. People simply ask, "What makes these actions 'bad'?" Or they make jokes. "Oooh, am I doing something 'bad'?" as though the thing we were talking about was something merely mischievous rather than harmful or even deadly to others. A better answer to the question "Why not steal?" is that you owe it in love to respect the dignity and worth of the people from whom you would be stealing. We owe our neighbor—all our neighbors—the same treatment we would wish to receive from them. And every sin, no matter how small it may seem, hurts us or hurts a neighbor, a neighbor who would be as angered and sorrowful as we would be at experiencing injustice. The question is whether we can start seeing others the way God sees them—as infinitely important, infinitely valuable, even with all their faults and sins, just like we are.

At the heart of the Law is love. Love is what motivates us to restrain ourselves in certain ways and to exert ourselves beyond what is strictly required. Love is what should motivate the discipline it takes to develop the skills and virtues. When you love basketball or love music, you practice and practice because developing excellence in the skill gives you joy; it makes you more like the basketball players or musicians you admire. When you love others, you begin by obeying the Law (no fouling other players or sour notes) and practicing the virtues every day: no lying, no gossip, not giving in to your selfishness or your appetites every time they flare up, honesty with others, small acts of kindness or compassion, patience, going out of your way to help.

Starting Small, Starting Now

You do not start playing basketball in the Final Four. So too you generally do not start developing the virtues by feeding all the starving children in sub-Saharan Africa. Someday, you may play in the Final Four, and someday, you may be called upon to feed the poor in Africa. For now, you might start by showing kindness and understanding to that strange, odd neighbor down the street whom everyone else shuns or by helping other people in your community. Right now, there might be very little you can do to help people half a world away, except pray for them. And you should. But right now, today, you can help people in your community, in your classroom, and in your own house. It may not be dreamy and romantic, as in the movies, but truth be told, helping starving children in Africa or homeless people on the streets of New York is never as gloriously romantic as the movies suggest it would be either. A great deal of what it means to love is to get used to putting in the work. It begins with discipline and humility. You learn the skill; you take the coaching; you listen to what people who know more than you have to teach. Eventually you will have mastered the skill or acquired the virtue and will take great joy in it.

The first time you get a base hit in baseball feels wonderful. But that magic feeling will not last. To get the joy of the game, you need to practice and play, and sometimes lose, and pick yourself up and play some more. So too, the first time you serve soup to homeless people in a soup kitchen might make you feel wonderful. But the feeling rarely lasts. The real joy comes after you have gotten past the fake romance, seen the lives of these people fully and honestly, and learned how to be a help to them in their trouble. If this were easy, everyone would be doing it. If love were easy, the world would be full of it.

While it is true that the Law can become a burden and the enemy of love, this is due mostly to our fallenness. We human beings have amazing ingenuity when it comes to turning good things to bad ends. We split the atom, and what do we do with that knowledge? Almost immediately we harness it to make the most powerful bomb ever devised. It would be ungrateful, and more than a little foolish, for us to blame God for making atoms or giving us minds with which to discover how to split them. We could use that knowledge and that power to benefit others (as we have since then). The discipline we give ourselves and encourage in our communities is needed if we are not to become selfish maximizers of our own self-interest. The virtues begin in love, the love of the person and the desire to serve the person's good, but they must spread out from there until they envelop the entire person: mind, heart, and body.

Review Questions

1. What are the limits of law as a force for good in our lives, and why is law nevertheless a great help to us? Can you supply an example of a law or regulation or common practice that was helpful to you in becoming a better student, athlete, artist, or employee?

2. How are skills and virtues alike? How are they different? Which kind of quality seems to be harder to gain?

3. Does it seem to you that the theological and cardinal virtues name real human qualities that a person either has or does not have but can nevertheless be measured by? Or are they more like the various optional skills and abilities that we gain along life's way, such as speaking this or that foreign language, playing this or that instrument, and being good at this or that academic subject? Defend your answer.

4. How would a Christian answer the question, "Why not steal?"

5. Discuss the paradox that love, though difficult to practice, brings great joy to the person who loves well.

Put Out Into the Deep

One of the most important texts in the tradition of the virtues is the *Rule* written by St. Benedict of Nursia (ca. 480—ca. 545). This brief compilation of rules for monks is in part a handbook for an abbot and in part a spiritual guide for the monk. It is so full of wisdom and interwoven with passages from Sacred Scripture that it has been treasured as spiritual reading by monks and laity alike. The text is available online at *osb.org/rb*. We recommend that you choose a chapter from the *Rule* whose title intrigues you and read it in light of this chapter's discussion of law and love, asking yourself how the rule or practice in question could help you in your quest for happiness.

CHAPTER 9

Faith and the Virtues

And they came to Bethsaida. And some people brought to him a blind man, and begged him to touch him. And he took the blind man by the hand, and led him out of the village; and when he had spit on his eyes and laid his hands upon him, he asked him, "Do you see anything?" And he looked up and said, "I see men; but they look like trees, walking." Then again he laid his hands upon his eyes; and he looked intently and was restored, and saw everything clearly" (Mk 8:22–25).

The miracles of Jesus are marvelous in many ways and offer lessons suited to various situations in life. As we discussed in chapter 1, Jesus more than once restored sight to the blind and used physical blindness as a metaphor for interior and moral blindness. In this miracle, we see Jesus heralding the sacraments of the Church. The people of Bethsaida had faith that Jesus' touch would heal, but instead of responding to their plea in the terms they had framed it—they "begged him to touch him"—he used his saliva to convey the grace of healing. Not only does the touch of Jesus heal, but the water from his mouth heals, just as the water of our baptismal fonts now heals our sinfulness. Moreover, he did not heal all at once, but in two stages, so that century after century of Christians would know that our conversion and growth in holiness does not typically happen all at once, but takes multiple touches from Jesus: in the sacraments, in the graces he provides in prayer, in the illumination he gives in his Word, and in the help provided by the counsel and example of other people.

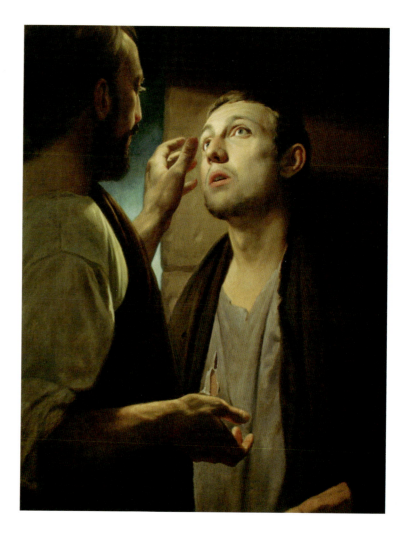

Andrey Mironov, Christ and the Pauper, Healing of the Blind Man. *2009. Oil on canvas. Private collection.*

Throughout this second volume of *Why Believe?,* we have been concerned with the question of our happiness. We know that we will be made happy in this life only to the extent to which we become the kind of person we want to be and the kind of person others need us to be: trustworthy, kind, thoughtful, helpful, in a word, reliable. We have also seen that the way the Church talks about human character is in terms of the virtues. Now it is time to address the virtues directly and to learn more about prudence and justice, the two moral virtues that are most important for our daily lives. Yet we have also seen that the road to happiness begins with the recognition of our sinfulness and lack of virtue. And so, we are confronted with a great puzzle. If we are not yet virtuous, then we do not have the desires of a virtuous person. But the virtues are gained only by doing the virtuous deeds that we do not yet fully want to do. How can we break into this circle? Aristotle thought that if people are not raised the right way in a community that nourishes the virtues they will not develop them. On this basis, some of us could look at ourselves and say, "Well, I guess I missed my chance." Is that the whole story? No. The Christian message is that there is hope, a hope born of faith in God's love.

A Faith that Inspires Hope

What drives the engine of personal growth and moral reform? The Christian answer is love: God's love for us. We know that the love of friends and family can empower us to be and to do more than we thought possible. To an outsider, the prospect of taking care of a severely disabled child may look daunting, perhaps even impossible. Yet if you ask the family members of this child, "How do you do it?," they will look at you in bewilderment and say, "He is my brother. I love him." That is all the explanation they need.

How is love to be measured? How can it be demonstrated by logical proof? Love is not contrary to reason, but it is one of those features of the world that we have a hard time putting into words. Often the writers who come closest to expressing it adequately are poets, playwrights, and novelists, not theologians or psychologists. If you want to understand human love, you do not read this book, you read the novels of Jane Austen or the poetry of John Donne, or you watch the plays of William Shakespeare. Here we talk about love. The poets portray it. And scripture explains it. Love, immeasurable, ineffable, is the object of faith.

Faith is reason reaching out beyond itself to realms it cannot capture in its usual categories. "Faith and reason," St. John Paul II memorably declared, "are like two wings on which the human spirit rises to the contemplation of truth; and God has placed in the human heart a desire to know the truth—in a word, to know himself—so that, by knowing and loving God, men and women may also come to the fullness of truth about themselves" (*Fides et Ratio*, 1). The "truth about ourselves" is that

For many people, faith in a God of love is a prerequisite for believing in human love.

we are made for love by God, who, we learn in the Gospels, is love. The nihilism of a Friedrich Nietzsche does have a partial truth to it, in that we have indeed been created by God "from nothing" (*ex nihilo*) and, when we turn away from the love of God and others, we return to nothing. If we are not anchored firmly in love, it becomes difficult to avoid the conclusion that life is meaningless. It is when we are giving and receiving in love that the temptation to nihilism seems most absurd and least threatening. It is when we are most obsessed with ourselves that the specter of meaninglessness looms large.

We need faith, then, to believe in love. We need faith to believe that love is possible in a world where we violate the law of love as often and as pitilessly as we do. Thus, for us, faith must also be faith in the possibility of forgiveness and reconciliation. Faith in a God of love is not contrary to faith in human love. Indeed, for many people, faith in a God of love is a prerequisite for believing in human love. It is easy to become cynical, especially when people who say they love you disappoint you, as they sometimes will. The first question we must ask ourselves, then, is not whether we believe in God; the first question is whether we believe in love. Because if we cannot believe in love, then we will never believe in a God of love. And that is the God in whom Christians believe.

Can we say "I believe in love" in a world which seems unloving? For this we need faith, the kind of faith which generates hope for something more, something better, which opens the door to the acceptance of love.

We love because God has loved us first (see 1 Jn 4:19). If we have to say, "I am not sure about 'God,' but I do believe that my mother loves me and that I love her, and that I love my friends, and that building these relationships, sharing life with these people, and expanding our circle of love to include as many people as possible in the communion we enjoy is what makes life meaningful," then this is a good first step. Grace does not violate nature, it perfects it. God's love is not mutually exclusive with human love. The more we enter into true human love (as opposed to the selfish dispositions we often call love), the closer we get to understanding the God of love.

The first step in the moral life is to care enough to make the sacrifices necessary to set out on the road to developing the virtues. So, we begin with faith—faith which gives birth to hope and love. Caring enough to make these sacrifices is made possible when we accept God's love for us.

Christians believe that God expressed this love for us by becoming man and suffering and dying on a cross. As St. Paul pointed out, one might be willing to die for a good person, a friend, or a loved one, but God was willing to die even for sinners, even for those who were crucifying him (see Rom 5:6–8). The Christian creed says even more: it claims that Christ is not gone, that his love endures, and that we can still encounter that embodied love in person, no less than the apostles did in the upper room when the risen Christ appeared to them. Opening ourselves up to God's love and receiving his grace in the sacraments serves as the foundation of a life of virtue.

Christ is not gone. We can still encounter that embodied love in person, no less than the apostles did in the upper room when the risen Christ appeared to them.

Becoming Wise

While the animating or moving force of the virtues is love, the guiding principle should be prudence or, to use a more common word, wisdom. In English, we too often associate prudence with being cautious or careful. Thus, when people hear that prudence is the prerequisite for the other virtues, it sounds strange, even contradictory. Being prudent seems to be the opposite of being brave.

Young firefighters are told by older experienced firefighters, "We don't want any *heroes* around here!" In fact, they are all heroes for what they do every day. Given how dangerous fire is, the firefighter's work requires that he almost always must steel himself against the very real prospect of pain. What then do the older, more experienced firefighters mean when they say this? They mean a firefighter should not go running into a burning building recklessly. For a firefighter to be courageous—and not foolhardy—he must run into the building at the right time, in the right way, and with the right equipment. He must find the mean between rashness and cowardice; it is there that virtue lies. Prudence finds that mean by enabling the firefighter to determine how best to fight a fire, and, more generally, by enabling us to determine the right course of action and to choose it. Should you run into a burning building to save a person trapped inside? If you are a frail 80-year old and the person inside is 300 pounds, likely not. If you are as strong as a linebacker and have some training as a volunteer firefighter, probably so. It is the judgment of prudence that is operative here.

In the case of an unwed mother's unexpected pregnancy, the virtue of prudence dictates, first, that terminating the life of the child is out of the question because no innocent human being is ever to be killed.

Prudence is a wisdom that rightly assesses the various situations and circumstances of life in light of the principles or norms that guide human action in general. It is not, for that, the same as "moral relativism" or "situation ethics." If Jewish refugees show up at the door fleeing the Nazis, then we must do everything we can to help, whether we feel like it or not. What exactly is to be done may take some puzzling out. But the prudent person will apply the general principle that innocent human life is to be protected to these circumstances and make the judgment, "I have to help these people as best I can." So too, in the case of an unwed mother's unexpected pregnancy, the virtue of prudence dictates, first, that terminating the life of the child is out of the question because no innocent human being is ever to be killed. Deciding whether to raise the child or offer her for adoption will require an additional judgment of prudence. Helping the Jewish refugees and bringing the baby to term will also require courage. The decision has to be made, acted upon, and its likely consequences embraced, and each of these steps may require that we conquer our fears. Even having the presence of mind to make the judgment will require courage. The virtues are interconnected; we need all of them together to be happy.

The German philosopher Josef Pieper (1904–1997) described prudence as "the art of deciding wisely." "The prudent man," he explained, "acknowledges the obligations contained in objective reality." He "approaches each decision with his eyes open, in the full light of knowledge and faith. He discerns reality objectively, sizes up a factual situation for what it is, and weighs the real value of things." Many citizens of Calcutta passed by the homeless every day and barely saw them. Mother Teresa saw the image of God lying there on the street. Who saw more clearly? Who weighed the real value of things? That person is prudent, Pieper wrote with admirable concision, "who directs the choice of his will according to his insight in a situation and in the true reality of things as God has created them."

Yet prudence, like every other virtue, is similar to athletic or artistic skills in this: it needs to be developed. Your wise grandmother was not born that way. She became wise over the years because she learned from her experiences. If we think Mother Teresa went into the slums of Calcutta with a shining halo around her head simply knowing what to do in every situation, we would be mistaken. She had to learn (in fact, one of the first things she did was to take lessons in nursing). She made mistakes, and she learned from those mistakes, offered herself back to God's care, and persevered.

If we want to become wise like our grandmother or Mother Teresa, we must find wise people, watch what they do, and listen to what they say.

How do we become wise in the way that many grandmothers or Mother Teresa did? We watch, listen, and learn. If we want to be wise, we must find wise people, watch what they do, and listen to what they say. Theology teachers can teach the general principles of the moral life, but the wisdom that is prudence is an art of applying those principles to specific circumstances. Hence prudence requires experience, usually lots of it. And many of those experiences will be painful ones. None of us in this life is perfect, so we will make mistakes. And venturing out into new areas beyond our current experiences, we are more likely to make mistakes. The good news is that learning from our mistakes is one of the most effective ways of developing prudence. Too often people try to hide their mis-steps or shy away from difficult assignments where they might make a mistake. It is from taking risks and shouldering new responsibilities, even if we fall short of perfection, that we gain the experience that makes us prudent.

It is from taking risks and shouldering new responsibilities that we gain the experience that makes us prudent.

Jesus instructs us to be perfect as our heavenly Father is perfect (see Mt 5:48). But this means we should desire to be perfect with the perfection of our heavenly Father, not act as though we must create our own sort of perfection. Christ did not come and die on a cross for the perfect. He came to give hope to those who fall short. If going into a Catholic church were a public proclamation of sinlessness, no honest person would go. But since the Church preaches that we go to gain forgiveness of our faults and to be renewed in grace, even the worst sinner who earnestly desires to live a better life belongs there, because the earnest desire to live a better life is already evidence of God's grace at work. So, if you hear that call, follow it, whatever your sins and no matter how badly you feel about yourself. You may not believe that anyone could love you, but God does anyway—you may as well accept it. Granted, once you open that door, God will want to clean the whole house of your soul, and that may hurt a bit. But we know from St. Paul and others that Christianity is not supposed to be comfortable (see, for instance, Heb 12:4).

Becoming Noble

"While prudence is the cornerstone of the cardinal virtues," says Pieper, "justice is their peak and culmination. A good man is above all a just man." Whenever the scriptures wish to single out someone as especially noble—St. Joseph, for example, foster father of our Lord—the word used is "just" or "righteous" (see Mt 1:19). God is often called a just God, and we who are made in his image are called to become just as well.

We say that someone who is just gives to each person his or her due. With the virtues of temperance and fortitude, the balance or mean between the extremes of too much and too little is relative to the person making the decision. How much alcohol is too much? It depends on who you are and the situation you are in. The balance with justice, however, is not in the one deciding. The objective measure, measuring what is owed to another, is something we discover out there in the world. We do not create it. Our task is to discern the inherent worth of the thing—what is appropriate or fitting—and then act accordingly. It would not be fitting to give someone a gold medal merely for showing up to work on time, nor, conversely, to punish an employee for not being able to guess his duties in the absence of being told them directly. The owner of a company can buy and sell machinery for the warehouse, but he is not allowed to buy and sell the human workers. When the workers become nothing but another entry on the company's accounts no different from inventory, cash on hand, and sales receipts—when they are not treated as persons but as objects or things—then they are not being treated justly.

What I owe because of the intrinsic value of the thing may not be the same as its market value; it is not the same as what someone might be willing to pay for it. Some things we call priceless no amount of money will buy. Other things we call priceless cost nothing. Life is priceless. Love is priceless. Justice involves discerning the true value of things and acting accordingly. It may mean giving the right amount of money; it may mean offering no money at all when doing so would cheapen a generous deed. It will mean helping those less fortunate than you and being faithful in your relationships.

When it involves human persons, justice sometimes goes beyond what is strictly owed. Theologians like St. Thomas Aquinas included under the virtue of justice other virtues such as compassion and liberality. You are not required to invite guests into your home, but you do. You are not required to pay for a poor student's dinner, but you do. If you have ever worked as a waiter or waitress at a restaurant, you have perhaps seen the virtue of liberality when someone gives you a nice, big tip, not to make herself look important, but because she notices that you work hard and probably need it. This virtue's name comes from the Latin word for freedom. The liberal man is free from his money's power and thus able to give it away without regret to those who deserve it.

If you have ever worked as a waiter or waitress at a restaurant, you have perhaps seen the virtue of liberality when someone gives you a nice, big tip, not to make herself look important, but because she notices that you work hard and probably need it.

When writing about the nobility of the people in the little village of Le Chambon in France where over 5000 Jews were hidden from the Nazis and rescued during the Second World War, historian Philip Hallie was led to observe that "habit is by definition not inborn." Hallie's historical study had taught him one of the most important lessons that we learn from the tradition of the virtues, that it takes work to gain a good habit "and to make it firm enough to resist the temptations of fear and greed and cynicism." Hallie added a fascinating commentary on the importance of striving for greatness:

> The Italian novelist and essayist Natalia Ginzburg has made a distinction between *piccolo virtù*, *little virtues, like thrift and caution, and the great virtues, like compassion and generosity. She has urged us to stop drumming self-serving penny wisdom into the heads of our children—they will learn it, she says, with a little prodding and by using their own common sense. In fact, the little virtues are commonsensical. They protect our hides— that is their main function. If all we do for our children is pound into their heads reasons for protecting their own hides, their second nature will be as wide as the confines of their own self-seeking skins. One's life is usually about as wide as one's love. But if we make the often-impractical great virtues part of their lives, their second nature will be as wide as their love.*

A youth volunteer hands out supplies in Kanchanaburi, Thailand.

It is a much greater good for a whole team to win than it is for a single player to win accolades for her performance.

This is a valuable reflection, and it can be still more valuable if we ask ourselves "How wide is my love?"

In the last analysis, the virtue of justice is measured by the requirements of the common good. When we are devoted to the common good as our own highest personal good, we are like the soccer player who cares only about whether her team wins and is entirely indifferent to whether she scores a goal. That kind of disposition is extremely worthy or noble because it is a much greater good for a whole team to win than it is for a single player to win accolades for her performance. And we should note, too, that the noble soccer player is also the happiest soccer player when her team wins. The good in question—victory—is a common good; she cannot call it "mine" unless it also belongs to the whole team and is therefore "ours." Because human life is a cooperative affair, defined by our friendships and relationships, justice is the noblest virtue. It is a disposition to strive for common goods, goods like truth and friendship that we are able to enjoy because they are shared with others.

Justice is a disposition to strive for common goods, goods like truth and friendship that we are able to enjoy because they are shared with others.

Becoming Christ-Like

Thinking of justice as giving others their due, people sometimes make the mistake of assuming that justice is contrary to mercy. Although the just person knows how to show the proper appreciation for good deeds, in both words and actions, he or she is neither shocked nor overly troubled when others fail or are unjust. The just person recognizes injustice and has the wisdom to correct it.

Justice is not something a robot or a computer program could determine mathematically in place of a human being. Although it is true that if you steal a stereo from someone, justice requires restoring the stereo or one of equal value, many injustices cannot be so easily resolved because they may involve something unquantifiable, such as what kind of relationship you owe someone. The goal of justice among persons, given the reality of human nature, is reconciliation and restoration of communion. And so justice may require mercy or forgiveness. Human beings make mistakes. Two things are therefore necessary along with clear standards of justice if we are to maintain the fellowship within a community. The first is that we must learn to forgive others when they fall short of the standard, as we too will need to be forgiven when we fall short. Every day we ask God to forgive us "as we forgive those who trespass against us." The second is that we will sometimes need to break the vicious cycle by which people exact retribution for harm they have suffered.

Human beings make mistakes. We must learn to forgive others when they fall short of the standard, as we too will need to be forgiven when we fall short.

The justice of God actually causes me to trust, and this is why. To be just is not only to exercise severity in order to punish the guilty. It is also to recognize right intention and to reward virtue. I expect as much from God's justice as from his mercy. It is because he is just that he is compassionate and filled with gentleness, slow to punish, and abundant in mercy, for he knows our frailty. He remembers we are only dust. As a father has tenderness for his children, so the Lord has compassion on us.

St. Thérèse of Lisieux (1873–1897)

Let us say you are an employee who stocks shelves at a local business and your boss is a person who thinks the way to inspire people is to verbally abuse them in front of others. One day, he bawls you out. Perhaps you made a mistake, but not one to justify such abuse, so you are angry. But you need your job, so you cannot quit or answer back to your boss. You cannot pay it back to the person who did the injustice. What often happens then? You go out into the world frustrated and angry, and you unload that anger on someone else. You yell at your mother or at the clerk at the check-out counter. This merely adds to their bad day, so they in turn inflict it upon someone else: husband, children, or other customers. The only way the cycle can be broken is if there are people willing to be circuit breakers. These people, when they have injustice done to them, either demand justice from the wrongdoer or, if this is not possible, resolve at least not to inflict it upon others. They break the cycle by repaying evil with good.

In embodying these three dispositions—upholding firm standards of justice, while always seeking mercy and reconciliation and refusing to perpetuate injustice—you make yourself more and more like Christ. Indeed for Christians, the goal of all the virtues is to become more Christ-like. The virtues enable us to live the fundamental admonitions to love God and love our neighbor both in the tedious everydayness of our lives as well as when things are in crisis and become complex and confused. We cooperate with God's love and grace to make prudence, temperance, courage, and justice "second nature" to us because we have been bidden by Christ to love our fellow human beings as he has loved us. We are even told we must love our enemies. Did not Christ do the same? God has not asked us to do anything he has not done himself. He is not asking us to make sacrifices greater than his own.

There are two passages from the Second Vatican Council that John Paul II quoted in nearly every one of his encyclicals. The first declares that it is "only in the mystery of the Incarnate Word that the mystery of man takes on light" (*Gaudium et Spes*, 22). But what does Christ reveal? What light does he shed on "the mystery of man"? The second passage favored by the Pope, several sentences later, reveals that,

> the Lord Jesus, when He prayed to the Father "that all may be one…as we are one" (Jn 17:21–22), opened up vistas closed to human reason, for He implied a certain likeness between the union of the divine Persons, and the unity of God's sons in truth and charity. This likeness reveals that man, who is the only creature on earth which God willed for itself, cannot fully find himself except through a sincere gift of himself (Gaudium et Spes, 24).

Charity reaches out to embrace others and to form them into a community having a likeness to the union of divine persons in the Holy Trinity. We do that when we make a sincere gift of ourselves to others in true friendship founded upon virtue.

It is not merely that the Triune God serves as a model for us to imitate, however. To live the moral life is, on the Christian understanding, to participate in the life of God. When we live a life formed by the virtues, animated by faith, hope, and love, we become like Christ—Christ for others. We no longer look around and ask, "Where is God? Why is God not taking care of these people?" We say instead, "God is here. I wish to make him present in and through me just as he becomes present in and through the material elements of the sacraments."

When we become like Christ, we see the Law not as the commands of an angry master given to those he rules, but as the kind instruction of a loving Father to his children. And the children of the household do what the Father asks not from fear of punishment, but out of love, because they are co-heirs of the household like the Son. Embracing God in love rather than fear is made possible for us by the gift of God's own Holy Spirit; thus, to live the moral life, on the Christian understanding, is to enter into the Trinitarian life of God. This is what it means to be truly human, to be remade into the image and likeness of God. And the more we become like Christ, the more we become the reliable friends and sons and daughters we all long to be.

Review Questions

1. Can you think of times when the example of a parent, teacher, coach, or friend led you to take an important step forward in the pursuit of virtue? Explain.

2. Have you ever witnessed someone coming alive to the love of God for the first time? How did his or her life change as a consequence? If you do not know of someone in your own circle of friends and family, you may appreciate reading or listening to one of the conversion stories available on FORMED.org.

3. Prudence requires seeing reality for what it is. How might outside influences in our lives (media, friends, and so on) affect our judgments? Have you encountered a friend making a bad judgment because of peer pressure or cultural pressure? What is required to stand firm in support of the truth when pressure to conform mounts?

4. Although justice is commonly described as giving others their due, it is actually a much broader virtue. What are some of the ways you have witnessed people acting in a noble or generous manner and how did those deeds express the broader aspects of justice? If you wish, you may draw your answer from the life of a saint.

5. Explain how the moral life for Christians is an imitation of Christ and a participation in the Trinitarian life of God.

Put Out Into the Deep

For a lucid introduction to the virtues that situates the moral life within the context of our pursuit of happiness and uses contemporary examples, see Steven J. Jensen, *Living the Good Life: A Beginner's Thomistic Ethics* (Catholic University Press, 2013).

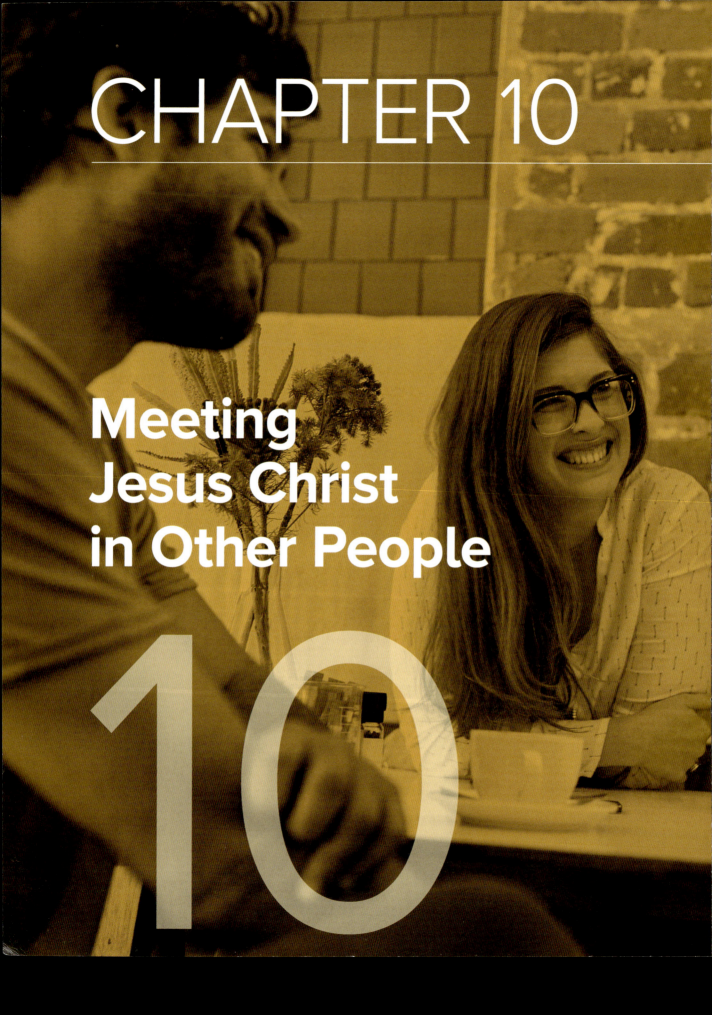

CHAPTER 10

Meeting
Jesus Christ
in Other People

10

A Foundation for Charity

Christ calls us to love one another as he has loved us (see Jn 13:34). When thinking about love, the first people that come to mind might be relatives, friends, or someday a spouse. But Christ means the love called charity, which he wishes us to have for both God and others, even people we do not like. In fact, Christ says to love our enemies with charity (see Mt 5:44).

But how can we love people whom we do not like, let alone enemies, or find Christ in such people? People we do not like often do frustrating things. Enemies do terrible things. For that matter, relatives, friends, and spouses can also do frustrating or even terrible things. The love of family, friendship, or married love can grow cold without charity to strengthen it.

Say we granted all this. Yes, charity is possible. Yes, Christ commanded charity. Yes, charity is necessary to support our other loves. Still, is there anything attractive about the love called charity? If charity involves loving enemies, why would Benedict XVI say that "joy is intimately linked to love"?

To find an answer, we do not start with the hardest form of charity, the love of enemies, but at the foundation, that is, charity to God and self. As Benedict XVI recalls, St. John wrote that "God loved us first" (see 1 Jn 4:10), so the only reason we are able to love our neighbor is because God "loves us, he makes us see and experience his love" (*Deus Caritas Est*). Once we understand how God has loved us, it is easier to see how charity to others could be a source of adventure, wonder, and joy.

With the help of the great Spanish contemplative nun St. Teresa of Avila, we can better understand how God has made and loved us. In *The Interior Castle*, she invented an analogy for how each of us is made in the image and likeness of God. She likened the soul to a castle or house with many rooms. The deepest interactions between God and the self take place in the very center where God lives. No matter how large, magnificent, and spacious we imagine the house to be, it is nicer than that. Teresa said that on this subject, our imagination cannot exaggerate. It has more rooms than we can imagine, with outdoor gardens and fountains and so many other amazing things that "you would want to be dissolved in praises of the great God who created the soul in His own image and likeness."

Take a moment to picture your soul, a unique country more incredible than anything you can imagine. Envision epic mountain ranges or white sandy beaches on a deep blue sea. Imagine lawns, meadows, forests, waterfalls, caves, footpaths, and avenues. Picture the house set in the very heart of this magnificent country. See the garden and tree-house; the pools, decks, balconies, and patios; the fireplaces, fire-pits, and grills; the big kitchens, workshops, libraries, the window-seats, the spiral staircase, wide sofas, and soft beds. Whatever you picture, it is nicer than that. Somewhere inside God is waiting. And the amazing thing is that this country is you.

Using imagination and memory to picture the soul as a marvelous place and speaking with God there is a kind of prayer which Teresa strongly recommended. If we took her advice, we might experience four possible outcomes.

First, exploring and appreciating our own remarkable country can be a foundation for a relationship with God. Psalm 139 says "I praise you, for I am wonderously made" (Ps 139:14). God waits here to talk and enjoy this magnificent place with us. And we may find ourselves wanting to speak with him.

Second, as our relationship with God grows, it can reduce loneliness. Since Christ is most fully present in the eucharist, and meets us in his Word, other sacraments, and other people, it can seem that, unless we are physically present in church or with other people, we are essentially alone. But in fact, God is also with and in us, knowing and loving our inner country more than we do. Long before Teresa wrote *The Interior Castle*, Augustine marveled how God is more "interior" to us than we are to ourselves. According to Teresa, someone who continues to meet God in his own country begins to stop feeling alone.

Third, as we begin to appreciate our country, it builds true self-worth and confidence in God. Take the analogy of the soul as a country, imagining sin to be like litter on the beach. Are there sins, blindspots, and weaknesses like pieces of litter all over the beach? Sure. Take the analogy further, imagining achievements and good deeds like extra furniture and buildings in our country. Would it not be nice to produce achievements like deck-chairs or add buildings like a food pantry for the poor? Sure. But we do not need to remove litter or add extras to make the country wonderful. God already made it wonderful. He does not say, "I will only love this beautiful country after you have removed all these sins littering the beach." He does not say, "I will only love this beautiful country after you have added extra good deeds." The only reason to remove litter or add anything is because the country is already so wonderful, a place worth taking care of and improving.

St. Teresa of Avila (1515–1582) was a reformer of the Carmelite order in Spain. The recipient of many extraordinary visions and graces, she was led by Christ to devote herself to assisting other women—and some men—to embrace a rigorous monastic life devoted to contemplative prayer. The autobiography she wrote under obedience, called The Book of Her Own Life, *is a major spiritual classic. She is a Doctor of the Church, and her feast day is October 15.*

Take the analogy one last step. Many people doubt or do not know the splendor of their country and God's love for them. So they look to achievements, money, fame, power, or romance to give them self-worth. Yet if we secretly suspect our country is worthless, it does not matter how much we do or how much money, fame, and power we have. At the end of the day, we feel stuck with a place nobody wants or likes. Even romance fails us. If we do not like our country, we will not want to show it to others. We fear guys or girls will not want to be with us if they really know us. It is hard to receive attention for something we do not value. Worse, if others treat our country poorly, we might let them, because we ourselves do not value it.

When we do see and value our country as God does, we gain confidence in God. Knowing that our worth and God's love are not conditional upon removing sin or adding good deeds, nor found in external goods like money and fame, we begin to trust God. As Benedict XVI said, God "loves you for what you are, in your frailty and your weakness, so that, touched by his love, you may be transformed." Secure in God's love and certain he has made us in his image and likeness, we can work peacefully with him to make a wonderful country even better.

Fourth, once we value our soul as God does, we can begin to value others rightly and love them with charity. St. Thomas Aquinas wrote that the love we have for ourselves is the root of charity to others. Christ commands us to treat others as we would wish them to treat us (Lk 6:31). Christ similarly commands us to love our neighbor as ourselves (Mt 22:39; Mk 12:31). If we want to know how to love others, we first need to know how we should love ourselves. Teresa's analogy of the soul to a beautiful country has just answered this question. In learning to value our own soul as a place made in God's image and likeness and home to him, we discover how to value other people.

For anyone who has ever wanted to have an adventure, charity to others is an invitation to explore. Are you astounded by the natural wonders and magnificent house in your own soul? Adventures and wonders await you in the new countries of other people. God awaits you as well, and based on your experience of him at home, that promises to be very exciting.

Sin is like litter on the beach of our soul. We do not need to remove the litter to make the beach wonderful; God already made it wonderful.

Learning Charity

Charity asks us to explore and appreciate the inner countries of other people made and loved by God. To make this exploration, we need guidance about the activity of charity, what to expect and what to keep in mind.

To love with charity, it helps to understand that it is an activity with special characteristics. First, we learn some kinds of activities through practicing. We are designed to love. So, unlike learning the violin or playing football, we are all born with a talent for charity, given a special infusion of charity through baptism, and aided continually by God's grace to practice charity. But like violin and football, we still need to practice to get good at charity. Like violin and football, we start out in life with no idea of how to practice charity, and no idea how to start. We need to apprentice ourselves to mentors who are better at the activity than we are and can help us start, improve, and move forward when we make mistakes or reach new levels of ability. We find such mentors in the saints as well as in good men and women who help us apply the example of the saints to our particular circumstances.

To love with charity, we need to apprentice ourselves to mentors who are better at the activity than we are: the saints.

Second, some kinds of activities cannot be appreciated until one gets good at the activity. Like playing the violin or playing football, we cannot experience how good charity is, until we have put time and practice into it. We have to get the hang of the violin, of playing football, and of practicing charity, to appreciate it. It is important to remember this, because at the beginning, we can feel it is all just playing boring scales, doing tedious push-ups, or the equivalent. We have to keep our eyes on the prize and be patient until we get a little bit better at the activity.

Third, some kinds of activities cannot be reduced to simple programs such as "How to Become a Top Violinist in Three Simple Steps" or "Ten Rules for Becoming History's Greatest Football Player." Some activities have only basic principles, allowing for participants to exercise creativity and contribute new ways of engaging in the activity. Violinists interpret old melodies in new ways or write new music; football players invent new plays and set new records. Similarly, the Catholic Church gives basic guidelines through her moral teaching. But within these basic rules, there are hundreds of ways to practice charity. That is why the saints are so different from each other. They are married, single, priests, and religious brother and sisters. They care for the poor, write poetry, work as scientists, practice law, cure the sick, or climb mountains. With charity, there are only the basic guidelines of the Church's moral teaching. After that, there is much freedom to experiment.

So there is no recipe for charity. The best thing is to launch into the activity, keeping the Church's basic moral guidelines in mind, looking for mentors in the saints and good men and women we know, and knowing that it takes time and practice to begin getting the hang of it. Every explorer makes mistakes, but you do not get good at exploring except by exploring, and you do not find new mountains or sail the new seas of other people's countries except by getting out there.

So there is no recipe for charity. The best thing is to launch into the activity, keeping the Church's basic moral guidelines in mind, looking for mentors in the saints and good men and women we know, and knowing that it takes time and practice to begin getting the hang of it.

Two Helpful Principles for Practicing Charity

Pay Attention

The last section pointed out that there is no recipe for practicing charity. This makes a lot of sense if we recall Teresa's analogy of the soul being like a country. If we visited a foreign country with a long list of all the things we think it needs, we would likely get it wrong. People, like places, are unique and have their own peculiar needs. What people need most of all from us, before we do anything, is our attention. Benedict XVI made this point: "Going beyond exterior appearances, I perceive in others an interior desire for a sign of love, of concern. . . . Seeing with the eyes of Christ, I can give to others much more than their outward necessities; I can give them the look of love which they crave" (*Deus Caritas Est*, 18). According to John Paul II, charity implies concern, tenderness, compassion, openness, availability, and "interest in people's problems" (*Redemptoris Missio*, 89).

Mother Teresa (1910–1997) was a religious sister and teacher before following a call from God to serve the poor in Calcutta, where she founded the Missionaries of Charity. Much of their work focuses on charity to people with physical poverty, but Mother Teresa said that the poor includes anyone who is suffering: "poverty means, first of all, to be hungry for bread, to need clothing, and to not have a home. But there is a far greater kind of poverty. It means being unwanted, unloved, and neglected." According to Mother Teresa, this greater poverty afflicts both rich and poor. Everyone needs attention. Mother Teresa observed, "I often ask for gifts that have nothing to do with money. There are always things one can get. What I desire is the presence of the donor, for him to touch those to whom he gives, for him to smile at them, to pay attention to them."

As the Father has loved me, so have I loved you; abide in my love. If you keep my commandments, you will abide in my love, just as I have kept my Father's commandments and abide in his love. These things I have spoken to you, that my joy may be in you, and that your joy may be full. This is my commandment, that you love one another as I have loved you.

John 15:9–12

The beginning of this chapter examined Teresa of Avila's analogy to show that the foundation of charity is seeing ourselves as made in God's image and likeness. That was the foundation for relationship with God, the end of loneliness, true self-worth and confidence in God, and charity. Appreciating the self as made by God helps with charity to others in two ways.

First, we become better able to know and appreciate others as made in God's image and likeness. When we see ourselves as God sees us, we realize that each of us has years of suffering, joy, questions, and desires. We have dozens of rooms, gardens, and pathways, uniquely mirroring some aspect of God. We cannot be understood and appreciated in ten minutes or even ten days; it takes time and attention. And the same is true for other people. Donations, food, shelter, medical care, job training, and the like can be very helpful. But what other people need first is "loving personal concern" (*Deus Caritas Est*, 28). People need to see themselves as God sees them, and we can help by showing the same loving personal concern we would want to receive.

Second, we become better able to help people. When we know we are made in God's image and likeness and loved by God, it becomes easier to work on sin or do good deeds. We do not have to earn God's love. Other people also need to know that they are loved and have true worth. If they do not believe that, they become completely discouraged. We can show them the same loving encouragement God shows us, loving people despite their sins or faults, helping them gain true self-worth and confidence in God.

Be Open to Receiving Charity

Another thing to keep in mind as we begin the practice of charity is the importance of receiving charity. Receiving charity from other people sounds so pleasant, we might think it is better to say, "No, no, serve me last!" and go to the back of the line. We might even feel unworthy of receiving charity. Nevertheless, letting others love us is a way to practice charity.

According to Aquinas, we are called to imitate God in two ways: first by imitating his goodness and second, by imitating the way he helps people to do good. So when we practice charity, we imitate God's charity. And when we help someone else to practice charity, we imitate the way God helps people to practice charity. Aquinas actually said the second way is better: "it is a greater perfection for a thing to be good in itself and also the cause of goodness in others, than only to be good in itself." God does not want us to remain students, but to join him eventually as teachers of charity. God is a master of charity, "a master, who not only imparts knowledge to his students, but gives also the faculty of teaching others."

It is good to teach others to practice charity. One of the best ways is to provide opportunities by being open to receiving charity. And the best opportunities are those where we help others to exercise loving personal concern towards us. This means letting people get to know us. Our inner country is the most important and valuable thing about us, not our donations or services. Allowing people to see and appreciate our country is the gift of our self. As Teresa's analogy reveals, the self is the most precious thing God has given us, and therefore the best thing we could give.

Of course, allowing people to know us can carry a cost; it allows for rejection and hurt. People can be blind to the beauties of our country or use what they know against us. This is why it is so important to turn inward to God and renew our vision of our own worth as made in the image and likeness of God. If we turn frequently to Christ, he can repair damage, renew energy, and help us engage once again in the practice of charity, even receiving charity and allowing people to know us. Those who do have eyes to see and appreciate the splendor of our country will gift us in ways we cannot imagine.

The Gifts of Charity

Our ability to love others comes from God; our attempts at charity must come from his initiative. It is very important, therefore, to sustain all our attempts in charity through frequent conversations with God in our own country. As the chapter noted earlier, the activity of charity demands practice, asking for help, and persevering, knowing we might not enjoy charity before we get the hang of it. Charity demands time and attention to others. It comes with the risk of being hurt. These challenges can weaken our confidence in God or lead us to doubt our own worth. And if we do not trust God's love or value our own soul, it is impossible to help other people trust God's love and value their own souls. All the good we do and all the good we are comes from God. To share God's love, we have to revisit how he first loved us by making us and living within us.

Aquinas called God a master of charity: in addition to saints and other good men and women, we need help from the greatest mentor of all, God himself. We see how important it is to talk with God, asking him to inspire, comfort, and help us, when we consider how many people have a "distressing disguise." Mother Teresa used this phrase to describe how the poor can appear. Although other people are made in the image and likeness of God, they often appear in distressing disguises. They look or act in disturbing ways. Our enemies have the worst disguises. To us they seem terrible; their true worth is completely hidden. Sometimes our relatives, friends, or spouses appear disguised. We have to turn to Christ within us, in our own country, to ask for faith to believe that there is something great behind those disguises, to ask for grace to look past those disguises. And Christ helps us; the more we turn to him, the more he helps us look past our own disguises to see our inner worth and his closeness to us. He does the same when we turn to others.

What do we lose if we decide charity is not for us? First, we miss out on experiencing the beautiful countries found in other people. We may damage their countries. We may miss out on the possibility of attention, appreciation, and charity from other people.

Second, since we are all connected through Christ, hurting or ignoring other people's countries actually causes damage and neglect in us. Benedict XVI put it like this: "Our lives are involved with one another, through innumerable interactions they are linked together. No one lives alone. No one sins alone. No one is saved alone. The lives of others continually spill over into mine: in what I think, say, do and achieve. And conversely, my life spills over into that of others: for better and for worse" (*Spe Salvi*, 48).

Third, we miss out on sharing a certain kind of life with God. If you have ever been interested in something like the violin or football, you know how enjoyable it is to share this interest with a friend. God is a master of charity and a master creator. He will not force us to take an interest in the countries he has created. But if we do not, we miss out on sharing the core of his life.

What are the gifts that come from the practice of charity? First, charity helps us have better relationships. Charity helps us look past disguises, and that can be a huge support when it is hard to love relatives, friends, or a spouse.

Second, charity is a source of joy and wonder. Aquinas wrote that doing good to others can be a source of pleasure. Once we start to practice charity, Christ's friends become our friends, and there is pleasure in doing good things for our friends. Also, being a source of goodness gives pleasure. If you have ever scored a goal, played music exceptionally well, written an outstanding report, or done anything really well, you know how it feels to recognize that a good thing came from you. Sometimes when practicing charity, we make mistakes; other times we do it well, and it is tremendous to realize that God has mentored us to a point where we can show real charity. Additionally, wonder comes when we encounter some great new thing beyond experience or understanding. Because charity is an adventure into the unique and incredible interior worlds of other people, we can expect to experience wonder frequently.

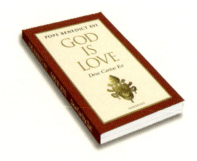

Deus Caritas Est, or God is Love, published on Christmas Day 2005, was the first of Benedict XVI's three encyclicals. It offers a stirring reflection upon true and false love, as well as an exhortation to perform acts of charity and mercy.

Finally, there is the joy of charity itself. It is hard to describe what is so great about playing the violin or football to someone who has never played. The best we can do is show them great musicians or athletes playing. But watching a touchdown is nothing like scoring a touchdown. Similarly, it is hard to describe how great it is to practice charity. The life of a saint can give us a glimpse, but really, you must experience the practice of charity to know its value.

This chapter began by exploring the foundation of charity in the love of God and self. When we understand our own worth and the gift God made to us by creating us so wonderfully, we can begin to understand the true worth of other people behind their disguises. Rooted and strengthened in the love God has for us, we can explore the incredible interior castles of other people, meeting Christ again and again in each one. We can receive charity from others, sharing with Christ, saints, and other people an indescribable experience. Like playing in a symphony or on a football team, it is greater than anything one of us alone could experience.

Charity Rediscovered: Caryll Houselander

Caryll Houselander (1901–1954) was a British writer and artist. Although many failed to give her loving personal concern in her early years, she later experienced charity, and in turn, spent the rest of her life finding Christ in others.

As a child, Caryll suffered both great illness and great loneliness. Only the eucharist and one family friend ever gave her comfort. Her only sibling went to boarding school, and her mother went travelling. Her father gave her spending money and left her alone. Around the age of eight, she suffered some kind of nervous breakdown. For months, she endured fevers, difficulty in breathing, increasing weakness, and tremendous anxiety. Caryll grew so weak, she was believed near death. A priest was called to give her last Holy Communion. For a moment she lay still, then suddenly she sat up, and asked for her toy soldiers. She was completely better.

But then her parents, who had been fighting for years, now separated. In a room at the top of the house where she kept a picture of Christ, nine-year-old Caryll promised never to love again: "I would belong only to myself." She continued to live with her mother, and they became very poor as her mother struggled to earn an income. She was frequently sick and had to change schools four times. One year, when Caryll was sixteen and finally returning to school after a long illness, her mother suddenly demanded she end her education and return home permanently. The reason? To help run her mother's rental property. Caryll could not afford to buy nice clothes or go out. Gradually, she lost all her friends.

During this time, some Catholics were rude to her. Snapping one day, she left the church, saying she would never go back. She was seventeen. The one thing Caryll needed most, loving personal concern, was the one thing she most lacked. Christ's presence in the eucharist had been her deepest love, and now she left behind her that great consolation.

Houselander attended art school and tried to support herself through odd jobs, including baby-sitting, house-cleaning, and doing sound effects at a theater. She was always hungry. She got evicted. She tried many different religions, still torn by her love for the eucharist. She had an affair with an older divorced man who dropped her for someone else. In her free time, she used to walk around London for hours. Near the end of her affair, she had an experience which changed her forever: "I was in an underground train, a crowded train in which all sorts of people jostled together. . . . Quite suddenly I saw with my mind, but as vividly as a wonderful picture, Christ in them all. . . . I came out into the street and walked for a long time in the crowds. It was the same here, on every side, in every passer-by, everywhere Christ."

Then, she met a young man preaching about Christ in a public park. The young man was Frank Sheed (1897–1981), one of the greatest Catholic speakers of the 20th century. He married Maisie Ward (1889–1975), and together they founded a major Catholic publishing house called Sheed and Ward. They befriended Caryll, and she returned to the Catholic faith in 1925.

Thinking about the first time she met Frank Sheed, Houselander later wrote: "It was the Catholic Church being Christ; not waiting for the people to come in, but coming out to the people. . . . Christ following His lost sheep of whom I was one." For so many years, no one had paid attention to her. In a dark time, the Sheeds befriended her. Impacted by this and her experience in the train, Caryll began to seek Christ in other people. She soon started a work called Loaves and Fishes to help people who struggled to find jobs and pay bills. Loaves and Fishes had no office or not-for-profit status.

It was just Caryll and friends keeping an eye out for opportunities to help. She coordinated this quiet charity for over twenty years.

Caryll also created original artwork and woodcarvings for churches, and with Maisie Ward's encouragement, began to write. She wrote and illustrated hundreds of stories for children. Some of her spiritual books published by Sheed and Ward were best-sellers and led thousands to contact her for advice. Her replies were full of encouragement and good questions; she made people feel comfortable discussing what mattered to them.

Caryll Houselander lived through the London bombings of World War II. She served as a nurse and was one of many who stayed on the rooftops during air-raids to spot fires and dispatch fire-fighting teams. Some of the raids lasted an hour, some went on for more than eight hours. The bombings terrified her; sometimes her mouth dried up so completely she could not talk. Hurrying home one time from the hospital, she suddenly saw a bomb flying through the air. She dropped face-down to the ground as the glass windows around her exploded into fragments. No one could believe she was alive when the blast ended.

One of the worst raids came when Caryll was working one night:

> Our London barrage had been going on for hours, German planes coming over, in batches of a hundred at a time, in relays all night, and the barrage, which meant a non-stop, ear-splitting thunder of gun-fire going all the time. I was in a hospital helping give First Aid to the wounded and got sent to a ward where there were patients who had been operated on that day and so could not be moved down to the parts of the hospital considered a little more safe. . . . I was told to go to the ward and keep those poor patients (who could not move an inch) from being afraid. On the way upstairs

I realized that my mind was quite empty and that there was not one thought in it with which to reassure anyone.

But, as she climbed the stairs, she began to feel accompanied by the Communion of Saints. Entering the hospital ward, Caryll found she was able to talk with the patients and comfort them through that long, frightening night.

After the war, a psychologist friend arranged for Caryll to work with children suffering trauma. She spent hours teaching art, making toys with them, and listening. Others were amazed by the change in children who spent time with her. The psychologist said later that Caryll had "loved them back to life."

Caryll Houselander died of breast cancer in 1954. Her last year was one of continual pain, but she still managed to write letters, carry out her Loaves and Fishes work, and illustrate a Stations of the Cross. Caryll was devoted to Christ in the eucharist and in other people. She had learned, to use John Paul II's words, that "the vocation of every human being is to receive love and give love in return." Maisie Ward wrote this about her: "the discovery of the unknown Christ in man, by men in whom also He secretly dwells, was the chief achievement of her own spiritual life, the chief adventure in which she tried to engage all who came to her for help."

Review Questions

1. What is the "interior castle" according to Teresa of Avila, and what are four possible outcomes of praying about it in conversation with God?

2. Charity is an activity with three special characteristics. What are these characteristics and why is it important to keep them in mind?

3. How is "paying attention" important for charity?

4. How can "receiving charity" be a form of charity?

5. What are three gifts the practice of charity gives to human life?

6. What is the connection between charity to self and charity to neighbor?

7. Suppose a classmate has done something to you that you really did not appreciate—perhaps it was a prank, or a rude or inconsiderate action, or saying something behind your back, or posting something on social media that reflects badly on you. Describe a charitable response to such an action.

8. In his third encyclical, *Caritas in Veritate* (2009), or *Charity in Truth*, Benedict XVI stressed the essential link between charity and truth. Must an action be true to be charitable? Does the exercise of charity require that we be truthful? Is helping someone to understand the truth an act of charity? Are we convinced that the highest truth is that God is love and that we are called to love him and to imitate his love by our love for others? What would it mean for us to take this truth to be the highest truth?

Put Out Into the Deep

If you would like to know more about Mother Teresa, a great place to start would be with a slim volume on her written by Malcolm Muggeridge called *Something Beautiful for God* (Harper & Row, 1971). Muggeridge (1903–1990) was a famous British journalist and television personality whose encounter with Mother Teresa profoundly changed his life. His eyewitness testimony to her holiness is by turns humorous, insightful, and deeply challenging.

CHAPTER 11

We will
ABOLISH
ABORTION

Sign up for the FREE app at
WWW.ABOLISHABORTION.COM

True Communion

11

Christ founded the Catholic Church as his bride, his body, and a temple of the Holy Spirit (CCC 787–797). The Church exists in this earthly world with visible members and structures, but the Church is also a "spiritual reality" and "bearer of divine life" (CCC 770). The previous chapter explained how we can find Christ in others. Nowhere is this more possible than in the communion of his members and friends, the Catholic Church. In the Church, we have a glimpse of the life prepared for us in heaven.

But some do not experience the Church as a glimpse of heaven or a home for the lonely. Some see her more as a purveyor of guilt. Some are shaken by the shameful behavior of historical or contemporary Catholics. As the last chapter mentioned, Caryll Houselander's departure from the Church was partly due to the behavior of insensitive Catholics. But she did return to the Church. Why do Catholics go back? Or stay? Why do others join? Their connection cannot be driven by a love for guilt, nor a naïve belief that Catholics are nice, perfect people who never let you down. What do they see in the Catholic Church?

The Story of Alec Guinness (1914–2000)

Alec Guinness entered the Catholic Church in 1956. A British-born actor, Guinness featured in over 150 film, television, and stage productions, including *Hamlet; Romeo and Juliet; Macbeth; Murder in the Cathedral; The Importance of Being Earnest; Tinker, Tailor, Soldier, Spy;* and *Star Wars*—you may have seen him as Obi-Wan Kenobi. As a child, Guinness moved more than thirty times with his single mother to escape unpaid bills. When he was five, his mother entered a violent and unhappy three-year marriage. The first kindness Guinness knew came from former performers, one a dancer, another a gymnast. Guinness soon began staging performances and attending plays. When Guinness was nineteen, he determined to try for a full scholarship to the Royal Academy of Dramatic Art and to ask an experienced actress to help him prepare. Guinness's first lesson was not promising. "O, for a Muse of Fire!" he began.

"O my God!" his teacher exclaimed, burying her face in her hands. It was not a promising start. Once, after weeks of training, his teacher told him: "I can't teach you. . . . Forget about the professional theatre."

> "I can't forget the theatre. I want you to go on teaching me," Guinness pleaded.
>
> "You're wasting your time and mine. And your money."
>
> "I don't care!" cried Guinness. So, his teacher persevered. In fact, when Guinness ran out of money, the actress insisted on free lessons.

The day of the audition came. But when Guinness arrived, he learned the scholarship was not being

granted that year. "I turned away," said Guinness. "And felt despair." Walking away, he met up with a friend who told of another school offering a scholarship and holding auditions that same day. Guinness had to run; he was one of the last twenty people in line. Before five judges, he went through his prepared pieces, won the scholarship, and quit his job to become an actor. Through theater, he met and married Merula Salaman in 1938. They had a son named Matthew and were married over sixty years.

For years Guinness had no religion. Growing up, he received little help to sort out his needs and questions at home, where "nothing was certain and promises were made only to be broken." He explored many faiths, but it never occurred to Guinness to step inside a Roman Catholic Church. One night, during a World War II air raid, Guinness took shelter at the home of a friend who introduced Guinness to belief in the eucharist. He gave Guinness a copy of St. Francis de Sales's *Introduction to the Devout Life*, which the actor kept for the rest of his life.

When Guinness's eleven-year-old son Matthew became ill with polio, Guinness began visiting a small Catholic church after work. One day he prayed to God, "Let him recover, and I will never put an obstacle in his way should he ever wish to become a Catholic." Three months later Matthew was able to walk; by Christmas he was back to playing soccer.

The Guinnesses were seeking a better school for Matthew when a friend suggested a Catholic institution. Guinness began to object, and then he remembered his bargain.

Matthew went to the Catholic school and entered the Church a few years later. That summer, his father took a wandering bicycle ride which ended up near a Catholic church. He went inside, met a priest, and said he might like to enter the Church. As Guinness began to learn about the Church, so many things made sense that he wondered if the priest was holding something back. Guinness decided to visit the weirdest Catholic thing he could imagine, a Cistercian monastery. His bedroom was ugly; the bathroom smelled strange. The breakfast was baked beans and flabby bacon on wet toast. Some of the religious brothers were odd, some interesting and funny. Early one morning, as Guinness later wrote, he went to the chapel, full of the sound of small bells being rung for the consecration of the eucharist:

> the great doors to the East were wide open and the sun, a fiery red ball, was rising over the distant farmland...there was an awe-inspiring sense of God expanding, as if to fill every corner of the church and the whole world....the regularity of life at the Abbey, the happy faces that shone through whatever they suffered, the strong yet delicate singing, the early hours and hard work...if this was the worst that Rome had to offer, it was pretty good.

A year later, Guinness entered the Catholic Church. Soon Merula also entered, joining Guinness for their first Christmas as Catholics in Sri Lanka where he was filming *The Bridge on the River Kwai*. They went to Mass "in a little church, open at the sides to palm trees and the sound of surf breaking on a hot, white, sandy beach, with tropical birds flitting over the heads of the congregation." Guinness had experienced both physical deprivation and the poverty of loneliness. But now, as he put it, "like countless converts before and after me, I felt I had come home."

Converts like Guinness see Christ, beauty, truth, goodness, and peace, when they see the Church. Communion with Christ is communion with the Church, his body, and with its members, Christ's friends. In the Nicene Creed, we profess our belief in the communion of saints, a reality which connects us to Christ.

> *If I have one regret...it would be that I didn't take the decision to become a Catholic in my early twenties. That would have sorted out a lot of my life and sweetened it.*
> *—Alec Guinness*

The Communion of Saints

To be a Catholic is to be connected to a wide multitude of people, the communion of saints. The communion of saints is made up of three kinds of followers of Christ: those in heaven, including officially canonized saints; those in purgatory; and those on earth.

The first part of the communion of saints includes those who have died and are in heaven with Christ. Whatever your personality or experience, you are bound to find a mentor among these people, especially those who have been officially canonized as saints. For the passionate, there is an Augustine or Teresa of Avila. For the born leaders, there is a Paul, Joan of Arc, or Ignatius of Loyola. For the thoughtful, take Thomas Aquinas or Catherine of Siena. Their words help us to know them; their lives inspire.

Moreover, these saints are not simply historical models. They accompany us now. Just as we ask friends, we can ask the saints for their prayers and support. The saints are particularly attentive and sympathetic to our needs and struggles. When we talk to them, they hear us. Chapter 3 of the first volume of *Why Believe?* pointed out our profound need for friendship. Christ said, "I will not leave you desolate" (Jn 14:18). Founding the Catholic Church was one of the ways he gave us friends to help us come close to him. All Christ's followers in the gospels had to be introduced to him by others; after Christ ascended, all his followers needed help from other followers to persevere.

Another part of the communion of saints includes those in purgatory, friends of Christ who have died and are undergoing a transformation necessary to be fully united with him. Whatever this transformation looks like, both the delay of being fully united and the transformation itself are causes of suffering. As the last chapter explained, it is good for us to love, particularly to love the suffering. Prayer for the dead can help their transformation and console them. Maybe they are in heaven and do not need our prayers. But maybe they do. It is a gift to be able to help those who have died; prayer connects us to the friends we miss.

One convert particularly drawn by the communion of saints was George Lathrop (1851–1898). Lathrop was a novelist and poet; at one time he served as associate editor for *The Atlantic*. His wife, Rose Hawthorne Lathrop (1851–1926), was the daughter of Nathaniel Hawthorne, author of famous works like *The Scarlet Letter*. George and Rose Hawthorne Lathrop were quite well-known when they entered the Catholic Church in 1891. Their conversion shocked many, but, as George explained, one of his reasons for wanting to be Catholic was precisely the communion of saints: "it links together the religious souls of all periods, whether now on earth, or in the world beyond."

The third part of the communion of saints includes all the baptized, whether lay or consecrated, who are attempting to follow Christ through the Catholic Church on earth. This part helps us to seek Christ, by offering a living teaching authority or Magisterium, physical help, and a shared and transformed life.

Revelation 5:8 presents the saints in heaven as linked by prayer with their fellow Christians on earth.

The Earthly Church Offers Us Its Guidance and Help

We are fallen, limited human beings. We make mistakes, have blind-spots, forget things, and experience difficulty sorting out our ideas and emotions. In Christian life, we can turn to the scriptures for help. We can turn to the Church's Tradition. But if you have ever learned a skill, instrument, or sport, you know that it is particularly helpful to have a person who knows the field, as well as the challenges of the current situation, and who can help you to understand and grow. It is the same with the Church. Christ knew how difficult it is for us to gain proper perspective. So, in addition to scripture and Tradition, he gave us the Magisterium, a living pope with bishops and priests, earthly guides to help us navigate scripture and Tradition in the context of our current situation.

In addition to scripture and Tradition, God gave us the Magisterium, a living pope with bishops and priests, earthly guides to help us navigate scripture and Tradition in the context of our current situation.

When the Magisterium teaches, we can hear and see the teachers. As body-soul creatures, who learn through experience and interaction with other people, we need this third way to understand Christ's teaching. We are sorrowfully aware that popes, bishops, and priests can and do sin. Sometimes, like Guinness's teacher, they do not want to help for reasons of weakness or sin; but like Guinness, we must demand their help. In the fourteenth century, St. Catherine of Siena had to convince the reigning pope to shoulder his responsibilities to lead and teach. Many times, however, the Church's official teachers have been wise and generous. In the sixteenth century, St. Teresa of Avila wanted to determine whether Christ was helping her develop a new insight into prayer or whether her imagination was simply out of control. So, she wrote what she experienced and let the Church help her know if her experience could be reconciled with the teaching of Christ. She did not have to pursue Christ alone. The Church is full of sinners, but if you have questions, you will find a living Magisterium guided by Christ and Catholics who want to help you.

Christ and his saints help us, and one way is by inspiring earthly members of the communion of saints to provide us with tangible care. Tangible care is a hallmark of the Catholic Church.

The Catholic Church on earth is also able to give us physical help. Much of our life, we are vulnerable and dependent—as children, as elderly, and when we are sick or sad or poor. Christ and his saints help us, and one way is by inspiring earthly members of the communion of saints to provide us with tangible care. Tangible care is a hallmark of the Catholic Church. One of the things which drew Rose Hawthorne Lathrop to the Church was the visible witness of so many women rolling up their sleeves and caring for people. Wherever there is a need, there are Catholics trying to help. From the earliest days, Christians tried to help widows and orphans. John of God worked with the mentally ill. Peter Claver entered slave ships to comfort the captives. John Bosco and Mary Mazzarello ministered to at-risk young people. Catholics have been founding schools, hospitals, and meal centers for centuries. They provide medical care, comfort the dying, and visit the imprisoned. They minister to the homeless, refugees, women unexpectedly pregnant, victims of human trafficking, and people in areas of natural disaster. Are these Catholic teachers, doctors, volunteers, priests, and religious brother and sisters holy? Not necessarily: they are sinners like everyone else, somewhere on a path to Christ, just as we are. To encounter the earthly Catholic Church is to encounter a very mixed group of people. But we all need help during this life, and when you need help and look, you will find Catholics ready to assist you.

The Earthly Church Offers Us a Shared Life

The Catholic Church on earth is able to share a transformed life. Where there is the Catholic Church, time and space are transformed. For example, it is interesting that the weekend developed around Sunday, not, for example, around Wednesday or Thursday. If governments and businesses give time off, fifty-two times a year, at the very same time each week, it is because where the Church is or has been, there lingers the understanding of Sunday as special. Sunday commemorates both God's creation of the world and Christ's recreation of the world through his death and resurrection. Where the Church is or has been, Catholics aim to make their worship special. They dress up or prepare the best music and flowers. They try to take time off from work and make time for prayer. They do fun restful things: they take naps, read, and go for walks. They do special things with their family and friends: they cook brunch, go to the beach, and play games.

The continued presence of feasts like Christmas confirms how profoundly the world has been changed by its encounter with Christ and the Church. The impact of the Church is seen in traditions around the world. Where there are Catholics, there are May evenings where people set out flowers before pictures of the Mother of God or crown her statue with wreaths of flowers. They carry her image outdoors, during the day with a brass band playing, or at night along a country lane lit by jars full of candles. The feast of the eucharist follows, Corpus Christi, where Catholics take the eucharist out into the streets with music and flags. In some places, they make carpets of flowers for the eucharistic procession; they hold neighborhood foot-races, perform plays, and create life-size games of chess. In August, the Church celebrates the Assumption of Our Lady; in some places Catholics celebrate this feast day by making a pilgrimage to a special church or shrine dedicated to Our Lady. They carry their packs, meet new people, walk hundreds of miles, work up incredible appetites, tell stories, and camp under the stars or sleep in hospitable pilgrim hostels. All through the year, people experience the same fellowship on pilgrimage to other holy places like Lourdes in France, Guadalupe in Mexico, and Baclaran in the Philippines.

The Impact of the church is seen in traditions around the world. (Top Left) Petal and flower carpet for Corpus Christi celebration in Spain. (Top Right) In New Orleans, a king's castle is used to celebrate the end of Mardi Gras and the beginning of Lent. (Lower Left) The day before All Saints' Day, children get the gratuitously fun and silly experience of running around in costumes and eating as much candy as they want. (Lower Right) In Poland, children dress in traditional costumes and sing Christmas carols.

On All Saints' Day, the Church celebrates all those friends of Christ who rejoice with him in heaven. The prior evening is the eve of All Saints' Day, also known as "Halloween." And there are still vestiges of the joy of this feast. Once a year, children get the gratuitously fun and silly experience of running around in costumes and eating as much candy as they want. November 2, All Souls' Day, ushers in a month of prayer for the dead. The liturgical year ends with the Feast of Christ the King, and a new church year begins with Advent.

Where the Church is or has been, there are people preparing for Christ each December with evergreen wreaths holding purple and rose candles, hymns like "O Come, O Come Emmanuel," and special penance services. Then comes Christmas with its caroling parties, pageants, trees, wreaths, and garlands, lights in the windows, gifts, special cakes and cookies, eggnog and wassail, party clothes, a wide cast of mythic characters surrounding the feast, and at the center a Christmas nativity scene with a small child Jesus. On New Year's Eve and the next day, every Catholic Church ushers in the new year by celebratings the feast of Mary, the Mother of God.

The year moves into Lent, involving pancakes, parties, and King Cake with a prize inside on Mardi Gras, the night before Ash Wednesday. Ash Wednesday brings fasting and ashes on the forehead to remind us of the four last things: death, judgment, heaven, and hell. Lent is marked by purple in the churches, retreats and missions, penance services, parish fish fries, two fun breaks with St. Patrick's Day and St. Joseph's Day, care for the poor, and long green palms carried on Palm Sunday as the Church remembers Christ's entry into Jerusalem on the way to suffer and die. A few days later, on Holy Thursday, the Church commemorates Christ's Last Supper, representing that same sacrifice once again at Mass, and thanking Christ for founding two sacraments, the eucharist and the priesthood. The church is full of flowers and candles. The priest gets down on his knees to wash feet as Christ washed the feet of his disciples. The words prayed before the washing of the feet are, "Where there is charity and love, there God is." At the end of the Mass, the eucharist is removed from the tabernacle and taken to the "altar of repose," a place set apart and decorated with flowers, plants, and candles to represent the Garden of Gethsemane where Christ prayed the night he was arrested. In many churches, people sit with Christ until midnight. Then the eucharist is removed from the church, the holy water poured out, and the candle in the red glass tabernacle lamp blown out. When people enter the church on Good Friday, they do not genuflect. Or they stop awkwardly in the middle of genuflecting when they remember that the tabernacle is empty. The priests enter silently at the Good Friday liturgy. They lie full length on the ground remembering how Christ died for us. People hear the scriptures recounting Christ's death; they kiss replicas of the cross on which Christ died.

Where charity and love are, there God is.
Christ's love has gathered us into one.
Let us rejoice and be pleased in Him.
Let us fear and let us love the living God.
And may we love each other with a sincere heart.

Ubi Caritas, antiphon for Holy Thursday

On the evening of Holy Saturday, a change begins for the Church. At home, parents lay out Easter clothes. Parents or bunnies fill baskets full of candy and hiding decorated eggs. Outside the church, the priests light a bonfire, called the "Easter fire." As little red-gold sparks fly up into the air, a brand-new, specially painted wax candle, the "Easter candle," is lit from the fire. People light their candles from one another's and walk into the darkened church where they hear the very first reading of scripture: "In the beginning, God created the heavens and the earth" (Gen 1:1). The story of salvation is told from Genesis to Abraham to Moses, through the Psalms and prophets, to St. Paul and, finally, to the Gospel on the resurrection. This is the night Christ rose from the dead; this is the night the Church receives anyone who has

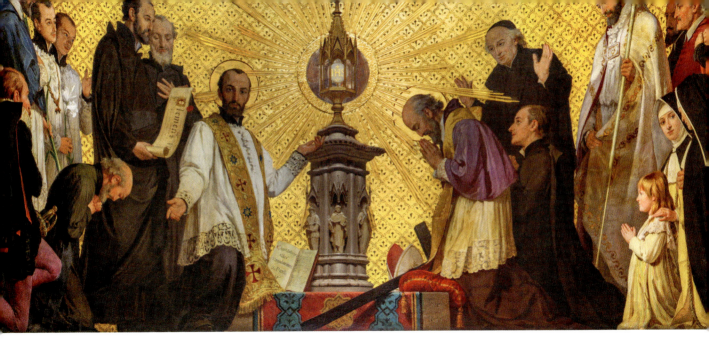

The Church's life starts with the eucharist;
It is a life which impacts every aspect of
life on earth.

asked to be baptized or confirmed. "Glory to God in the highest," the people pray; the lights shine out on a church full of flowers. Before the new Catholics profess their new faith, all the people pray over them: "Holy Mary, Mother of God, pray for us. Saint Michael, pray for us. Holy Angels of God, pray for us. Saint John the Baptist, pray for us. Saint Joseph, pray for us." And this is happening all over the world. In magnificent European basilicas with vaulted ceilings, in the churches of Nigeria, Brazil, and Australia, and in Jerusalem's Church of the Holy Sepulchre over the place where Christ died and rose to give us life, new Catholics are embarking on a shared life in Christ.

These last few paragraphs have described the transformation of time and space within the Roman rite in certain parts of the world. Within the Roman rite there are many other traditions, and within the Church, there are many other rites, with ancient liturgies and traditions surrounding life in Christ. What they all share is a transformation of time and space, involving both body and soul, in a life lived with others seeking Christ. It is a life which impacts every aspect of life on earth.

The Church's life starts with the eucharist; it flows into the streets in eucharistic processions. It flows into the streets through people like Rose Hawthorne Lathrop, who loved Christ in the eucharist and Christ in the poor. After George Lathrop's death, she founded a home to care for people with incurable cancer. Joined by other women, this work eventually gave birth to the Hawthorne Dominicans, providing free palliative care to those suffering terminal cancer and unable to pay their medical bills.

The Church on earth is on pilgrimage, on the way to Christ. The Church is full of sinners, but if you want a rich shared life of true communion, you will find Catholics willing to walk with you.

Explore the Church

If the Catholic Church is this kind of home, why do some experience it as a purveyor of guilt? There are many responses to this question, but this chapter will make just a few. First, a person who experiences the Church only as an enforcer of rules may want to consider the arguments of the previous several chapters on law, grace, virtue, and charity. The concept of sin and guilt can be very difficult for people who struggle with self-loathing and doubt God's love for them. They can take sin as further proof that they are worthless, or that God rejects them, rather than seeing sin as it truly is—an obstacle in the relationship between a splendid child and a loving father. People with a proper understanding of their own worth and God's love find it easier to acknowledge their sin with peace and to welcome the help of the sacrament of Reconciliation and the Church's moral teaching as means to find Christ. So, if the Church's moral teaching seems oppressive, then it would be well to investigate whether one has a proper sense of one's own worth and of God's love.

Second, if a person experiences the Church only as an enforcer of rules, then it would be good to seek out experiences of the communion of saints. Most aspects of life in the Church are not mandated. No rule says you must cook Sunday brunch, go on pilgrimage, attend a eucharistic procession, have a Lenten fish fry, or set up a Christmas nativity scene. Rose Hawthorne Lathrop cared for incurable cancer victims, not because she was forced to, but because she wanted to. Most aspects of Catholic life are the gestures of loving and happy creativity, the hopeful outpouring of people seeking Christ in the company of his bride, the Catholic Church. The commandments of Christ are few compared with everything we can say, do, and think. If we tallied all possible words, thoughts, and actions, only a tiny percentage would actually be considered sins. Christ's moral teachings are like the boundaries of a green field as wide as a universe. The boundaries serve simply to keep us within reach of a relationship with Christ; within the field there is almost an unlimited range of movement.

Christ's moral teachings are like the boundaries of a green field as wide as a universe; within the field there is almost an unlimited range of movement.

It often happens, however, that people's only experience of the Catholic Church is those moral boundaries, the minimum requirements of life in Christ. Their experience is like a car-owner who knows only this about his car: that it will not run without gas. There is a sort of rule about needing gas to get the car going. But would he know what it means to own a car? We would have to ask, "Wait! Have you never gone on a road-trip? Never rolled your windows down and sang really loudly to your favorite song? Never run out for pizza? Never tinkered around with the engine? Yes, the car needs gas, but there is more to the car than that." If the Catholic Church appears only like a moral enforcer, get to know it better. Learn about the saints, reconnect with the beloved dead, ask questions of Catholics and seek their help, and look for the incredibly varied aspects of the true communion that Catholic life offers.

Experiencing the Catholic Church only through its moral boundaries is like a car-owner who only knows his car will not run without gas.

Another objection raised early in the chapter concerns the lack of holiness in Catholics—including laity, religious, priests, bishops, cardinals, and even popes. Few things are more disturbing than meeting a Catholic who lacks interest in Christ or whose actions violate fundamental Catholic principles and the demands of charity. If one has suffered at the hands of other Catholics, it can be easy to move from blaming things on the particular faults of individual Catholics to blaming the Church. The Church is holy in her union with Christ, given the means of holiness, and called to be holy. At the same time, the Church's earthly members are sinners at every stage of closeness to or distance from Christ. Since the Church is ultimately Christ's bride and body, to be angry at the Church is to be angry at Christ. If this is your experience, take a look at Chapter 13 on suffering. Christ wants and expects you to ask him about what you have suffered. Consider also what Caryll Houselander learned. If you have suffered at the hands of Catholics, seek, pray for, and find some Catholics who have truly embraced Christ and his Church. Catholics were one of the reasons Houselander left the Church, but Catholics Frank and Maisie Ward showed her a different aspect of the Church. And finally, turn to the Christ in the eucharist.

This is the advice of J. R. R. Tolkien, author of *The Lord of the Rings*. When his son was suffering depression and sagging faith, Tolkien sympathized and tried to advise him. According to Tolkien, if we find it difficult to believe in the Church, we will want a reason to leave. Bad Catholics seem like one of these reasons. Tolkien knew plenty of bad Catholics, and in fact, Tolkien admitted to being part of the reason behind his own son's difficulty with the Church:

> *I fell in love with the Blessed Sacrament from the beginning— and by the mercy of God never have fallen out again: but alas! I indeed did not live up to it. I brought you all up ill and talked to you too little. Out of wickedness and sloth I almost ceased to practice my religion .... I regret those days bitterly (and suffer for them with such patience as I can be given); most of all because I failed as a father. Now I pray for you all, unceasingly.*

Tolkien was a sinner who failed his son, as we fail each other every day. No one joins the Church to find perfect people; people join it to find Christ. And so Tolkien advised his son that the only cure for struggles with the Church is connecting to the eucharist.

People enter or remain in the Church because they believe it was founded by Christ and is guided by the Holy Spirit to preserve Christ's teaching and provide the sacramental life we need to be united to Christ. People are drawn most powerfully by Christ in the eucharist. And they enter and remain because the Church is a home, in which there are people who are willing to help you make sense of reality, to care for your needs, and to walk with you on pilgrimage to Christ. Alec Guinness remarked, "If I have one regret (leaving aside a thousand failings as a person, husband, father, grandfather, great-grandfather and friend—and my lazy, slapdash, selfish attitude as an actor) it would be that I didn't take the decision to become a Catholic in my early twenties. That would have sorted out a lot of my life and sweetened it." If we look upon the Church with the eyes of faith, we too will find what Guinness, Tolkien, Houselander, and so many other grateful Catholics have experienced through the ages: true communion.

Review Questions

1. Do you know anyone who became a Catholic or returned to the practice of the Catholic faith? What were the reasons?

2. What is the communion of saints? How do the saints support our life in Christ?

3. Why can it be hard to accept advice or guidance from others? What virtues or qualities in ourselves or in priests, bishops, and the pope would make it easier to accept the help of Christ through the teaching authority of the Church?

4. Have you ever felt inspired or supported by other members of the Catholic Church? This can include saints, friends or relatives who have died, and Catholics you have heard of or know personally. How did they inspire or support you in your Catholic faith? Did they reveal anything about Christ to you; if so, what?

5. Have you ever experienced the shared Catholic life and the transformation of time and space as described in this chapter? Or in other ways? What was the experience? What aspects of that experience struck you? Did it support you in your Catholic faith or reveal something about Christ? If so, what?

6. Where there are Catholics, there is a life transformed. What are some ways at home, school, or parish we could carry on this transformation of time, space, and shared life?

Put Out Into the Deep

Anyone interested in going deeper into the relationship between Christ and the Catholic Church can begin with the excellent introduction found in Benedict XVI's short work *The Apostles* (Huntington, IN: Our Sunday Visitor, 2007). This book compiles a series of Wednesday audience addresses which Benedict XVI gave between March 15, 2006 and February 14, 2007. In twenty-one brief chapters, Benedict helps the reader go deeper into scripture to understand why Christ founded the Church. Individual chapters dedicated to each apostle and to figures like Paul, Stephen, and the women who followed Christ, make *The Apostles* both a clear introduction to the nature of the Catholic Church and a fascinating exploration of some of the New Testament's most compelling figures.

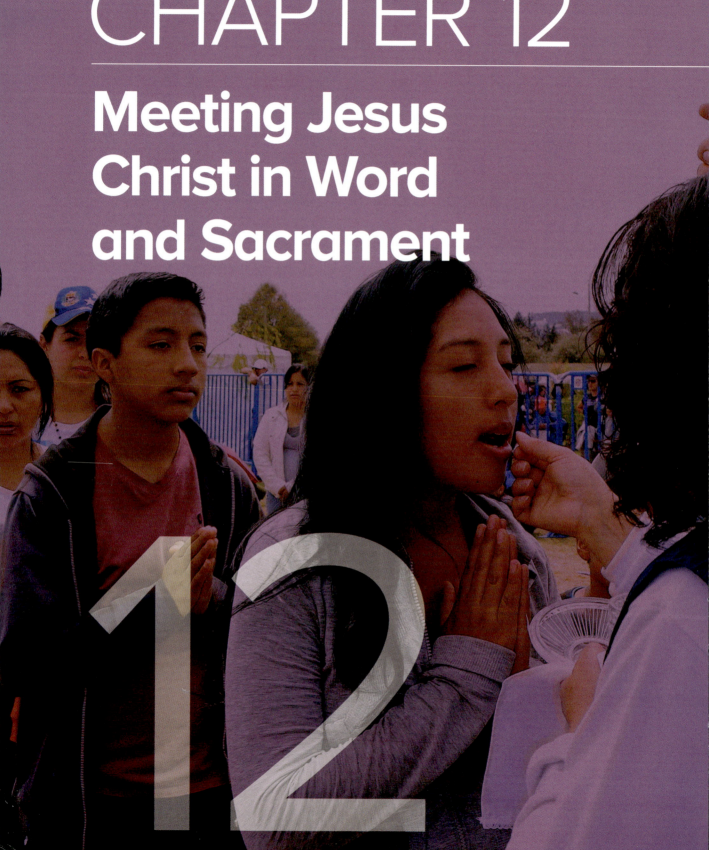

CHAPTER 12

Meeting Jesus Christ in Word and Sacrament

Francis-Xavier Nguyên Vân Thuân (1928–2002) was born in Vietnam as the oldest of eight children in a Catholic family. Ordained a priest at the age of twenty-five, he went on to serve at a parish, hospital, and prison, earn a church law degree, and mentor other priests. Later as a bishop, Vân Thuân recruited dozens of young men to study for the priesthood, founded youth associations, and helped to found a Catholic radio station. In 1975, Vân Thuân became bishop for Saigon, the capital of South Vietnam.

1975 was a very difficult year for Vân Thuân's country; it was the final year of the Vietnam War. North Vietnamese communist troops captured South Vietnam that April. Thousands tried to flee; many more died. With the new government came severe restrictions on the practice of the Catholic faith. Soon Catholic schools were closed, the religious brothers and sisters disbanded.

On August 15, 1975, Vân Thuân began a prison sentence that would last thirteen years. He realized, "I was losing everything." Nine of those years he spent in solitary confinement in a windowless cell. The heat and humidity were intolerable. Sometimes the lights burned day and night; for other long stretches of time, there was total darkness. At first, no one spoke to Vân Thuân. It was unbearably sad and lonely. Throughout his imprisonment, Vân Thuân found it difficult or even impossible to pray: "Many times, I cried like Jesus on the cross: 'My God, why have you abandoned me?' Yet, I know God did not abandon me."

Vân Thuân tried to engage his guards in conversation; he began telling them stories and teaching them English and French. Slowly he made friends with them. One day a guard asked Vân Thuân, "Can you teach me a Latin song?" Vân Thuân taught him the "Veni Creator Spiritus," or "Come, Holy Ghost," a song sung at Vân Thuân's ordination as a priest and consecration as a bishop, the same song often sung or recited during the sacrament of Confirmation. One morning in Vân Thuân's windowless prison, he suddenly heard singing. He lifted up his head, and these were the words he heard: "Pour love into our hearts and uphold the weakness of our body with your perpetual strength. Drive our enemy far away and give us the gift of peace."

Vân Thuân wrote later: "I would never have believed that an atheistic policeman would learn this entire hymn by heart, much less that he would start to sing it every morning ... I realized that the Holy Spirit was using a communist policeman to help an imprisoned bishop pray when he was too weak and depressed to be able to pray."

In 1989, Vân Thuân was transitioned to house arrest. Again, he made friends with his guard, who allowed him to write spiritual books, took Vân Thuân by night to administer the Anointing of the Sick to people, and brought priests to see him, as well as seminarians whom Vân Thuân trained and secretly ordained. The guard was expected to spy and report on Vân Thuân. One day, he gave up because he could not think of anything to write. But Vân Thuân urged him, "You have to write! If you don't write, you'll be replaced."

"But I don't know what to write!"

"Then I'll write the report," said Vân Thuân. The police were so impressed by the quality of the report that they rewarded the guard with a bottle of orange liqueur! Happy with the success, Vân Thuân and his guard celebrated with a toast.

In 1991, Vân Thuân was permitted to visit Rome, but then refused entry back to his home in Vietnam. So, Vân Thuân stayed in Rome, where he later served as president for the Church's Pontifical Council for Justice and Peace until his death in 2002.

Throughout his imprisonment, fellow prisoners asked Vân Thuân the reasons for his hope. His guards asked, "Does God really exist? Does Jesus?" Vân Thuân would never have been able to comfort his fellow prisoners or befriend his guards if he had not been meeting Christ in word and sacrament.

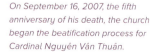

On September 16, 2007, the fifth anniversary of his death, the church began the beatification process for Cardinal Nguyên Vân Thuân.

Meeting Christ in the Word

Jesus Christ, the son of God, the "Word," was made flesh and became a man for our sake (see Jn 1:14). Just as God made himself accessible to us, so, too, God made his words accessible to us through the medium of human language. God inspired and guided human authors to capture his divine word in human words, sentences, stories, histories, prayers, letters, and personal accounts. Christ once asked his apostles if they wanted to leave him. Peter replied, "Lord, to whom shall we go? You have the words of eternal life" (Jn 6:68). When Vân Thuân was imprisoned, he made a small book of scripture verses. He had no paper at first, but the police gave him notepaper to answer their questions. From this supply, he slowly set aside enough paper to make a tiny notebook holding over three hundred sentences which Vân Thuân could remember from the scriptures. As Vân Thuân put it, "The words of Jesus possess a substance and depth that other words do not, whether they be philosophical, political, or poetic. The words of Jesus are, as often defined in the New Testament, 'words of life.'" Vân Thuân knew he needed the word of God to survive.

The word of God also nourished Vân Thuân's fellow prisoners. Some prisoners managed to smuggle a copy of the New Testament into the prison, dividing and memorizing the text. If guards were heard approaching, they buried the precious texts under the sand of the floors. At night in the darkness, prisoners could be heard reciting from memory. To hear the words of Christ, to hear the story of his suffering in that dark place, was to be in the presence of Christ himself.

Vân Thuân and these prisoners knew that the Bible provide a personal, life-giving, and transformative contact with Christ. According to Benedict XVI, in the scriptures,

> God speaks ... God answers our questions ... with human words, he speaks to us personally. We can listen to him; hear him, come to know him and understand him. We can also realize that he can enter our life and shape it, and that we can emerge from our own lives to enter into the immensity of his mercy.... In his Word, God is speaking to each one of us ... he speaks to the heart of everyone: if our hearts are alert, and our inner ears are open, we can learn to listen to the word he personally addresses to each of us.

The word of God is never exhausted. All aspects of human experience are addressed in the scriptures. Here God speaks to us about our experience of the wonders of creation in the Genesis account, where the "Spirit of God was moving over the face of the waters," and where God looked on everything he had made and saw that "it was very good" (Gn 1:2, 31). God speaks to our wonder in passages like this: "How great is the house of God!... The stars shone in their watches, and were glad; he called them, and they said, "Here we are!" They shone with gladness for him who made them" (Bar 3:24, 34).

God speaks to our wonder in passages like this: "How great is the house of God!... The stars shone in their watches, and were glad; he called them, and they said, "Here we are!" They shone with gladness for him who made them". (Bar 3:24, 34)

God illumines our human condition and its remedy in the stories of the fall and Christ's own passion and death. The search for love is found in the story of Isaac and Rebecca, Tobit and Sarah, Ruth and Boaz, and in the Song of Songs where "love is strong as death …. Its flashes are flashes of fire, a most vehement flame. Many waters cannot quench love, neither can floods drown it" (Song 8:6–7). Betrayal, repentance, and forgiveness wind through the stories of Cain and Abel, David, Peter's denial of Christ, and the conversion of Paul. Courage, fidelity, and God's help are on display in the stories of Noah, Abraham, Moses, Joshua, Gideon, Esther, Judith, Susannah, the Maccabees, and the Acts of the Apostles. The experience of suffering is voiced in the words of Job and Jeremiah. Guidance is found in Proverbs and the epistles of the New Testament. Hope can be discovered in the form of words concerning the kingdom of God:

> *Everyone who thirsts, come to the waters; and he who has no money, come, buy and eat! Come, buy wine and milk without money and without price (Is 55:1).*

> *Have no anxiety about anything, but in everything by prayer and supplication with thanksgiving let your requests be made known to God. And the peace of God, which passes all understanding, will keep your hearts and your minds in Christ Jesus (Phil 4:6–7).*

> *'Behold, the dwelling of God is with men. He will dwell with them, and they shall be his people, and God himself will be with them; he will wipe away every tear from their eyes, and death shall be no more, neither shall there be mourning nor crying nor pain any more, for the former things have passed away.' And he who sat upon the throne said, 'Behold, I make all things new' (Rev 21:3–5).*

The source of hope in Christ and his life are revealed in the Gospels. There Christ teaches, heals, loves, and suffers for us. And Christ is found in the Psalms.

As Benedict XVI wrote, "In the Psalms we find expressed every possible human feeling set masterfully in the sight of God; joy and pain, distress and hope, fear and trepidation: here all find expression" (*Verbum Domini*, 24). We see in the Psalms expressions of joy, praise, and thanksgiving. For example, Psalm 84 rejoices: "Blessed are the men whose strength is in you, in whose heart are the highways to Zion" (Ps 84:5). Psalm 18 marvels how God "brought me forth into a broad place; he delivered me, because he delighted in me" (Ps 18:19).

But we also see in the Psalms expressions of grief and rage. For example, Psalms 25, 56, and 69 speak of being lonely and afflicted. Psalms 27, 38, and 55 speak of feeling abandoned by parents or friends. Psalms 69 and 137 express anger against enemies. Psalms 10, 13, 22, 42, and 44 directly ask God, "Where are you?" The Psalms show us that God knows the human experience: to be fallen in a fallen world, to be frightened, to suffer, to feel resentment and rage, and to wonder how to broach such urgent questions with God. God made us, knows us, and loves us. He wants our real self to come to him. But we often hold back some part of our self, the parts we are ashamed of—our sins, our doubts, or our frustration about problems in our life. We do not realize that God already knows about these parts; he is neither scandalized nor repelled by them. In fact, our weakness draws his concern and sympathy. The Psalms give us the words to express our experience and share it with God. Even as the psalmist in Psalm 39 exclaims that he is crushed by God's blows, even as he brokenly begs God to "remove your stroke from me," he also says staunchly to God, "My hope is in you" (Ps 39:10, 7). When we do not know how to talk to God, the Psalms teach us to pray.

We can deepen our encounter with Christ in scripture in several ways. To read or memorize passages, to ponder and revisit them, to imagine the scene, to compare passages to other parts of scripture, to listen to what Tradition and the living Magisterium can teach us about the scriptures, and to talk personally with Christ about his word, all these are ways to meet Christ in the words he addresses to each of us. Just like Vân Thuận and his fellow prisoners, we find what the Church has found: "the force and power in the word of God is so great that it stands as the support and energy of the Church, the strength of faith for her sons, the food of the soul, the pure and everlasting source of spiritual life" (*Dei Verbum*, 21).

We can deepen our encounter with Christ in scripture.

Juan Fernández Navarrete, Bautismo de Christo, c. 1567, Oil on panel. Prado National Museum, Madrid, Spain.

Meeting Christ in His Sacraments

Christ also meets us in his sacraments, beginning with Baptism. This foundational sacrament frees us from sin, makes us adopted sons and daughters of God, and members of the Church, the body of Christ. Christ commanded his apostles to go and make disciples of all nations, baptizing them in the name of the Father, Son, and Holy Spirit (see Mt 28:19–20; Mk 16:15–16). This sacrament was so important for Christian life, that Christ, who had no need to be freed from sin and was already the son of God, modelled for us the importance of Baptism by going to his cousin John to be baptized in the Jordan River (see Mt 3:13). The sacrament of Confirmation continues what is begun in Baptism, uniting a person more deeply to the Church and granting him the gift of the Holy Spirit (CCC 1285). At Pentecost, the apostles received the gift of the Holy Spirit and began their ministry by baptizing almost three thousand people (see Acts 2:41). The apostles continued their ministry, praying for the baptized, as Paul does in Acts 19, "that they might receive the Holy Spirit… Then they laid their hands on them and they received the Holy Spirit" (Acts 8:15–17).

The rite of Baptism relates how God prepared the human race to encounter him in this sacrament:

> At the very dawn of creation your Spirit breathed on the waters, making them the wellspring of all holiness. The waters of the great flood you made a sign of the waters of baptism, that make an end of sin and a new beginning of goodness. Through the waters of the Red Sea you led Israel out of slavery, to be an image of God's holy people, set free from sin by baptism. In the waters of the Jordan your Son was baptized by John and anointed with the Spirit. Your Son willed that water and blood should flow from his side as he hung upon the cross. After his resurrection he told his disciples: "Go out and teach all nations, baptizing them in the name of the Father, and of the Son, and of the Holy Spirit." Father, look now with love upon your Church, and unseal for her the fountain of baptism. By the power of the Spirit give to the water of this font the grace of your Son. You created man in your own likeness: cleanse him from sin in a new birth to innocence by water and the Spirit.

"This is our faith," the bishop tells those about to be confirmed. "This is the faith of the Church."

Whether we are transformed by Baptism and Confirmation depends partly on our response to this encounter with Christ's grace. But, incredibly, receiving the grace itself does not depend on our level of commitment to Christ, the quality of our faith, or our personal holiness. This is the ultimate reason the Church makes these sacraments available for infants. As John Henry Newman wrote: "Baptism placed you in this blessed state. God did not wait till you should do some good thing before He blessed you. No! He knew you could do no good thing of yourselves. So He came to you first; He loved you before you loved Him; He gave you a work which He first made you able to do." Vân Thuân was once amazed to learn of some Hmong people who wished to receive Baptism and Confirmation. They had no priests, churches, or schools, but they had heard of Christ through a radio station. They knew they would meet Christ in Baptism and Confirmation. They desired this encounter so much that they were willing to make a twelve-day march on foot through the mountains to find the closest church.

We meet Christ also in the sacrament of Reconciliation. One way that Christ manifested his divinity was by claiming the power to forgive sins. He forgave sins multiple times in the Gospels (see, for example, Mk 2:5, 10; Lk 5:20–24). Although Baptism frees us from sin and joins us to

Christ's body, we still have the power to sin and turn from Christ and His Church. Christ had to reconcile with people who had already been baptized, such as Peter after he had denied Christ (Jn 21:15–18). We need ongoing conversion; we need ongoing forgiveness. Christ extended this to his followers, and he gave his apostles the power to forgive sins: "As the Father has sent me, even so I send you.... If you forgive the sins of any, they are forgiven; if you retain the sins of any, they are retained" (Jn 20:21–23). Through the sacrament of Reconciliation, everyone can gain direct access to Christ and his saving mercy, everyone can be forgiven, reconciled, and strengthened to grow in relationship with Christ, just as Peter was on the shores of the sea of Tiberias.

Through the sacrament of Reconciliation, everyone can gain direct access to Christ and his saving mercy, everyone can be forgiven, reconciled, and strengthened to grow in relationship with Christ, just as Peter was on the shores of the sea of Tiberias.

The act of expressing sorrow privately to Christ and asking his forgiveness connects us to him. But there is a particularly powerful encounter with Christ in the sacrament of Reconciliation. We encounter Christ in a special way when we hear him say through his ordained priest: "God, the Father of mercies, through the death and resurrection of his Son, has reconciled the world to himself and sent the Holy Spirit among us for the forgiveness of sins; through the ministry of the Church, may God give you pardon and peace, and I absolve you from your sins in the name of the Father, and of the Son, and of the Holy Spirit." When we repent and confess our sins to a priest through the sacrament of Reconciliation, we speak directly to Christ. Fr. Walter Ciszek, a priest imprisoned for his faith like Vân Thuân, treasured the chances for Reconciliation which came occasionally in the prison camps. People came, not to confess to Ciszek, but to Christ. And they did indeed meet Christ through this sacrament.

François Mauriac (1885–1970) was a French journalist and writer of fiction and plays. He won the Nobel Prize for literature in 1952. A life-long Catholic, he wrote a book entitled Holy Thursday, *which revealed what the eucharist and other sacraments meant to him.*

François Mauriac once pointed out that priests, even the pope, need to meet Christ in the sacrament of Reconciliation: "the man before whom we kneel, kneels in his turn...he hears our sins but confesses his own." Priests cannot give themselves the sacrament of reconciliation. In order to receive the sacrament himself, Ciszek had to wait until another priest was imprisoned with him. There were some risks because Ciszek was forbidden to administer the sacrament of Reconciliation. Sometimes Ciszek heard the confessions of other priests who had been pressured into spying on fellow prisoners. Ciszek knew he was risking his life when he secretly offered the sacrament of Reconciliation to these priests. What if they turned him in? Yet, Ciszek said: "We heard their confessions and they heard ours...we could not bring ourselves to turn anyone away from the grace to be gained in the sacraments or in listening to the word of God. We all had our failings; each of us knew only too well how much we depended upon God and his grace." All Christ's followers, including priests, bishops, and popes, are sinners. All need and have received an incredible gift in the sacrament of Reconciliation: as Mauriac put it, forgiveness, peace, and a blank page.

But the deepest sacramental encounter with Christ is found in the eucharist, Christ's own body and blood, Christ made present to us through the Mass. Chapter 12 of volume I on "The Bread of Life" explained how God paved the way for this sacrament through key events in the Old Testament and finally through Christ's own teaching. The Church has always taught how we can encounter Christ physically, hidden behind the qualities of what looks like bread and wine, but truly present in his body, blood, soul, and divinity.

From the apostles at the Last Supper, to the disciples on the road to Emmaus, to the present day, Christ's followers can know him in "the breaking of the bread" (Lk 24:35). The eucharist welcomes us in moments of joy. Converts Alec Guinness and Msgr. Ronald Knox

(1888–1957) found themselves so eager to see Christ sometimes that they literally ran to church to visit the eucharist. The eucharist welcomes us in moments of doubt and discouragement. J. R. R. Tolkien once told his son, "Out of the darkness of my life…I put before you the one great thing to love on earth: the Blessed Sacrament....There you will find romance, glory, honour, fidelity, and the true way of all your loves upon earth."

Similarly, Caryll Houselander once wrote to a friend,

> We need comfort, sympathy, love, as well as wisdom and practical help and cure; in fact, we not only need help, but that someone should be as concentrated on us as we are on ourselves, supporting us, loving us, feeling deeply for us, every second of the day and night. Well, Our Lord is the only one who can answer that need. If you go often to visit the Blessed Sacrament, and pray in the presence of the Blessed Sacrament, tell Our Lord in your own words, or your own tears, or your own dumbness, that you can hardly suffer it. Ask Him to help; you can be perfectly certain that He Will.

Leonardo Da Vinci, The Last Supper, 1490s, Tempera and gesso, Convent of Santa Maria delle Grazie, Milan, Italy.

The eucharist transforms us. Receiving the eucharist healed Caryll Houselander when she was a child sick with emotional pain.

Jesus healed Thérèse of Lisieux in a similar way. The youngest of the family, a child who had lost her mother, Thérèse suffered incredible anxiety for years. She cried often; she cried if she hurt someone; she cried for having cried: "I was really unbearable because of my extreme touchiness." As an adolescent, Thérèse could see no remedy. And then, one Christmas after Thérèse had received the eucharist at Midnight

Mass, the family went home. Her father was annoyed to see Thérèse's older sister still babying Thérèse by putting out her "magic shoes" full of presents. "This will be the last year!" he said irritably, just the kind of thing to make Thérèse cry. But Thérèse was changed. She found she could sit cheerfully by her father to open her presents. The family thought it was too good to be true. But, as Thérèse wrote later, receiving the eucharist had changed her: "the work I had been unable to do in ten years was done by Jesus in one instant." This seems like a small thing, but for Thérèse it was enormous. There is nothing we need too small or insignificant for Christ to care about or cure through his presence in the eucharist.

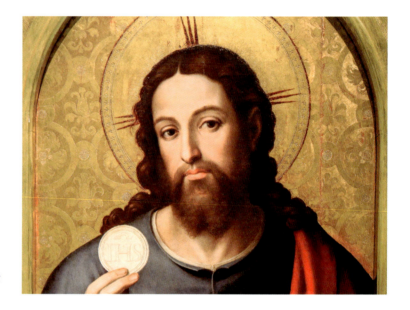

Jesus helps us in and through the eucharist when no one else can.

Jesus helps us in and through the eucharist when no one else can. In prison, Ciszek went for years without holy communion: "I prayed to God, I talked to him and asked for help and strength, I knew that he was with me. All this I had, and yet I could not have him in my hands, I could not have his sacramental presence. And the difference to me was very real." Later in the prison camps, when it became possible to celebrate Mass and hide the eucharist among the prisoners, Ciszek wrote:

> *You cannot explain all this, I know, to those who do not believe. Even for many Christians, I fear, the notion of the Blessed Sacrament as the bread of life is somehow only a poetic or symbolic phrase used by Jesus in the Gospel. Yet what a source of sustenance it was to us then, how much it meant to us to have the body and blood of Christ as the food of our spiritual lives in this sacrament of love and joy. The experience was very real; you could feel its effects upon your mind and heart, upon your daily life.*

Only the powerful presence of Christ in the eucharist explains the remarkable change in Ciudad Juaréz, Mexico. Between 2008–2010, the city was considered one of the most dangerous in the world, with drug and gang-related violence leading to arson and forty deaths per day. Desperate, one of the parishes began eucharistic adoration in 2013, and the annual murder rate plummeted. "Only Jesus is going to save us from this, only Jesus can give us security" said parishioners, and they were right. As Vân Thuân wrote, "At all times, and especially in times of persecution, the eucharist has been the secret of the Christian life, the food of witnesses and the bread of hope."

When Vân Thuân was arrested, he had nothing but a rosary in his pocket. The next day, he was allowed to write friends for things he needed, like toothpaste and clothes. He added, "Please send me a little wine as medicine for my stomachache." They knew what he meant. With the supplies came a bottle of wine labelled "medicine for stomachaches" and some small pieces of unleavened bread hidden inside a flashlight so Vân Thuân could celebrate Mass. Every day, Vân Thuân poured three drops of wine and one drop of water into the palm of his hand to celebrate Mass secretly. Each day he met Christ on the cross and "confirmed with all my heart and soul a new pact, an eternal pact between Jesus and me."

Just as Ciszek and his fellow prisoners found comfort in the eucharist, so too did Vân Thuân's fellow prisoners. They were divided in groups of fifty, sleeping on wooden boards in a common room, each prisoner allowed no more than twenty inches of sleeping space. At night, Vân Thuân would celebrate Mass from memory and distribute communion. Vân Thuân wrapped the eucharist in a small paper packet, hidden in his pocket. Every week, during the mandatory all-prisoner meeting, Vân Thuân and other Catholic prisoners would pass the small packet to the other prisoner groups. In this way, every prisoner group was allowed to

In 2013 the annual murder rate plummeted in Ciudad Juaréz when one of the parishes began eucharistic adoration.

"Surely goodness and mercy shall follow me all the days of my life; and I shall dwell in the house of the LORD forever" (Ps 23:6).

have the eucharist with them at night: "Everyone knew Jesus was in their midst. At night, the prisoners would take turns for adoration. With his silent presence, the eucharistic Jesus helped us in unimaginable ways."

The word of God prepares us to encounter Christ in the sacraments. The sacraments return us to the word of God, as Benedict XVI explained: "From the two tables of the word of God and the Body of Christ, the Church receives and gives to the faithful the bread of life" (*Sacramentum Caritatis*, 44). Thus, the Mass is the "source and summit of the whole Christian life," (*Lumen Gentium*, 11), uniting and fulfilling all the ways we meet Christ through word and sacrament.

Why would Christ arrange for us to encounter him through the medium of human language, through physical means like water, oil, bread, and wine, through people and the audible verbal confession of sin to a human priest, the verbal audible pronouncement of words, and the physical laying on of hands? That he did so is clear from scripture. Perhaps the reason is simply because he made us body-soul creatures. God chose to give us bodies and called it very good; Christ took on a body for our sake. It makes sense that he would help us encounter him in ways which match how he made us.

Psalm 23 teaches us about the kind of God who made us. He is a God found in baptism: "The LORD is my shepherd, I shall not want; he makes me lie down in green pastures. He leads me beside still waters. He restores my soul." He is a God found in confirmation: "Thou anointest my head with oil." He is a God found in reconciliation: "He leads me in paths of righteousness for his name's sake. Even though I walk through the valley of the shadow of death, I fear no evil; for thou art with me; thy rod and thy staff, they comfort me." He is a God found in the eucharist: "Thou preparest a table before me in the presence of my enemies." Like Vân Thuân and all others who have met Christ in his word and sacrament, the followers of Christ can say, "Surely goodness and mercy shall follow me all the days of my life; and I shall dwell in the house of the LORD forever" (Ps 23:1-6).

Review Questions

1. Using this chapter and others in *Why Believe?*, explain the scriptural origins for the sacraments of baptism, confirmation, reconciliation, and the eucharist.

2. Do you experience meeting Christ in the scriptures through personal reading or the readings at Mass? What stories or passages have inspired you? What have you learned?

3. Many different ways have been developed over the centuries to help us explore the scriptures and meet Christ there. Some of these ways include the following: Lectio Divina, praying the *Liturgy of the Hours*, reading the scriptures according to the "Four Senses of Scripture," and reading an annotated version of the scriptures which allows one to read its cross-references to other related parts of scripture. If you have used these methods, how have they been helpful?

4. Why might some people experience difficulty in receiving the sacrament of reconciliation? What might be ways we could understand or explain it so as to make it easier for people to experience Christ's mercy through it?

5. If the eucharist is the source and summit of Christian life, what might be some ways we can cultivate a love for the Mass and the eucharist in our own lives, at home, at school, and elsewhere?

6. At times Vân Thuận was unable to pray. Sometimes, we, too, experience no consolation or comfort in our prayer. How can scripture and the sacraments help us through such times? How can we support others in similar difficulties?

Put Out Into the Deep

John Paul II's *Ecclesia de Eucharistia* (2003) explores the importance of the eucharist for many aspects of Christian life, including the love of others, the Church, and the other sacraments. With personal stories from John Paul II's own experience and a fascinating reflection on Mary's connection to the eucharist, this encyclical provides an excellent starting-point for anyone interested in delving into the Church's teaching on the eucharist and other sacraments.

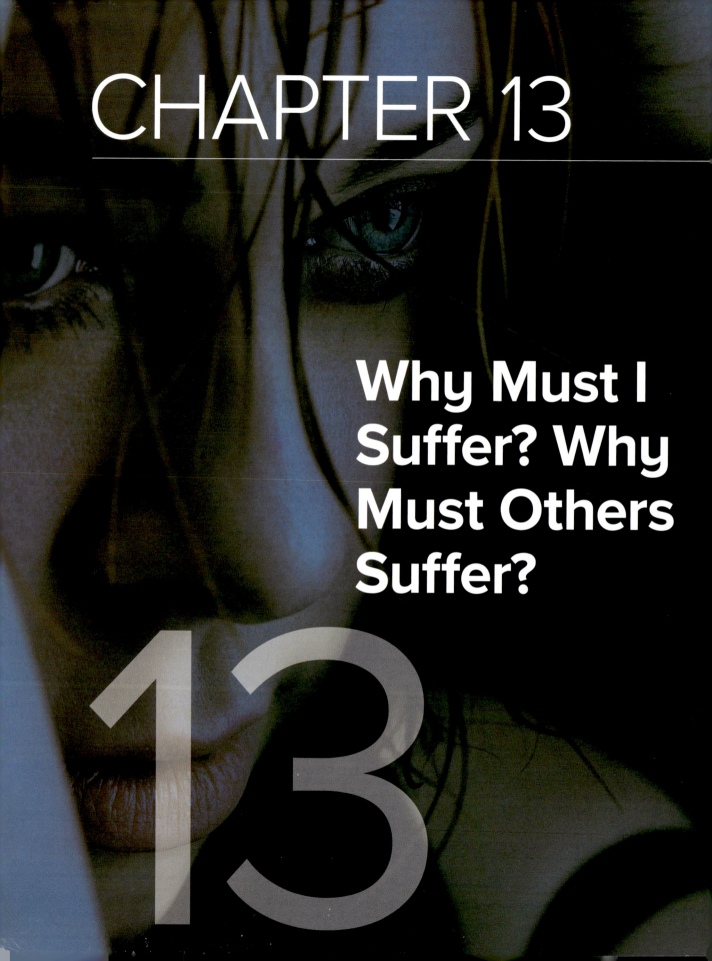

CHAPTER 13

Why Must I Suffer? Why Must Others Suffer?

13

Suffering is a mystery. Every attempt to understand it brings up baffling questions about God. If God is good, why do innocent people suffer? If God is all-wise, could he not find some way to preserve our freedom and end suffering at the same time? If God is loving, could he not develop some better, less painful method of teaching us virtue and wisdom? It is true that Christ suffered. But, as C. S. Lewis once replied when he was suffering, "Does that make it easier to understand?" Each truth provokes another question. Every attempt to explain suffering brings us back to the fact that suffering is a mystery. Hardest of all to understand is the idea that Christ invites us to redemptive suffering.

Given a choice between suffering and escape, many would choose escape. People try to bury themselves in work, volunteering, or distracting themselves with fun activities. They try romance, shopping, substance abuse, or even sleeping as much as possible. But if you have tried any of these methods, you know their limitations. Such methods bring only temporary escape; soon enough you find you need new and increased doses of escape.

Suffering is hard. And it is hard to read about suffering because words on the page are limited in their power to comfort or to illuminate mystery. This chapter can only point to what sufferers before us have learned from Christ.

This chapter will tell what we know about suffering in two parts. The first part describes how suffering entered the world and how Christ came to end suffering, beginning with certain kinds. The second part explores how Christ suffered to end suffering by transforming it into a kind of charity and by inviting us to join him in practicing the charity known as redemptive suffering.

Christ Came to End Suffering

St. Thomas Aquinas described evil as the absence of some good thing that ought to be there and suffering as being stuck with this absence and knowing it. Pain is the absence of health; cruelty from other people is the absence of the right understanding and respect they should have for us as made in the image and likeness of God. Ultimately, suffering is loss. This loss came into the world through the original sin of Adam and Eve. By trusting the word of the serpent over the word of God, Adam and Eve lost the good relationship they had with reality. They lost their good relationship with others. In the Genesis story, we see them suddenly blaming each other. They lost their good relationship with themselves, becoming ashamed of how they appeared. They lost their good relationship with God: they hid from him.

Christ came to end sin and the terrible suffering it inflicted on the human race. We do not see God telling Adam and Eve that suffering builds character. We see him promising a "seed" which shall bruise the head of the tempting serpent (Gen 3:15). We do not see Christ telling the blind, the lame, and the sick that "what doesn't kill you makes you stronger." We see him healing their suffering; we see him weeping over the death of Lazarus and raising him from the dead. Revelation teaches us that God is good, wise, and loving, and that he made us good. If suffering meant that God hated some of us or that some of us were bad through and through, he would not invite all of us to join him in paradise. But we know that he wants everyone to be saved and come to a knowledge of the truth (see 1 Tim 2:4). If suffering were good in itself, there would be suffering in paradise. But we know that in heaven every tear will be wiped away (see Rev 21:4).

Christ wants to restore us to the good relationships we once enjoyed. He began by dying to save us from sin. Our personal sin creates suffering. As we have noted, sin puts us into a state of war with ourselves, others, the world, and God. Sin comes with the same kind of torments, restlessness, and fear that addictions do. Christ wants to liberate us from sin and the suffering it causes. The call to redemptive suffering does not include the suffering of sin. Christ came to free us from this suffering. In addition, he came to free us from certain kinds of suffering, the hellish kinds of suffering to which sin leads: the suffering of isolation, of not valuing the self, and of not seeing God as our father.

The Suffering of Isolation

One result of personal and original sin is the loss of relationship with others, that is, the suffering of isolation. Loneliness is perhaps the most difficult part of suffering. Many people have no one to comfort or help them. Even when there are people to help, suffering can still awaken a terrible feeling of isolation. Sometimes it seems as if no one notices, understands, or cares. We are embarrassed for our suffering. We feel an expectation to appear tough or look happy, as if people would reject us for our suffering because they do not want to be bothered with it. But Christ wants to free us from isolation. As we saw in chapter 10, Christ wants us to experience loving personal concern.

Christ did not suffer in isolation. We might think it would be braver to say, "No, no, I don't want to bother you; I'll go off into the distance and suffer alone." But Christ did not seem to think that was good. He specifically asked Peter, James, and John to stay with him in the Garden of Gethsemane (see Mt 26:37; Mk 14:33). He let Simon of Cyrene help him carry the cross (see Mt 27:32; Mk 15:21; Lk 23:26). He let his mother, his disciple John, and other women watch at the foot of the cross (see Mt 27:55–56; Mk 15:40–41; Lk 23:49; Jn 19:25–26). Christ rejected the expectation that we should try to hide our sufferings. He did not suffer alone. He does not let us suffer alone: he suffers with us and he gives us the means to escape isolation.

Guiseppe Cesari, The Agony in the Garden, 1597–98, Oil on canvas, Uppark-National Trust, South Harting, United Kingdom.

Not valuing the self as God does can also lead to shame. Sadly, some people experience guilt, even after they have been forgiven of their sins.

The Suffering of Not Valuing the Self

Another result of personal and original sin is a loss of right relationship with ourselves. Not valuing the self as God does leads to self-loathing; it can lead us to seek self-worth through means which ultimately fail, such as wealth, fame, power, romance, or endless activity. Not valuing the self as God does can also lead to shame. Sadly, some people experience guilt, even after they have been forgiven of their sins. They fail to see what chapter 10 stressed: God loves them independently of anything they do or fail to do.

If we do not value ourselves as God does, we can also fail to exercise charity to ourselves. This leads to further sufferings. Too often we forget that Christ made the whole of us. He asks us to love God with all our strength, heart, mind, and soul (see Mt 22:37; Mk 12:30; Lk 10:27). He asks this because he wants to have a relationship with the whole of us. Instead, we reject some part of the human person; we reject the body or the soul, we reject the intellect, or at other times we scorn the emotions. Following this trend, we often fail to exercise charity to some part of ourselves. We do not eat well, and so we experience physical suffering. We are stressed because we are being a perfectionist about some project. We do not try for opportunities because we fear to make mistakes, and so we experience emotional and mental suffering because we have not been exercising and caring for our gifts of intellect and will to make thoughtful, creative decisions. Or we do not make time to turn to God interiorly or receive the powerful support of the sacraments, so we get discouraged, restless, and it becomes easier to sin. We suffer because we have not been caring for our spiritual needs.

Exercising charity to ourselves is particularly important in the context of redemptive suffering. The most important aspect of caring for our spiritual needs is recognizing that we need an ongoing relationship with Christ and that he wants to have one with us because we are wonderful in his eyes. Because they know that redemptive suffering is good and selfishness is bad, however, people might be inclined to undertake sacrifices far beyond their capabilities and at great cost to themselves, without the benefit of talking to Christ and the advice of good men and women. Such sacrifices often backfire, leaving us exhausted, resentful, and less likely to attempt sacrifices in the future. Redemptive suffering does not ask us to hurt ourselves to love others. When the saints sacrifice supports to their needs, they do so in the context of conversation with Christ about making the sacrifice and about how he will meet their needs in other ways. Christ does not want us to suffer because we fail to value ourselves as he does. Christ came to restore our right relationship with ourselves, and he gives us the means to do this.

The Suffering of Not Seeing God as our Loving Father

The worst result of personal and original sin is loss of right relationship with God. Failure to see God as our loving father leads to fear and despair. When C. S. Lewis's wife died, part of his suffering was the terrible fears it raised about God. If God lets us suffer, can he be good? Or can it be there is no God? Are we helpless in a terrible world? Lewis experienced fears which many sufferers have felt. If God is not a real and loving father, then we are truly lost.

C. S. Lewis (1898–1963) was a member of the Church of England, and a British professor and writer. He wrote several books on suffering including The Problem of Pain *and* A Grief Observed. *He is best known for writing* The Chronicles of Narnia.

But Christ came to end the suffering which comes from this confusion about God. Christ does this in many ways. Often he gives experiences which comfort and help us to understand, as Lewis came to recognize when facing extreme sorrow. In his words, it was like being "a man in total darkness. He thinks he is in a cellar or dungeon. Then there comes a sound . . . waves or wind-blown trees or cattle half a mile away. And if so, it proves he's not in a cellar, but free, in the open air." Lewis realized that we make mistakes, we forget things, we have blind-spots and ignorance. What we see at one moment in time is not necessarily how things are in general. Lewis felt abandoned or attacked by God. But realizing his own weakness gave him incredible hope that God might be closer and more loving than it seemed. Lewis was on his way towards relief from the suffering which comes from not seeing that God is our Father.

Human weakness was also the means by which God regained his priest Walter Ciszek, whom we met in the last chapter. Fr. Ciszek (1904–1984) was a Jesuit priest serving in Poland in the late 1930s. He was arrested when the Soviet Army invaded. His captors wanted him to sign a false confession saying his priestly work was an attack on the government. After five years of torture, he signed the false confession. His captors then offered Fr. Ciszek a choice: cooperate as a spy or be killed. Fr. Ciszek tried to delay his decision, but as time passed, he lost all hope. He even lost his faith in God. He realized that if he wanted to get his faith and hope back, he would have to depend completely on God. This terrified Fr. Ciszek, because, as he later wrote, "we believe that we depend on God . . . but we are afraid to put it to the test. There remains deep down in each of us a little nagging doubt, a little knot of fear which we refuse to face or admit even to ourselves, that says, 'Suppose it isn't so.' We are afraid to abandon ourselves totally into God's hands for fear he will not catch us as we fall." In the darkest moment of his life, Fr. Ciszek had to face his fear and doubt about whether God loved him like a father.

Fr. Ciszek brought back to mind some old memories of God. Without any certainty that God existed or loved him, he then tried to pray. For the first time, Ciszek learned "total trust in his love and concern for me and his desire to sustain and protect me." Fr. Ciszek felt his anxiety and tension diminish; he experienced a feeling of liberation, confidence, and happiness. The next time he met with his captors, they again threatened him with death. But Fr. Ciszek felt very differently. He was still afraid to die. But nothing is as frightening as uncertainty about whether God is taking care of us, and Fr. Ciszek had just been spared from that kind of suffering. Redemptive suffering does not include the suffering of separation from God. Christ came to restore our relationship with God, and he gives us the means to discover how God is a loving father.

"We believe that we depend on God . . . but we are afraid to put it to the test. There remains deep down in each of us a little nagging doubt, a little knot of fear which we refuse to face or admit even to ourselves, that says, 'Suppose it isn't so.' We are afraid to abandon ourselves totally into God's hands for fear he will not catch us as we fall."
—Father Walter Ciszek

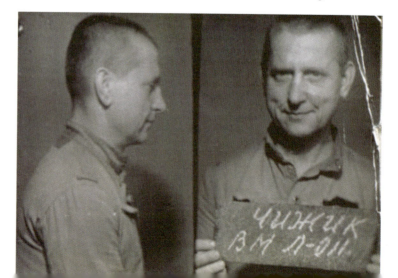

Christ Gives us Means to Escape Hellish Suffering

We have seen that Christ came to end the worst aspects of suffering which began with original sin: personal sin, isolation, not valuing the self as God does, and not seeing God as our father. Now we want to know more about how he does so. We have just seen the personal experiences of Christ's healing that helped C. S. Lewis and Fr. Walter Ciszek during their darkest hours. But the Christian life offers many additional responses to suffering that may be called ordinary channels of grace. To liberate us from sin and experience forgiveness, Christ gives us baptism and reconciliation. He gives us ways to grow strong against the false promises of sin, such as the Mass, eucharistic adoration, and other forms of prayer.

To liberate us from isolation, he lives within us; he raises up people like Teresa of Avila to teach us to find him within us. He founded the Church and instituted holy orders and holy matrimony as two sacraments for building communion among the people of God. He gives us the communion of saints. He inspires holy men and women to care for each other, from priests bringing the anointing of the sick and married couples founding hospitals, to religious brothers caring for those with psychological sufferings and religious sisters comforting the dying, just as Christ himself showed loving personal concern for the suffering.

To help us see our true worth and discover God as a loving father, Christ gives us the sacraments, which heal our blindness to this reality. Christ gives us the scriptures, which speak ceaselessly of our worth in his eyes. This is especially true of the Psalms, which as chapter 12 explained, give us the words to bring our whole self to God and discover him as a loving father. Christ taught his disciples to pray, beginning with the words "Our Father." He has raised up holy men and women over the last two thousand years to repeat his teaching that we are made in his image and likeness and totally loved by a compassionate Father. He gives special devotions, such as the Sacred Heart and Divine Mercy, which help people remember that God is merciful and loving. Besides sacraments, revelation, and his own loving influence, Christ gives us the example of saints as well as regular sufferers like Lewis and Ciszek to help us reconnect to God. In all these ways and more, he walks with us in our suffering to free us from the losses which came into the world through sin.

What remains mysterious is why Christ did not end suffering all at once. Christ healed many people during his ministry, but he did not heal everyone. It is a mystery why he allows the losses from original sin to continue between the Incarnation and when he comes again. But perhaps we can gain a little more understanding if we consider how Christ had an additional goal for suffering. He definitely wanted to end the suffering this chapter has just described. But he also wanted to end suffering as we know it by transforming it into a kind of charity.

A young Nigerian boy suffering from malnutrition. Christ healed many people during his ministry, but he did not heal everyone. It is a mystery why he allows the losses from original sin to continue between the Incarnation and when he comes again.

Christ Transforms Suffering

The last section explored how original sin led to the loss of right relationship with others, self, and God. Christ worked directly to end these sufferings specifically by suffering and dying. Christ also led a counter-attack on suffering by transforming it into a means of relating to others, self, and God.

Christ chose to suffer freely because he loved God the Father and he loved us and wanted to save us. To ask us to join him in redemptive suffering is to ask if we, too, would like to love in this way. Redemptive suffering means to join our sufferings to Christ's so that we share in his suffering and become his partners in charity. When we join our suffering to Christ's, we become his partners in helping people find perfect and everlasting happiness.

Redemptive suffering might intimidate us. But we should keep in mind that redemptive suffering is the most difficult kind of charity. As explained in chapter 10, charity takes practice. When we take on great sacrifices for others without prayer and without considering our duties to ourselves, our efforts can backfire. It is not a good idea to compete in the Super Bowl without prior practice and coaching; similarly, it is not a good idea to undertake the hardest form of charity without prior practice, prayer, and consultation with others. Furthermore, charity to others begins with charity to self, which means taking care of the kinds of suffering described in the beginning of this chapter. If we do not love ourselves enough to deal with sin, isolation, valuing the self as God does, and seeing God as our father, we will not be in a good position to love others. We will not be in a position to help them escape the worst kinds of suffering because we ourselves are still trapped in those prisons. The foundation for redemptive suffering is working with Christ in the right order to free ourselves first, and then others, from the sufferings born from sin.

So what does redemptive suffering look like? Imagine something free of the sufferings of sin and rooted in a deep connection to God's grace and mercy. Imagine something free of isolation, done instead with the support and company of others, including God, friends, and the communion of saints. Envision something free of self-loathing, undertaken with a deep sense of one's own worth. Finally, picture something done in complete certainty that God is near us, protecting us and loving us like a father.

We almost need a new word to describe whatever kind of suffering this would be. If we can imagine redemptive suffering, a form of love free of all those burdens, we can better understand St. Paul's mind-boggling words: "We are afflicted in every way, but not crushed; perplexed, but not driven to despair; persecuted, but not forsaken; struck down, but not destroyed; always carrying in the body the death of Jesus, so that the life of Jesus may also be manifested in our bodies" (2 Cor 4:8–10). It becomes easier to understand how holy men and women willingly join Christ in redemptive suffering and, moreover, seem joyful about it. They do endure difficult things; they do experience fear and sadness. But these sufferings are freed from the hellish burdens of sin, isolation, self-loathing, and dread of God, and they are endured for love. This is a very different kind of suffering than what most of us are used to. This is redemptive suffering, suffering liberated and transformed by Christ into a form of charity.

Making Experiments in Redemptive Suffering

Who would want to attempt redemptive suffering? Because redemptive suffering is an advanced form of charity, anyone interested in redemptive suffering should start back with chapter 10. But if we have been practicing charity and desire to practice redemptive suffering, how do we actually begin?

Begin with small experiments. Begin by talking with God about something you are already suffering. Consider someone you want to help, either someone you actually know or anyone who needs help. Talk with God and consult a good and mature man or woman about your idea and develop a length of time to offer your suffering, joining it to Christ's suffering to help this person. When Fr. Ciszek was facing death and struggling with his faith, he did not say, "What a great thing I can offer for others!" He had to focus on finding God his father, not making a sacrifice far beyond his capabilities. So start with a small kind of suffering, not the worst suffering you are enduring, and a limited amount of time. For example, "I will offer my sore throat for five minutes, joining it to Christ's suffering to help my friend who is sick." God will help your friend in the way he needs most (but a way that may not look like what you expected).

Any kind of suffering can be joined in this way to Christ's suffering. We might not be able to do anything tangible for people we love, but we can always offer suffering. For example, you break your leg in May. What good is that? It means discomfort and a wasted summer, not able to work or swim or do anything you were planning to do. But if you say, "I hate this, but, for maybe ten minutes, I want to join it to Christ's suffering as a way to love," your suffering mysteriously begins to help in unimaginable ways. Christ joins it to his own suffering, using it to comfort your friend or protect your future spouse or transform your enemy. He uses it to end war or disease; he uses it to save people from despair and bring them to eternal life. Suddenly, the event of your broken leg has power. Before the coming of Christ, suffering was made additionally worse by its feeling of total pointlessness. But redemptive suffering has meaning.

Your experiments in redemptive suffering are working if you see your relationship with Christ growing, along with a deeper sense of peace and his love for you. If you see yourself slipping into the old modes of suffering described in the last section or feeling exhausted or resentful, talk with Christ about a simpler, more manageable experiment or even pause experiments until your relationship with Christ is stronger.

If your experiments are working, you could talk with Christ about making voluntary sacrifices. Again, you would want to commend your inspiration to Christ in prayer and take counsel from a mature man or woman of faith about the timing and nature of the sacrifice. Redemptive suffering is a way to love. Christ does not want us to undertake a sacrifice which looks loving but is done apart from loving conversation with him and apart from loving awareness of our own needs. Evaluate these experiments again by the same means. Through God's grace, there is no more powerful way to love others than to suffer for them by joining our sufferings to Christ's.

The Answer to Suffering

This chapter cannot resolve the mystery of suffering. Often, we find ourselves suffering and hate it. We want to know why God is allowing us to suffer. We do not receive an immediate answer. What we do receive is help to remove the unnecessary aspects of suffering: are you suffering from sin? From isolation? From self-loathing? From dread of God? Have you taken on something too hard for you without consulting God? Let us remove those burdens! Part of the reason Christ suffered was to end such burdens.

But after that? What about other kinds of suffering? Is there an answer? Yes, says John Paul II. When he wrote his encyclical on suffering, *Salvifici Doloris* (*On the Christian Meaning of Human Suffering*, 1984), he was presenting the teaching of the Church and sharing what he had learned from experience. By the time he wrote on suffering, both his parents and his siblings had died. He had endured a war and military occupation of his homeland. He had survived a car crash and a shooting, in which his would-be killer almost murdered him. John Paul II had suffered and would suffer more; he wrote that it is completely normal to want an answer to the meaning of suffering. In fact, Christ is expecting us to ask him. But as soon as a suffering person asks the question,

> *he cannot help noticing that the one to whom he puts the question is himself suffering and wishes to answer him from the Cross, from the heart of his own suffering. Nevertheless, it often takes time, even a long time, for this answer to begin to be interiorly perceived. For Christ does not answer directly and he does not answer in the abstract this human questioning about the meaning of suffering. Man hears Christ's saving answer as he himself gradually becomes a sharer in the sufferings of Christ* (*Salvifici Doloris*, 26).

So the path to understanding our suffering begins in taking our suffering—our fears, anger, resentment, and pain—to Christ. He is waiting for us to ask him about our suffering. Tell him in your own words. Speak as boldly as the Psalmist does. Christ does not want us to suffer alone. He promises that he is with us even if it seems otherwise. By his own suffering and death, he came to free us.

As we are restored to right relationship with others, self, and God, we are freed from certain kinds of sufferings and receive a capacity to suffer in a different way—to suffer difficult things for love of others. If these words are too difficult to hear right now, turn back to Christ. Take him your suffering, speaking as he did when he suffered. On the cross, Christ asked: "My God, my God, why have you forsaken me?" (Mt 27:46; Mk 15:34). He was praying the beginning of Psalm 22:

> *In you our fathers trusted;*
> *they trusted, and you delivered them.*
> *To you they cried, and were saved;*
> *in you they trusted, and were not disappointed (Ps 22:4–5).*

These consoling words are even more helpful to us when we remember that they were consoling to Christ himself in his hour of greatest pain and need.

The Path of Suffering: St. Dismas

For anyone suffering, St. Dismas is a powerfully comforting figure. In the most terrible circumstances, he walked the path of suffering and came to everlasting life. We know little about St. Dismas. He was one of the two thieves crucified with Christ (*see Mt 27:38; Mk 15:27; Lk 23:32–33; Jn 19:18*). Dismas is the name given to the thief who defended Christ. As far as we know, the crucifixion was their meeting-place.

> *One of the criminals who were hanged railed at him, saying, "Are you not the Christ? Save yourself and us!" But the other rebuked him, saying, "Do you not fear God, since you are under the same sentence of condemnation? And we indeed justly; for we are receiving the due reward of our deeds; but this man has done nothing wrong." And he said, "Jesus, remember me when you come into your kingly power." And he said to him, "Truly, I say to you, today you will be with me in Paradise" (Lk 23:39–43).*

A few hours later, Christ died. When they came to remove the bodies, the thieves were still living. To hasten death by shock, their legs were broken (*see Jn 19:32*). And so Dismas also died.

What an amazing journey he had made that day! Whoever walked the path of suffering so quickly and in such terrible circumstances? The one suffering Dismas did not have to endure was isolation. At Dismas' feet were John, Mary Magdalen, and the Mother of God, mother of the suffering. Next to Dismas was Christ. Not only was Christ nearby, but amidst one of the most painful methods of dying known to human history, he and Christ spoke to each other.

But Dismas had to endure so many other kinds of suffering. Dismas was a criminal, so it is likely he was still enduring the sufferings which come from habits of sin. He did not have the opportunities we have. He could not turn to the sacrament of reconciliation; he had few supports to help him escape sin and its torments.

What about valuing himself as God does? As far as we know, Dismas had no knowledge of Christ's teaching. Because he was a criminal, it is likely his life was full of experiences that told him he was of no value. He was sentenced to suffer crucifixion, the ultimate humiliation. Why would he have seen himself as a child of God? How could he have known of his inner country, of being made in God's image and likeness? What about the certainty of God's fatherly concern? There is no indication that he had any habits of prayer or any faith to give him hope on his last day.

C. S. Lewis took comfort in realizing that what he saw was not necessarily how things really are. How little time Dismas had to learn this! The other thief was full of hostility to Christ. To the average bystander, Christ was a failure and a fake. Would a god hang on a cross or let himself be spit on and criticized? Would he let others suffer? Fr. Ciszek had to do the most frightening thing of all: trust God despite a fear of being disappointed. How little time Dismas had to decide this! The other thief challenged Christ, and Christ did nothing. If he had any power, he did not show it. Imagine how disconcerting it could be to need to trust someone who looked as helpless as Christ did at that moment.

Dismas saw a broken man; he ran a terrible risk of being disappointed. He was suffering unimaginable physical pain and humiliation. But he did a remarkable thing. He asked Christ to remember him when he came into his kingdom. Who else has made such a great and speedy act of faith? Who else made it in such painfully difficult circumstances? And who else got such a magnificent response? Christ gave him a direct promise: today you will be with me in Paradise.

There was no time to make small experiments with redemptive suffering. Yet, without any clear understanding of redemptive suffering, Dismas was doing it. He was suffering with Christ. When we suffer with Christ, we are cooperating with him to save others. Those who love and suffer with Christ are already on the way to paradise.

St. Dismas is a patron for sinners and those close to despair. His feast falls on March 25, the feast of the Annunciation, the day Mary, mother of sufferers, first conceived Christ who suffered for our salvation. Dismas is a good one to think about when we are suffering. He had so little to help him understand his suffering and so little time to find an answer. Yet amidst terrible suffering, he found the answer. Now in paradise, Dismas has a particularly loving and personal concern for those who suffer. In our youth or middle age or old age, he says to the sufferer, "Take courage! Soon you shall be with us in paradise!" And then one day, he claims the honor of saying to the sufferer, "Today you will be with us in paradise!" Dismas is one who can say with the Psalmist, "we went through fire and through water; yet you have brought us forth to a spacious place" (*Ps 66:12*).

Review Questions

1. What are the four worst kinds of suffering brought into the world through original sin?

2. What are some remedies Christ gives to escape these kinds of suffering?

3. What is the difference between redemptive suffering and the hellish suffering which came into the world through sin?

4. What is redemptive suffering and how can we participate in it?

5. What are good things to keep in mind when attempting experiments in redemptive suffering?

6. Drawing on insights and stories from *Why Believe*?, from scripture, and from personal experience, what are ways to keep up hope when we suffer? What virtues are helpful for keeping close to Christ during times of suffering? What insights from stories of saints or passages from scripture comfort us and illuminate suffering?

7. Drawing on insights and stories from *Why Believe*?, from scripture, and from personal experience, what are good ways to interact with someone who is suffering? What is good to do or not do, say or not say? Are some ways better tailored to some kinds of suffering versus others? How can we grow in our ability to help the suffering and better adapt our interaction to the needs of particular people?

Put Out Into the Deep

If you are interested in learning more about Fr. Walter Ciszek's struggles, read *With God in Russia* (reprinted by Ignatius Press, 1997). This is the incredible story of how he survived twenty-three years in Russian prisons and labor camps, enduring cold, hunger, sixteen-hour work days, and daily threats to his life, while secretly carrying on his priestly ministry. Told in his own words, *With God in Russia* is a remarkable story of hope rediscovered in a seemingly hopeless place.

CHAPTER 14

The Last Things

14

Throughout *Why Believe?*, we have reflected on how our lives are like a story. This theme has been taken up in many works of literature and dramatic theater, among them Pedro Calderón de la Barca's play *Life is a Dream* (1635). In this play, King Basilio dabbles in astrology to foretell the future. The stars seem to predict that the king's unborn son Sigismund will grow up to murder his father and rule as a cruel and vicious tyrant. To prevent this tragedy, Basilio imprisons his son from birth in an impenetrable tower. Trespassers are killed without a trial.

When the play begins, Basilio has decided to test whether his son will be as evil as the stars predict. He arranges for his son Sigismund to be drugged and brought to the palace. There Sigismund will wake to be treated as the royal prince. Depending on how Sigismund behaves with his new freedom and identity, Basilio will decide whether to free his son or imprison him forever.

Sigismund has spent his life in miserable captivity, not knowing who he is. It is not surprising that he is enraged and resentful. Sigismund wakes to his new role in the palace, and things quickly spin out of control as he kills one servant and tries to kill another, attempts rape, challenges his cousin, and eventually threatens his father Basilio. Certain that the stars had been right, Basilio orders that his son be drugged again and returned to prison. When Sigismund next wakes, he finds to his horror that he is again chained. Told that the palace was all a dream, Sigismund sinks into a hell of despair.

But soon the nation is turned upside down. Rebels have discovered Sigismund's existence. They free him in an attempt to overthrow Basilio, and Sigismund finds himself the leader of a revolt. In the final act of the play, amidst a war tearing the country apart, Sigismund watches and thinks. He knows what it is like to end one kind of life and wake up in a hellish prison. Now that he is free again, how will this chapter of his life end? And what will follow?

As the play reaches a climax, Sigismund pushes forward to victory and has Basilio at his mercy. Then Sigismund does a surprising thing. He decides to forgive his father and make peace. Basilio tried to use the

Pedro Calderón de la Barca (1600–1681) was one of the greatest Spanish playwrights. The author of more than one hundred plays, Calderón won lasting fame for Life is a Dream, *a moving tale of failure and forgiveness. The play is notable for its cast of fascinating and complex characters: a father who has abandoned his daughter and hides his identity from her; a daughter who disguises herself to find her faithless lover; a faithless lover scheming to marry the princess; a princess with a sharp eye; a hilarious clown who wants to save his skin; a pack of rebels who will stop at nothing—all of them caught up in the struggle between Basilio and Sigismund.*

stars to predict the future, but no one can predict how a man will use his freedom. Rather than causing conflict, Sigismund goes on to resolve the conflicts among other characters. Everyone is amazed by the change. Noticing their surprise, Sigismund replies:

> *I believe now that all human lives are just like dreams. They come, they go.*
> *So quell disordered insolence and passion*
> *so that there be nothing after to condemn dreamer or doer in the part he played,*
> *whether Tomorrow's dawn shall break the spell*
> *or the last Trumpet of the Eternal Day,*
> *when Dreaming with the Night shall pass away.*

Life is not exactly like a story or a play. Sigismund learns that life is like a rehearsal for a real story, a real play. And what that real play looks like depends very much on how we play our role during the rehearsal of life. Sigismund woke up once to a hellish prison. He wants to wake to something better when his next chance comes.

Thinking about our story, its goal, and the meaning of death used to be a very popular topic for Lenten retreat conferences, which were sometimes called "The Four Last Things: Death, Judgment, Heaven or Hell." Although such reflection has become less popular in recent decades, it is surely no less timely. In this chapter, we will first explore why it seems harder now to talk about death, judgment, heaven, and hell, and then consider the Church's doctrine on these matters.

Worth Our Hope

What makes it so difficult to talk about death and what follows? One reason might be the powerful promise that earthly life can be everything we want. If we can make the world a better place, why worry about the afterlife? Focus instead on the here and now. Phrases like "Change the world!" and "A New Tomorrow" attract us: we feel smart, brave, and caring when we devote energy to perfecting the here and now. "Living the dream" also attracts the part of us which would love unlimited money, the pleasures of fame, and the interest of beautiful people. The dream of progress—that things are getting better and that, with a little more effort, we can make life everything we want—has been around for centuries and still captivates many today.

The German Enlightenment philosopher Immanuel Kant (1724–1804), for example, hoped for a world made better through political change. Believing that the French Revolution that began in 1789 would accomplish that change, Kant wrote an essay in 1792 called "The Victory of the Good over the Evil Principle and the Founding of a

Kingdom of God on Earth." By 1795, when it was clear that the French Revolution did not lead to a better world, but rather to war, rape, and thousands of deaths, Kant was writing a very different essay, one called "The End of All Things."

The example of Kant was one among several chosen by Benedict XVI as illustrations of the false dreams of revolutionary ideology in his encyclical *Spe Salvi (In Hope We Were Saved*, 2007). In that work and in several other of his major writings, Pope Benedict also explored the popular idea that science is the key to progress. With so many powerful inventions and discoveries, a better world seems just around the corner (*Caritas in Veritate*, 68–77). Blessed John Henry Newman considered a third idea: that education is the way to a better world. One thing these approaches share is the idea that human beings have the power to make their earthly life perfect. Benedict XVI and Newman offer some reasons why this idea is problematic. But even before we explore their reasons, we already have a certain instinctual sense that human beings lack the power to bring earthly life to perfection.

The French Revolution did not lead to a better world, but rather to war, rape, and thousands of deaths.

This intuition might account for the popularity of future dystopic literature. Not long after the rise of hope in Progress, we see stories beginning to question whether humans have the power to perfect earthly life. One recurrent them in such literature is that human beings are limited. We cannot predict human behavior, so we cannot predict whether, for example, war will destroy human society or demolish the earth, setting the stage for works like Walter Miller's *A Canticle for Leibowitz*, Lois Lowry's *The Giver*, Cormac McCarthy's *The Road*, or Suzanne Collins's *The Hunger Games*. We cannot predict natural or biological disasters, as in P. D. James's *Children of Men* or James Dashner's *The Maze*

Runner. We cannot foretell if scientific experimentation will backfire, as dramatized in Veronica Roth's *Divergent* series or Mary Shelley's *Frankenstein*. In these novels, as well as Aldous Huxley's *Brave New World*, George Orwell's *1984*, and Ray Bradbury's *Fahrenheit 451*, attempts to resolve problems and prevent future suffering end in the use of force with most of the costs paid by the most vulnerable members of society.

Benedict XVI and Newman help us to understand why attempts to build a perfect life could end so disastrously. First, we cannot predict the future, and even if we could hypothetically control the forces of nature, we cannot control human beings. The decision to live rightly is a decision which must be made freely by each person: "free assent to the good never exists simply by itself. If there were structures which could irrevocably guarantee a determined—good—state of the world, man's freedom would be denied, and hence they would not be good structures at all" (*Spe Salvi*, 24). Each person in every generation meets the good anew and must decide whether to embrace it. Any attempt by politics or science to guarantee perfect behavior would lead, as it does in dystopic novels, to a reign of terror.

We have a certain instinctual sense that human beings lack the power to bring earthly life to perfection. This intuition might account for the popularity of future dystopic literature such as Suzanne Collins's The Hunger Games.

A second reason attempts to build a perfect world fail is that human beings are wounded by original sin. Neither politics nor science can predict or prevent the possibility that a human being might choose evil. Nor is education an adequate means to lead someone to avoid evil and live well. Newman points this out in his essay "The Tamworth Reading Room," writing that "science, knowledge, and whatever other fine names we use, never healed a wounded heart, nor changed a sinful one." Understanding what is right does not mean we will do it. Because we are fallen, it is easy to give in to sin and hard to choose the good. We human beings need grace if we are to live well.

Dystopic literature also illuminates another reason for the failure of attempts to build a perfect world. Although many of those who cause the dystopic future are well-intentioned, the goods they achieve are limited. They are so focused on enforcing conditions which eliminate suffering or on pursuing luxury and security that they miss out on much more important goods. Other characters in these novels learn better goods and higher truths: to love to the point of sacrifice, to seek wisdom and understanding, to love learning, to value integrity and truth, that ends do not justify the means, that the innocent and vulnerable must be protected, and that it is good to be good, even if that goodness costs you your life. These goods are shareable; they are common goods. When a person gains one of these goods—love, integrity, wisdom—we are all better for it; we all gain something eternal.

Even if we could establish a perfect earthly life in the future, that state of affairs will not do any good to those who have already died. It will not bring them back or offer them happiness.

Furthermore, some dystopic novels have incredible characters loved by both other characters and the readers. Some of these characters die. This illustrates a fourth reason attempts to build a perfect earthly life are doomed. Even if we could establish a perfect earthly life in the future, that state of affairs will not do any good to those who have already died. It will not bring them back or offer them happiness. A hope which only helps some of us is no hope at all. The real happiness we seek must be a good so perfect it can never disappoint. Attempts to perfect earthly life are bound to end in defeat and disappointment, so long as humans are free and fallen. So what is worthy of our hope?

We need a life where humans beings are both free and healed from sin. Such a life needs to be permanent and peaceful, never boring, always fresh, ever ancient and ever new. It needs to be a life where goods do not pit us against one another, but instead are true goods available to all. It needs to be a life of true and loving relationships. These are the characteristics of the place and the life we call heaven.

Nevertheless, even if we had no illusions about building a perfect earthly life, we still might struggle to think about heaven, let alone death, judgment, or hell. Before he became Pope Benedict XVI, Joseph Ratzinger suggested that one reason we find it so difficult to face these topics is that they raise unsettling questions. Where will I go? What will happen to me? Where did they go? Will I ever see them again? Some of the oldest human stories address these themes. The ancient Mesopotamian *Epic of Gilgamesh* centers on Gilgamesh's search for eternal life. Many Greek and Roman stories turn on the death of friends and take heroes to the land of the dead.

The need to understand death is one of the deepest human needs. Christ said, "I came that they may have life, and have it abundantly" (Jn 10:10). We were born to desire life. We have to know what death means. Christ has given an answer to the question of death, and it is worth seeing what the Catholic Church tells us about this frontier we all must cross.

The Four Last Things

Death came into the world through the sin of our first parents, Adams and Eve. The Book of Wisdom explains further that "God created man for incorruption and made him in the image of his own eternity, but through the devil's envy death entered the world" (Wis 2:23–24). God did not intend for us to die. Jesus himself weeps at the death of his friend Lazarus (see Jn 11:35). Knowing how difficult and frightening death can be, Christ has given us multiple ways to take comfort in the face of death. Psalms 6, 23, 30, 56, 68, and 116 speak of how God will deliver us from death. Prayers as simple as "The Hail Mary" call for help at the hour of our death. A person close to death can receive Holy Communion in conjunction with a sacrament especially reserved for the sick or dying, the Anointing of the Sick. Someone dying will see the priest hold up the eucharist and say, "Jesus is the food for our journey; he calls us to the heavenly table." But Christ does more than comfort us at death. Just as Christ transformed certain kinds of suffering into love, he transformed the worst suffering of all, death, into love fulfilled. As St. Paul says, to die is "to depart and be with Christ" (Phil 1:23). This gives us a key to understanding the four last things. If we can understand heaven, Christ's teaching on death, hell, and judgment makes more sense.

What is heaven? Ultimately, the worst thing about death is not the changing of circumstances or loss of a particular place, but the loss of relationships. Characters like the superheroes Captain America and Wonder Woman or the characters in Natalie Babbitt's *Tuck Everlasting* know this. Even if we could live forever, with youth, health, and pleasure, living forever while your friends die would be an intolerable burden. Cardinal Ratzinger explained that the worst aspect of the afterlife for ancient religions was the fear that, after death, one would be "banished into a noncommunication zone where life is destroyed precisely because relationship is impossible." Heaven has to be more than living forever or even living in a better place. It has to solve the problem of the death of relationships.

We know our bodies will be resurrected, but, as Ratzinger wrote, "the detailed particularities of the world of the resurrection are beyond our conceiving.…the new world cannot be imagined." As body-soul creatures in space and time, we cannot help imagining and describing heaven like some kind of place. What Teresa of Avila says about the soul is true of heaven: whatever you imagine, it is nicer than that. But, ultimately, heaven is not about a where and when nor about changed living conditions: heaven is about a person.

Christ tells St. Dismas, "Today you will be with me in Paradise" (Lk 23:43). According to Ratzinger, the most important part of that sentence is the phrase "with me." Christ is defining heaven for Dismas. Paradise

---

from **The Rite of Commendation** (prayers for dying):

Deliver your servant, Lord, from every distress. **R.** *Lord, save your people.*

Deliver your servant, Lord, as you delivered Noah from the flood. **R.**

Deliver your servant, Lord, as you delivered Abraham from Ur of the Chaldees. **R.**

Deliver your servant, Lord, as you delivered Job from his sufferings. **R.**

Deliver your servant, Lord, as you delivered Moses from the hand of the Pharaoh. **R.**

Deliver your servant, Lord, as you delivered Daniel from the den of lions. **R.**

Deliver your servant, Lord, as you delivered the three young men from the fiery furnace. **R.**

Deliver your servant, Lord, as you delivered Susanna from her false accusers. **R.**

Deliver your servant, Lord, as you delivered David from the attacks of Saul and Goliath. **R.**

Deliver your servant, Lord, as you delivered Peter and Paul from prison. **R.**

Deliver your servant, Lord, through Jesus our Savior, who suffered death for us and gave us eternal life. **R.**

is not "a place standing in permanent readiness for occupation and which happens to contain the Messiah along with a lot of other people. …Jesus himself is paradise, light, fresh water, the secure peace toward which human longing and hope are directed." When Christ tells Martha "I am the resurrection and the life" (Jn 11:25), he means more than, "I raise people from the dead" or "You need my help." Martha has just said she believes Lazarus will rise from the dead someday. Christ responds that eternal life is more than an event. Eternal life itself is to be with Christ: "I am the resurrection and the life." To be with Christ includes Christ's body, the communion of saints. To be in heaven is to be with Christ, and through him, and in relationship with others. Being in heaven can begin before we die because, ultimately, one is in heaven to the degree one lives in Christ.

What, then, is hell? Hell is the converse: to be without Christ. Christ speaks about hell multiple times in the scriptures (see, for example, Mt 5:22–29, 10:28, 13:41–50, 25:41; Mk 9:43–48). We know that Christ forces no one to choose hell (see CCC 1037). So why would some people choose it? Again, we have to realize hell is not a place so much as the loss of relationship with Christ.

Hell is not a place so much as the loss of relationship with Christ.

Just as heaven can begin on earth before we die, hell can begin before we die. Christopher Marlowe's play *Dr. Faustus* tells how a man sold his soul to the devil in return for supernatural powers. Early on, Faustus distances himself from Christ and forms a plan to sell his soul. In a conversation with the devil Mephistopheles, Faustus asks how the devil was able to leave hell to talk with Faustus. He totally fails to comprehend Mephistopheles' significant response: "Why, this is hell, nor am I out of it." The devil, perpetually estranged from God, brings that estrangement—hell—with him wherever he goes.

If you were to ask around, "Who wants to have a deep and tremendous relationship with Jesus Christ?," you might see some hands raised and others left dangling. Some people would not volunteer. Some days maybe we would not volunteer. If lacking a deep relationship with Christ is hell, why do some of these people seem untroubled? Many people who lack a relationship with Christ seem happy. Are they?

The more we turn from Christ, the more strongly do we experience a state of life which eventually becomes hell after death.

In their more fortunate moments or seasons in life, they will tell you that they are. But life's challenges are never far afield, and the greatest challenges of all stem from our own sinfulness. Born fallen, we all sooner or later experience moments of suffering from our own sins. To experience such suffering is to know what life is like apart from Christ, to know what hell is. The more we turn from Christ, the more strongly do we experience a state of life which eventually becomes hell after death. We can try to distract ourselves from hellish problems without actually escaping. Or we can seek a deep and tremendous relationship with Christ. People who have such a relationship eventually find ways to shed these kinds of sufferings for a life of grace, communion, and connection to God, allowing themselves to receive his love and experience his protection. They begin to experience heaven.

What then are death and judgment? If hell and heaven can begin during this life, Ratzinger suggests that the main difference between life and death is that after death we emerge "into the light of full reality and truth…the masquerade of living with its constant retreat behind posturings and fictions is now over….The judgment is simply the manifestation of the truth." The judgment is a moment between

Jean Cousin The Younger, The Last Judgement, *c. 1585, Oil on canvas, Louvre, Paris, France.*

the self and Christ, a moment of complete understanding and honesty about the state of the relationship. For some people, death and judgment are a doorway from a partial relationship with Christ to a full one. Some will be overwhelmed with happiness; they will be in heaven. But some will be uncomfortable or repelled; seeing Christ face to face will not change how they felt about Christ during life or the accompanying self-loathing, isolation, and addictions of sin. Some will be divided, like St. Peter was, drawn to Christ but also crying awkwardly, "Depart from me, for I am a sinful man!" (Lk 5:8). That kind of person needs a transformation which the Church calls purgatory.

As Ratzinger explains, purgatory is not a place that can be described or a phase that can be measured in units of time. Nor is it a place where we earn our way into heaven by completing a lot of difficult tasks. The essential thing to understand about purgatory is that it is a "process of transformation in which a person becomes capable of Christ, capable of God, and thus capable of unity with the whole communion of saints." Our own experience of relationships on earth shows us the necessity of this transformation. Even our best relationships are complicated by sins and failings: we hold grudges, get jealous, speak without thinking, and do any number of things which get in the way of relating deeply. These things also complicate our relationship with God. How much we would love to be free of such things! Ideally, we would accept his grace during life to heal such failings. But it is also possible for someone who has loved God deeply and has tried with mixed success to be purified from sins and faults to be given the opportunity in purgatory to let grace finish the job.

If we have suffered at the hands of others, we can also understand that justice demands purgatory. It is good to forgive and to turn to Christ for peace. But it is also good to ask about justice. Sins can be forgiven; a bully, an abuser, a murderer, and a rapist can be forgiven. But we may ask whether forgiveness means acting as though these wrongs never happened, acting as though it is perfectly fine to bully, abuse, murder, or rape. It is not only natural but good for a victim to ask about justice. As Benedict XVI explained, "Grace does not cancel out justice. It does not make wrong into right. It is not a sponge which wipes everything away" (*Spe Salvi*, 44). Although we cannot know what God's final justice will look like, sinners will experience justice in purgatory; in purgatory sinners will come to appreciate the full impact their sins had on their victims. So purgatory offers both grace and justice. For sinners trying to love God, it offers the possibility of mercy and a transformation which makes us capable of a full relationship with God. For victims of the sins of others, it promises that there will be real justice for the wrongs we have suffered.

Although we cannot know what God's final justice will look like, sinners will experience justice in purgatory; in purgatory sinners will come to appreciate the full impact their sins had on their victims.

Why Think About the Four Last Things?

Anyone who has experienced the misery of sin, isolation, self-loathing, fear, panic, and separation from God has had a glimpse of hell. We all have a stake in escaping such a life. Moreover, Christ teaches that the only escape, the only heaven that would really be a heaven, is relationship with Christ and, through him, with all our brothers and sisters. Someday we are not going to be able to avoid the question, "Do you want that?" For some, a relationship with Christ may conjure up memories of being bored at Mass or falling asleep during prayers. Relationship with Christ does not strike everyone as something desirable.

But if heaven is relationship with Christ, it is vitally important to start thinking about it. Relationship with Christ is one of those things that demands practice and involvement over time. Play rehearsals are often boring or annoying; they do not give the flavor of what a successful play feels like. The early stages of relationship with Christ do not always indicate what heaven is really like. As St. Bernard of Clairvaux (1090–1153) expressed in his hymn *Jesu Dulcis Memoria*: "No tongue can tell, no letter can express it: only the one with experience is able to believe what it means to love Jesus."

To persevere, we need to cultivate our desire for God, our desire for heaven. According to Aquinas, "the more we think about spiritual goods, the more pleasing they become to us." So let's start thinking about them. Mother Teresa said, "The first step to becoming holy is to will it.... With a will that is whole I will love God, I will opt for him, I will run toward him, I will reach him, I will possess him. But it all depends on these words: 'I want' or 'I do not want.' I have to pour all my energy into the words 'I want.'" Life in the Catholic Church has been given to us as our stage for rehearsing for heaven. Personal prayer and prayer with the Church are the most powerful means for developing a desire for God.

The second most powerful means is to remember and be on the alert for all the glimpses of heaven, of a deep relationship with Christ. We can all experience such glimpses of what the philosopher Joseph Pieper called the "mystery of creation" and "the core of all things." C. S. Lewis notes that we cannot engineer this experience; it is always a gift. Anyone who has this experience "will want it again.... I doubt whether anyone who has tasted it would...exchange it for all the pleasures in the world." The experience combines powerful desire with peace and contentment; it can come with an impulse of joy and tears at the same time. It can happen in the common experiences of human life: watching the northern lights or a sunset, the sight of snow, mountains, or the sea, the birth of a child, hearing a haunting piece of music, looking at a human face, or winning a victory with our team. It can happen through the experiences we have in the Catholic Church: at the reading of a Psalm, at an Easter Vigil, during the singing of a hymn at Christmas, at eucharistic adoration, when being served by another, or listened to or loved or forgiven; while watching someone make a heroic sacrifice, in the sudden and wonderful resolution of a terrible situation or in the startling faith of someone suffering. Whenever we experience anything true, noble, good, beautiful, admirable, anything excellent or praiseworthy, we experience Christ. He is truth, beauty, and goodness; all good things flow from Christ, reflect him, and come as a message from him to show us what he is like. Remembering and recognizing such experiences as experiences of Christ can develop our desire for heaven, that is, for a relationship with Christ. Prayer may seem boring at times, but eventually a relationship with Christ takes on the character of the best moments we know in this life. As our relationship with Christ grows, those kinds of moments grow in number and duration, so that heaven begins before death.

Those who experience a glimpse of heaven are drawn to share it with others. They do not try to build earthly paradises; they know we are free and fallen. But they do tend to seek out ways to introduce others to experiences of heaven: they paint, write music, and perform plays; they take friends on wilderness hikes and camps in the mountains; they build schools, hospitals, and shelters for the poor; they seek cures for terrible diseases and try to find new ways to help those in need; they visit the imprisoned; they cook for the hungry; they listen, and they comfort the dying. When we love Christ, we care for others, not to build an earthly paradise, but because we love them as his sons and daughters.

Experiences of heaven remind us of the reason we want to think often about the four last things. The reason for thinking and praying about death, judgment, heaven, and hell is to fuel our desire for God and keep us oriented toward the final goal of our story. Like Sigismund, we will all wake someday. And when we do, we will want to hear these words: "Awake, O sleeper, and arise from the dead, and Christ shall give you light" (Eph 5:14).

Review Questions

1. Identify and explain Benedict XVI's two reasons for doubting the possibility of progress and that humans have the power to make earthly life perfect.

2. In what sense is heaven not a place so much as a person?

3. How does this illuminate our understanding of the Church's teaching on death, judgment, and hell?

4. In light of this chapter and others, what are other potential ways we can experience Christ and glimpses of heaven?

5. What are ways we can help others have this powerful and important kind of experience?

6. C. S. Lewis says glimpses of heaven are different than pleasure, although they can cause pleasurable emotions. In light of this chapter and others, think about ways we can distinguish between real glimpses of heaven which actually bring us in contact with Christ and experiences which only seem to do so or even lead us from him.

7. Benedict XVI criticizes political, scientific, and educational structures which would try to guarantee or compel a perfect life because they ignore man's freedom. At the same time, neither he nor the Catholic Church condemns law and legal structures. In light of this chapter and others, consider and propose an answer to this question: how does law, including the Church's moral teaching, support man's freedom and differ from attempts to guarantee or compel a perfect life?

Put Out Into the Deep

This chapter references Pope Benedict XVI's encyclical *Spe Salvi*, which is worth reading in its entirety. It begins with a moving consideration of St. Josephine Bakhita, who was born in Africa, captured, and sold into brutal slavery. Telling her story, Benedict XVI bluntly acknowledges that life is hard; for some it is terribly hard. We can face it only if "our goal is great enough to justify the effort of the journey" (*Spe Salvi,* 1). Do we have a goal great enough? This is the question Benedict XVI poses and answers in this challenging examination of hope and the four last things.

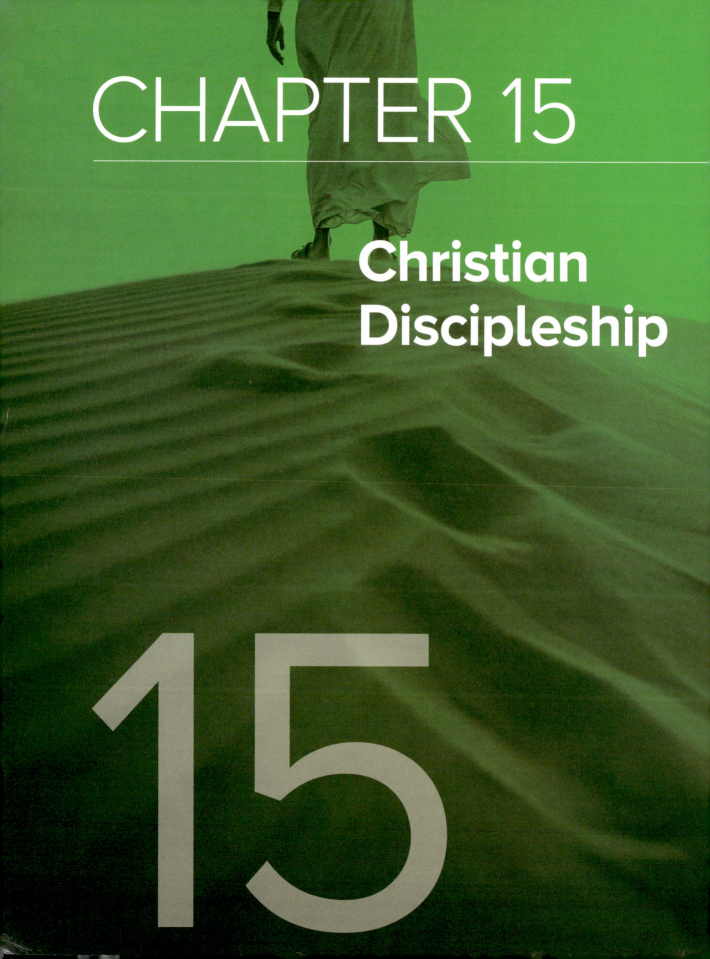

CHAPTER 15

Christian Discipleship

15

Our journey through *Why Believe?* began with a question Jesus asked his disciples some 2,000 years ago—a question he continues to ask us today: "Who do you say that I am?" This is not an abstract question, one only for priests, philosophers, and theologians to ponder or one that merely helps us get the right answers on a catechism test. Rather, it is a deeply personal question that is meant to lead us to a friendship with Jesus that shapes our entire lives. Indeed, for those who truly believe what Peter professed that day—that Jesus is "the Christ, the Son of the living God"—faith in Jesus is the starting point for the adventure of following him as a disciple.

But what does that mean? What does it look like to live as a modern-day disciple of Jesus? To shed light on this, we will go back in time to the first-century Jewish world in which Jesus lived and there learn what it meant for a disciple to follow a rabbi.

Follow Me

In the Bible, following a rabbi as a disciple was very different from modern classroom learning. On a college campus, for example, a professor gives lectures to students in a large hall; the students take notes, and they are examined on the material later in the semester. But in the university setting today, there is usually not an ongoing personal relationship and sharing of daily life between professor and student. To follow a rabbi, however, meant living with the rabbi and taking part in his whole way of life. A disciple might accompany a rabbi on his daily

James Tissot, Meal of Our Lord and the Apostles, *1886–1894, Opaque watercolor over graphite on gray wove paper, Brooklyn Museum, New York, NY, USA.*

routines: prayer, study, debating other rabbis, giving alms to the poor, burying the dead, going to court. A rabbi's life was meant to be a living example of someone shaped by God's Word. Ancient Jewish disciples studied not just the text of scripture but also the "text" of the rabbi's life.

Imagine spending three years not just with a wise, holy teacher, but with Jesus, the Son of God himself. That is what the original disciples of Christ had the chance to do. Jesus invited these men to live with him, share meals with him, pray with him, teach with him, serve the poor with him, and share life with him. This is the kind of apprenticeship the first disciples were seeking from Jesus when they asked him, "Where are you staying?" (Jn 1:38). With this question, they were not inquiring about Jesus's lodging preferences. They were subtly expressing their desire to stay with Jesus as a disciple stays with a rabbi. Similarly, when Jesus replied, "Come and see" (Jn 1:39), he was not asking them to come inspect his home. He was inviting them into a relationship.

This invitation marked the beginning of a life-shaping training for them. They would never be the same. When Jesus told the disciples, "Follow me" (Jn 1:43), he meant it not merely in the spatial sense of accompanying him in his ministry from one point to another. He meant it in the sense of spiritually walking in his footsteps, imitating his entire way of living—in other words, following him as a disciple. Over the course of many weeks and months, the disciples absorbed much from Jesus's way of living. They noticed the way he woke up early to pray, the time he had in solitude with God. They witnessed his compassion in helping the sick, the blind, the lepers, and others who were suffering. They were struck by his pressing need to go out to the peripheries, to those who were sinners, Gentiles, or social outcasts, and invite them into his Kingdom. They also observed the way Jesus debated his opponents, the way he taught the crowds, how he called people to repent, and how he offered them love and mercy. Over time, they began to absorb this way of life.

Even though Jesus lived 2,000 years ago, he is still alive today and we can encounter him personally—in prayer, in the Sacraments, in fellowship with others, and in learning about what he taught and how he lived.

According to one ancient Jewish saying, if you encounter a rabbi, you should "cover yourself in the dust of his feet and drink in his words thirstily." The expression probably draws on a well-known sight for ancient Jews: disciples were known for walking behind their rabbi, following him so closely that they would become covered with the dust kicked up from his sandals. This would have been a powerful image for what should happen in the disciple's spiritual life. Disciples were expected to follow their rabbi so closely that it was as if they would be covered with their master's whole way of thinking, living, and acting.

If we wish to follow Jesus as disciples, we will do the same. Even though Jesus lived 2,000 years ago, he is still alive today and we can encounter him personally—in prayer, in the Sacraments, in fellowship with others, and in learning about what he taught and how he lived. Through these practices we can be covered with the dust of our good Rabbi, Jesus Christ. By imitating his way of life, we will little-by-little be transformed, taking on the character of Christ.

The Four Habits of a Christian Disciple

The Bible underscores four key practices that marked the earliest followers of Jesus. We could think of these as the four key habits of a disciple—ways we regularly encounter Jesus anew. If we want our faith to be sustained long term, we need these four habits in our daily lives. According to Acts of the Apostles 2:42, the early disciples devoted themselves to:

1. The teaching of the Apostles,
2. fellowship,
3. the breaking of bread, and
4. prayer.

Although there are many creative ways one could sum up the various practices of a Christian disciple, following the biblical model is best. When the Church has summed up the Catholic faith, it has often turned to these four practices in Acts 2:42 as a way to present what it means to follow Jesus. In fact, the four pillars of the *Catechism of the Catholic Church* are based on them. So if we want a road map to help make sure we are on the right track in our relationship with the Lord, we can ask ourselves if we are growing in our understanding and living out of these four basic practices.

But there is more. If we want to keep the fire of faith burning, think of these four practices as logs we add to the fire. The more we grow in prayer, in fellowship with other disciples, in our devotion to the sacraments ("the breaking of the bread"), and in forming our minds with the revelation of Christ ("the apostles' teaching"), the more we encounter Jesus anew each day. We learn something new about Christ's teachings that challenges us. We sense in prayer his inviting us to take the step of faith. We experience his love and mercy in the sacraments. And we are strengthened by our fellowship with other disciples who encourage us in the faith and help bring the best out of us. If we want to grow as disciples and experience more of the transformation, forgiveness, and love God has in store for us, we want to make sure we follow these four practices the Bible singles out as the four habits of a disciple.

What we need to do often—even daily—is to lift our eyes from our present cares and preoccupations and set them, with the Psalmist, upon the far horizon, upon the hills from which we catch a glimpse of heaven.

The Teaching of the Apostles

As we saw in the last chapter, one of the biggest challenges of our modern age is that it focuses all our attention on this world, on what we can see. We become caught up in the pressures of life, worrying about what other people think of us, maintaining an image, pursuing the honors, riches, and pleasures of this world while being driven by a constant fear of missing out on what everyone else is doing. The secular environment induces us to focus on these present realities so that we forget the spiritual realities that govern the universe and matter most in our lives.

Yet our faith tells us the most important part of the universe is the spiritual reality, which is beyond our senses: the angelic beings that surround us moment by moment, the Holy Spirit who is present to us, the life of grace in our hearts, and our own spiritual souls that will last forever. Keeping these invisible realities in mind is far more important than keeping up with what is trending on social media. In our modern era that focuses just on this world—the honors, comforts, pursuits, and pleasures of this world—we easily lose sight of the most important realities: where we came from, where we are right now, and where we are going. What we need to do often—even daily—is to lift our eyes from our present cares and preoccupations and set them, with the Psalmist, upon the far horizon, upon the hills from which we catch a glimpse of heaven.

I lift up my eyes to the hills. From where does my help come?

My help comes from the LORD, who made heaven and earth.

He will not let your foot be moved, he who keeps you will not slumber.

Behold, he who keeps Israel will neither slumber nor sleep.

The LORD is your keeper; the LORD is your shade on your right hand.

The sun shall not strike you by day, nor the moon by night.

The LORD will keep you from all evil; he will keep your life.

The LORD will keep your going out and your coming in from this time forth and for evermore.

Psalm 121:1–8

With great effort, care, and attention, we need to raise our minds intentionally to the highest truths that God has revealed to us so that we can see our lives as they really are. God has revealed himself to us in his son, Jesus Christ, who is the Way, the Truth and the Life (see Jn 14:6). This revelation was handed on to the apostles and their successors through the Catholic Church, and the earliest disciples devoted themselves to forming their minds with this gift of God's revelation, which is expressed in the first point highlighted in Acts 2:42: "the teachings of the apostles."

We may ask, however, just what we should be doing to form our minds with this revelation of Christ?

First, there are two basic texts that should be a part of the regular diet of every Catholic disciple: the Bible and the *Catechism*. We should take time to read and study the Bible every day, for in it we encounter God's inspired Word. Many people read the newspaper or check their newsfeed or favorite websites every day. They do so, presumably, because they want to be aware of important things that may affect them that day. But the most important things are the truths of God, and they can and should affect us every day by shaping our outlook on life, informing our judgments, and guiding our choices. And they keep the flame of our relationship with Jesus burning. Even five minutes a day with the Gospel can be a tremendous help to our spiritual lives and our interior peace.

We also should take time to learn what is in the *Catechism of the Catholic Church*, which is the Church's official presentation of the faith. Knowing the Bible and the *Catechism* better will help us to see reality more clearly. While some people may think of faith as a leap in the dark, we should see these two important texts as a step into the light. They help us to see things as they really are and point us toward true happiness in life. As the Psalmist said with joy, "Your word is a lamp to my feet and a light to my path" (Ps 119:105).

Second, we can take time to learn about the lives of the saints. Whether it be saints of old, such as St. Augustine, St. Francis of Assisi, and St. Catherine of Siena, or modern saints, such as St. Therese of Lisieux, St. Mother Teresa of Calcutta, and St. John Paul II, these heroes of our faith stand as the truest representatives of Christ, and they inspire us to follow him by walking in their footsteps. When we encounter the witness of these men and women who have lived out the faith in an exemplary way, we gain examples of how we can put the faith into practice in our own lives.

When we take time to learn about the lives of the saints, we gain examples of how we can put the faith into practice in our own lives.

Fellowship

If we want to keep the fire of faith burning, there is a second practice we need to incorporate in our lives that is absolutely crucial: fellowship with other disciples. We cannot expect to grow in our relationship with Christ on our own. We need friends who are running beside us. They are not merely Christians in name or churchgoers who are passively going through the motions with their faith. Like you, they have inside them that spark of a disciple who has chosen to follow Christ and is striving for a deeper union with him. Do you have some friendships like this—friendships with other disciples who are seeking Christ's will for their lives, pursuing prayer, virtue, and holiness, earnestly struggling to be more and more like Jesus in all areas of their lives?

The Bible says that "iron sharpens iron, and one man sharpens another" (Prov 27:17). An iron blade cannot be made razor-sharp by a dull one. It takes one sharp blade to sharpen another. Similarly, we need fellow disciples in our lives so we can be sharpened by their example and pursuit of Christ. So important is Christian fellowship in the life of a disciple that the New Testament lists it as the second of the four key practices to which Jesus's earliest followers devoted themselves.

When making a charcoal fire, it is best to put all the coals together in one pile so that they feed off each other's heat. Together, each coal will burn stronger and longer than if it were isolated from the others. But what happens when one coal is separated from the other burning coals? It does not burn as strongly, and it will soon die out. The same thing happens when a disciple lacks fellowship with other committed disciples. When we do not have Christian friendships in our lives, our growth as disciples is likely to be stunted. We may even fall back into old bad habits or turn away from true discipleship, settling for mediocrity or lukewarmness in our faith.

Especially in a secular culture that is constantly luring us away from Christian values, we need brothers and sisters who help keep us on track by reminding us that we are not alone in our pursuit of Christ and that the effort and sacrifices we make in our total commitment to him are worth it. Our secular world is not going to offer that kind of encouragement. Quite the opposite. The world presents its many attractive honors, comforts, riches, shows, entertainments, pleasures, and pursuits as the fun and exciting kind of life. Meanwhile, Christian values like chastity, honesty, suffering for others, appreciating the blessing of children, living simply, serving the poor, and trusting God seem difficult and perhaps even boring.

If we are always surrounded by people who do not share these values with the same intensity as we do or do not share them at all, we become like that isolated coal. Our flame of faith is not likely to grow and may be at risk of dying out. We can certainly have friendships with people of different backgrounds. But having some regular fellowship with others who share our conviction in Christ is crucial. We need to live in joyful fellowship with other disciples who are striving after the same Christian ideals. We need to have regular contact with the other burning coals. It helps keep us on track, strengthens us in our most noble pursuits, makes us better, sharpens our swords, and continually re-enkindles the fire of our faith.

Having some regular fellowship with others who share our conviction in Christ is crucial.

Finally, while fellowship helps strengthen us in the faith, it is also a school of self-giving where we learn to grow in love. Jesus wants us to encounter him in the people in our lives. Through our daily interactions with others, we have countless opportunities to grow in kindness, patience, generosity, and self-control. We show our love for Christ by loving Jesus in our neighbors. According to many saints, a major sign of someone's increase in holiness is his or her growing in patient, generous, merciful love of neighbor. In fact, we grow in love of Christ through learning to love our neighbors—whether friends, family members, classmates, coworkers, or members of our local community—with all their quirks, needs, weaknesses, and faults. In so doing, we are simply learning to love others the way God loves us—freely, patiently, mercifully, and unconditionally, expecting nothing back.

Care for the poor is an essential part of what it means to be a disciple.

This is especially true regarding those in most need: the poor. When we grow in sacrificial love for the poor—whether the materially poor or the spiritually poor around us—we come to a deeper encounter with the Lord himself. Care for the poor is an essential part of what it means to be a disciple. As Jesus taught, "Truly, I say to you, as you did it to one of the least of these my brethren, you did it to me" (Mt 25:40).

Breaking of Bread

If you want to be healed of your weaknesses, then you will want to go to the sacraments. If you want to overcome your sins and grow in the spiritual life, then go to the sacraments as often as you can. If you want better friendships, a strong marriage someday, or a deeper understanding of God's plan for you, the graces offered in the sacraments can help you. Most of all, if you want to worship God, become more like Jesus and encounter him regularly in the way he most directly wants to transform you, then go to the sacraments often.

As we have seen repeatedly throughout the course of *Why Believe?*, the sacraments are not simply rituals we have to do to be good Christians or hoops we have to jump through because we happen to be Catholic. Rather, the sacraments are the most amazing events taking place every day in the whole world. They are not random rituals from our religion, but gifts given to us by the Lord Jesus so we can encounter him, the living God, today. Jesus himself established the sacraments, entrusting the graces of salvation to the Church, so they can be conveyed through these seven sacred acts. Through the sacraments, Jesus takes the treasures he won for us on the Cross some 2,000 years ago and applies them to our lives now. Through these ordinary, even daily occurrences, Jesus does his most profound work in our souls, turning sinners into saints one small step at a time.

Most of the sacraments either are received only one time (baptism, confirmation) or, if they can be received more than once, are received rarely (the anointing of the sick, matrimony, holy orders). But there are two sacraments we can receive frequently throughout our lives: reconciliation and the eucharist. We have discussed these sacraments from the perspective of their biblical roots and theological and personal implications. Now we will consider how a disciple makes them the very center of the Christian life.

Confession

The sacrament of reconciliation brings us right into the heart of our discipleship. As disciples of Jesus, we strive to imitate him and root out sin in our lives. But we always come up short and experience our own weaknesses and our inability to change. Two amazing things happen in confession.

First, we are freed. God wants to free us of our sins and all the uneasiness, guilt, and shame we might experience over what we have done. When we are truly sorry for our sins, God sees our contrite hearts. He is not sitting back angry, pointing his finger, and condemning us for our sins. Rather, he is like the father racing out to meet his prodigal son. Love makes him want to remove whatever obstacles keep him from being reunited with his son. That is the God we meet in confession. And how liberating it is to hear God, through the priest, tell us that our sins really are forgiven! "I absolve you of your sins."

So, no matter what you have done or how many times you have done it, and no matter how long you have been away from confession, know that Jesus is waiting for you in the sacrament of reconciliation. He longs to lift the burden of your sins and give you a new start in life.

But Jesus does not just want to forgive us. He wants to heal us. God does not merely issue a pardon, as though he were only a judge. He wants to get to the roots of our sins and cure us of our spiritual illnesses and wounds. He wants us to experience real change. In the sacrament of reconciliation, God gives us graces to avoid those sins in the future. We receive "an increase of spiritual strength for the Christian battle" (CCC 1496). This is one of the main reasons we desire to go to confession regularly. If we want to grow as disciples—if we want to access Christ's power to heal our weaknesses, overcome bad habits, and avoid falling into the same sins in the future—we should go to confession at least once a month.

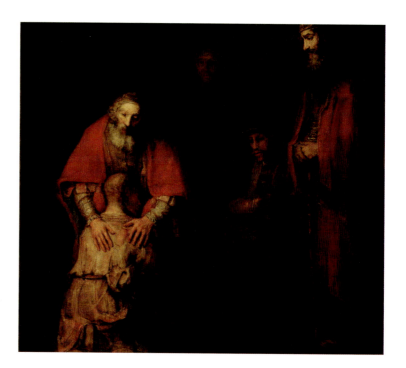

Rembrandt, The Return of the Prodigal Son, *c. 1668, oil on canvas, Hermitage Museum, Saint Petersburg, Russia.*

When we return to our pews after receiving holy communion, this is the most intimate time we have with our God—to talk to him from the depths of our hearts.

The Mass and Holy Communion

As disciples, we are called to imitate our Rabbi, Jesus Christ. But unlike other rabbis, Jesus does not merely offer us an example to observe from the outside. He actually abides within us. And we experience his abiding with us most profoundly at Mass when we receive Jesus himself in holy communion. Think about what this means: Our God loves us so much that he comes to us at every Mass under the appearance of bread and wine and then enters into us at holy communion. This is the most profound union we can have with our God here on earth. Do we approach this moment with sufficient seriousness? We become like the temple that housed God's presence in Jerusalem. Our God is dwelling within us.

When we return to our pews after receiving holy communion, it is not the time to look around and see who is at Mass or daydream about the football game in the afternoon. And it is certainly not appropriate to leave before Mass is over. This is the most intimate time we have with our God—to talk to him from the depths of our hearts. As he is lovingly dwelling within us, we should use these profound moments to tell him we love him, to thank him for the blessings in our lives, to pour out our hearts to him with whatever may be troubling us, and to quietly rest in his love and listen to him. This is the traditional practice of making "thanksgiving" after receiving the eucharist. We can take this time right after we receive communion and return to our pews. We might even stay after Mass for a few minutes to rest quietly with Jesus before rushing off to say hello to friends, grab a donut, or race to the car. We should let those intimate moments linger as long as we can.

Prayer

The fourth key habit of a disciple is prayer. Think of prayer as a conversation with a close friend—someone who knows you very well and loves you. As with any relationship, it is important to have time in conversation for the relationship to grow. And the more important the relationship, the deeper and more frequent that conversation should be. That is why Christians should take some time every day for prayer—time not just to say some prayers, but time for intimate conversation with the Lord, a personal encounter with our God.

But how does one begin to pray? Here are four simple things any ordinary Christian can do in conversation with God. These points can be summed up with the word "ACTS": adoration, confession, thanksgiving, and supplication.

The first thing we can do in prayer is *adoration*. This is the basic human response to God's gift of himself to us. We who are mere creatures acknowledge God as Creator. In response to God's goodness and love, we adore him—we worship him and pledge our love and our lives to him.

A second aspect of prayer is *confession*. Here, we refer not to the sacrament of confession, but to the daily practice of admitting our sins before God. As in any relationship, it is important to tell God that we are sorry for the ways we have hurt the relationship through our sins and failures to love. Taking time each day to consider what we have done wrong and what good we have failed to do helps us to express true sorrow for the ways we have fallen short in our relationship with God and neighbor.

A third form of prayer is *thanksgiving*. We should always express gratitude to God for his blessings, for the people in our lives, the ways he provides for us, the ways he helps us in our need, and how he supports us through our sufferings. Most of all, we thank God for the spiritual blessings he bestows on us through his work of salvation, from his becoming man and dying for our sins on the cross to the truth and graces he gives us through the sacraments and the Church.

Finally, *supplication*. This is simply presenting our needs before our heavenly Father. Supplication can take two forms. On one hand, we should always pray for others' needs. We can pray for the poor, the sick, and the suffering. We can pray for peace and justice in the world. We can pray for specific friends and family members in their particular needs for God's help. These kinds of supplications are known as "intercessory prayer." On the other hand, we should also pray for our own needs and intentions, whether it be asking God for help in our job, wisdom in how to handle a situation that troubles us, guidance in a decision, grace to overcome a certain sin, or comfort in time of sorrow. God wants us to come to him with our needs, and this is called "prayer of petition."

These four basic forms of prayer—ACTS—are found throughout scripture and the Christian tradition. We may speak to God aloud in a group, saying, "Thank you God for all your blessings!" Or we may whisper certain words on our own, "I love you God" or "Jesus, help me." Or we may simply speak to God in our heart, "Lord, I'm so sorry I did that. Please forgive me." Whether spoken aloud or silently in our hearts, these forms of prayer use words of praise, thanksgiving, sorrow, and supplication to carry out our life-long conversation with God.

A true disciple is committed to praying each day. Many Christian writers through the centuries have compared prayer to breathing. Just as we need to take in oxygen to survive, so we need to pray if we want to sustain the Christian life. When we do not take time for prayer, however, it may be an indication not so much of our busyness, but more of where our hearts really are. "For where your treasure is, there will your heart be also" (Mt 6:21).

Missionary Disciples

Soon you will be graduating and heading out into the adult world. For those of you who have turned eighteen, you are already adults in the eyes of the law. The years of childhood have come, or are swiftly coming, to an end.

The question presses upon you now more than ever: *what are you going to make of your life?*

The culture you are about to go out into, blessed and beautiful as it is in so many ways, is also, as we have discussed throughout these chapters, in many ways intent on separating itself from the life Christ invites us to live. This aspect of our culture makes it easy for you to conform. It does not ask much beyond your complacency as it leads you into choices that promise a false happiness.

But Jesus is inviting you, right now, on a very different and far more thrilling adventure. He wants you to be his close friend here on this earth and then be forever one with him in an even more intimate way in heaven. The adventure Jesus invites you on is specifically tailored to you. He has a work in mind that he wants you, and you only, to perform. The specific adventure he has in mind for you may, in the immediate term, mean a college career or a new job. But whatever form your adventure takes, Jesus will be there with you every step of the way, leading you on to a happiness that cannot let you down.

Friendship with Jesus puts us on a mission. No one in love can keep his heart from bursting forth to tell the whole world about his love. And the more we engage in the four practices of discipleship we have discussed in this chapter, the more we will fall in love with Christ and want to tell the world about him. You do not need to be a priest, religious brother or sister, or theologian in order to be an effective witness for Christ. If someone happens to watch a great movie and wants to tell others about it, he does not need to become a professional film critic to do so. Similarly, a married couple does not require a Ph.D. in marriage and family studies to tell others why family life is so wonderful. As Christians, we can speak simply from our experience of the marvelous things that we encounter, including the marvels of our relationship with God. When we experience God's love and fidelity, we, like Mary, spontaneously testify to our gratitude: "My soul magnifies the Lord, and my spirit rejoices in God my Savior, for he has regarded the low estate of his handmaiden" (Lk 1:46–48).

Though it may not realize it, the world is yearning desperately for the love that only Christ can give. Christ, in turn, desperately wants to give that love. But he wants to give it with and through you. With the tools of the Catholic education you have received and in a special way with the truths you have learned in *Why Believe?*, he wants you to help him embody that love and share it with the world.

References

Unless otherwise noted, quotations from Classical and Patristic texts are taken from standard texts available online, and quotations from the *Summa Theologiae* of St. Thomas Aquinas are from the Dominican Fathers edition, also online.

Chapter 1

C. S. Lewis, *Mere Christianity* (New York: Macmillan, 1952), 108.

Chapter 2

Miguel de Cervantes Saavedra, *The Adventures of Don Quixote*, trans. J. M. Cohen (New York: Penguin, 1950).

Christian Smith et al., *Lost in Transition: The Dark Side of Emerging Adulthood* (Oxford: Oxford University Press, 2011).

Chapter 3

Bill Moyers, *Healing and the Mind*, xi, based on the PBS special of the same name.

Robert Barron, "What Play Are You In? *The New Oxford Review* (December 2016).

Alan Jasanoff, *The Biological Mind: How Brain, Body, and Environment Collaborate to Make Us Who We Are.* Quoted from Steven Poole, "*The Biological Mind Review:* Identify Your Self," *The Wall Street Journal.*

Chapter 4

Antonio Damasio, *Descartes' Error: Emotion, Reason, and the Human Brain* (New York: Putnam, 1994).

Chapter 9

Philip Hallie, *In the Eye of the Hurricane* (1997; Middletown, Connecticut: Wesleyan University Press, 2001).

Chapter 10

"joy is intimately linked to love," Benedict XVI, "Message for the Twenty-Seventh World Youth Day," 2012.

All quotations from St. Teresa of Avila's *Interior Castle* are from the translation by E. Allison Peers (republished in 2007 by Dover Books, Mineola, New York).

God is more "interior" than we are to ourselves, *Confessions*, III, part 6, trans. F. J. Sheed, "You were more inward than the most inward place of my heart."

God loves you "for what you are," Benedict XVI, "Meeting with the Young People, Pastoral Visit to Turin," (2 May 2010).

Quotations from Mother Teresa are from LaVonne Neff, ed., *No Greater Love*, with a forward by Thomas Moore (Novato, CA: New World Library, 1997).

"the vocation of every human being," John Paul II, *Ecclesia in Asia*, 13.

"the discovery of the unknown Christ in man," Maisie Ward, ed., "Introduction," *The Letters of Caryll Houselander* (New York: Sheed and Ward, 1965), xi.

Chapter 11

"It links together the religious souls of all periods." The reference is from a letter, George Lathrop to Jeffrey Roche, 24 March 1891, cited in Diana Culbertson, ed., *Rose Hawthorne Lathrop: Selected Writings* (New York: Paulist Press, 1993), 33. The interpretation of Lathrop's letter is drawn from Charles Patrick O'Connor, *Classic Catholic Converts* (San Francisco, CA: Ignatius Press, 2001), 50. All other references to Rose Hawthorne Lathrop are drawn from Culbertson's book.

"Holy Mary, Mother of God, pray for us." The reference is from the rite for the celebration of the sacraments of initiation at the Easter Vigil, from the International Commission on English in the Liturgy, *The Rites of the Catholic Church*, vol. 1 (Collegeville, MN: The Liturgical Press, 1990), 149–150.

"I fell in love with the Blessed Sacrament." The reference is from J. R. R. Tolkien, Letter 250, to Michael Tolkien, 1 November 1963, in *The Letters of J. R. R. Tolkien*, edited by Humphrey Carpenter (Boston: Houghton Mifflin Company, 1981).

"If I have one regret." The reference is from Alec Guinness, *A Positively Final Appearance* (New York: Viking Penguin, 1999), 235–236. All other references about Alec Guinness are from his autobiography Blessings in Disguise (New York: Alfred A. Knopf, 1986).

Chapter 12

Early biographical details about Francis-Xavier Nguyễn Văn Thuận are drawn from two official sites dedicated to Cardinal Văn Thuận, http://www.duonghyvong.com/ and http://www.card-fxthuan.org/. Other references and quotations are drawn from Francis-Xavier Nguyễn Văn Thuận, *Testimony of Hope*, translated by Julia Mary Darrenkamp and Anne Eileen Heffernan (Boston: Pauline Books and Media, 2000).

"God speaks . . . God answers our questions." The reference is from Benedict XVI, "To the Members of the Roman Curia for the Traditional Exchange of Christmas Greetings," 22 December 2008.

Quotations for the rites of Baptism, Confirmation, and Reconciliation are drawn from the International Commission on English in the Liturgy, *The Rites of the Catholic Church*, vol. 1 (Collegeville, MN: The Liturgical Press, 1990).

"Baptism placed you in this blessed state." The reference is from John Henry Newman, "The Call of David," *Plain and Parochial Sermons*, vol. 8, sermon 4.

Quotations from Walter J. Ciszek are drawn from Walter J. Ciszek, *He Leadeth Me* (Garden City, NY: Image Books, 1975).

Quotations from François Mauriac are drawn from François Mauriac, *Holy Thursday* (Manchester, NH: Sophia Institute Press, 1991).

The reference to Alec Guinness and Msgr. Ronald Knox is drawn from Alec Guinness, *Blessings in Disguise* (New York: Alfred A. Knopf, 1986), 44.

"Out of the darkness of my life." The reference is from J. R. R. Tolkien, Letter 43, to Michael Tolkien, 6–8 March 1941, in *The Letters of J. R. R. Tolkien*, edited by Humphrey Carpenter (Boston: Houghton Mifflin Company, 1981), 53.

References

"We need comfort, sympathy, love." The reference is from Caryll Houselander, Letter to Mrs. Boardman, 22 January 1947, in *The Letters of Caryll Houselander*, edited by Maisie Ward (New York: Sheed and Ward, 1965), 145.

The reference to Caryll Houselander's sickness and cure is drawn from Caryll Houselander, *A Rocking-Horse Catholic* (London: Aeterna Press, 2015), 25.

Quotations from Thérèse of Lisieux are drawn from Thérèse of Lisieux, *Story of a Soul*, translated by John Clarke (2nd ed., Washington, DC: ICS Publications, 1976).

Quotations about Eucharistic Adoration in Ciudad Juaréz are taken from Patty Knap, "Mexican City Sees Stunning Drop in Violence as Adoration Increases," 1 February 2017, *National Catholic Register*.

Chapter 13

Quotations from C. S. Lewis are taken from *A Grief Observed*, with an afterword by Chad Walsh (New York: Bantam Books, 1976).

"As Msgr. Ronald Knox notes, not even Christ suffered in isolation." The reference is to Ronald Knox, "The Problem of Suffering," *A Retreat for Lay People* (New York: Sheed and Ward, 1955), 139.

Quotations from Fr. Walter J. Ciszek are taken from *He Leadeth Me* (Garden City, NY: Image Books, 1975).

"Holy Orders and Marriage as two sacraments for building communion among the people of God." The wording is drawn from the *Catechism of the Catholic Church*, paragraph 1534.

Chapter 14

"I believe now that all human lives are just like dreams." The reference is from Pedro Calderon de la Barca, *Life is a Dream*, translated and adapted by Adrian Mitchell and John Barton (Woodstock, IL: The Dramatic Publishing Company), III.3.

"Glory, science, knowledge, and whatever other fine names we use, never healed a wounded heart." The reference is from John Henry Newman, "The Tamworth Reading Room," section 3, available at newmanreader.org.

Quotations from Joseph Ratzinger are taken from *Eschatology: Death and Eternal Life*, translated by Michael Waldstein, edited by Aidan Nichols (2nd edition, Washington, DC: Catholic University Press of America, 1988).

"Jesus is the food for our journey." The reference is from the rite of Viaticum. See International Commission on English in the Liturgy, *The Rites of the Catholic Church*, vol. 1 (Collegeville, MN: The Liturgical Press, 1990), 857.

"Why, this is hell, nor am I out of it." The reference is from Christopher Marlowe, *Dr. Faustus* (New York: Dover Publications, 1994), Scene III, 13.

"The first step to becoming holy is to will it." The reference is from LaVonne Neff, ed., *No Greater Love*, with a forward by Thomas Moore (Novato, CA: New World Library, 1997), 54.

"Mystery of creation" and "the core of all things." The reference is from Josef Pieper, *Only the Lover Sings*, trans. Lothar Krauth (San Francisco: Ignatius Press, 1990), 23–24.

"Will want it again." The reference is from C. S. Lewis, *Surprised by Joy* (New York: Harcourt, Brace and Company, 1955), 18.

Rite of Commendation. Source: International Commission on English in the Liturgy, *The Rites of the Catholic Church*, vol. 1 (Collegeville, MN: The Liturgical Press, 1990), 866–67.

Chapter 15

Permission to republish materials adapted from Edward Sri, *Into His Likeness* (Ignatius Press and Augustine Institute, 2017) is gratefully acknowledged.

Art and Photo References

Cover St. Patrick's Cathedral at night, in Manhattan, New York. © Jon Bilous/shutterstock.com

P. 2 Sad father hugs his teen daughter. © Oleg Golonev/shutterstock.com

P. 5 © Restored Traditions. Used by permission.

P. 7 Rohingya refugees from Myanmar waiting for food aid in Kutupalong refugee camp near Cox's Bazar, Bangladesh. © Hafiz Johari/shutterstock.com

P. 8 She has problems with sore throat. © gpointstudio/shutterstock.com

P. 9 Jesus speaks to Zacchaeus the tax collector. Public Domain.

P. 10 Football coach training and teaching a football player. © digitalskillet/shutterstock.com

P. 15 Christ healing the blind. Public domain.

P. 16 Pretty girl taking a "selfie." © Jayme Burrows/shutterstock.com

P. 17 Woman praying in the church. © Milkovasa/shutterstock.com

P. 18 Human hands open palm up worship. © Artit Fongfung/shutterstock.com

P. 20 Madrid. Don Quixote statue. © JPF/shutterstock.com

P. 21 A pro-life demonstrator awaits the Supreme Court's ruling on abortion access in Washington, DC on June 27, 2016. © Rena Schild/shutterstock.com

P. 24 Laguna Beach, California - February 3, 2018 - Hands Across the Sand protest against Trump's offshore drilling proposal to expand off shore oil and gas drilling in coastal waters. © Steve Bruckmann/shutterstock.com

P. 27 Handsome young African American wearing casual sweater talking to his unrecognizable caucasian friend, listening to him with interest and attention. © WAYHOME studio/shutterstock.com

P. 29 Anxious worried girl thinking over problems in relationships. © fizkes/shutterstock.com

P. 30 PHILADELPHIA, PA OCTOBER 6, 2011 Two female Occupy Wall Street protesters holding sign protesting corporate greed. © Nick Tropiano/shutterstock.com

P. 31 Male beggar in hood showing "Seeking Human Kindness" Sign on cardboard. © Andrey_Popov/shutterstock.com

P. 33 In the underground laboratory, two clandestine chemists wearing protective coveralls and masks cook drugs. © Gorodenkoff/shutterstock.com

P. 34 3D Illustration of a magnifying glass over a paper background with focus on the word "me." © Olivier Le Moal/shutterstock.com

P. 36 Tall backpacker watching clear sunny spring daybreak over sea. © rdonar/shutterstock.com

P. 38 THE DEATH OF SOCRATES, by Jacques Louis David, 1787, French Neoclassical painting. Oil on canvas. © Everett-Art/shutterstock.com

P. 41 Busagazi, Uganda. May 3, 2017, Two little Ugandan children in rags sitting on a dirt floor in house. © Adam Jan Figel/shutterstock.com

P. 42 Back view backlight portrait of a single woman waching a sunset on the city with a warm light in the background. © Antonio Guillem/shutterstock.com

P. 44a Light brown wooden round dining table. © kibri_ho/shutterstock.com

P. 44b Love of mother and daughter © kikovic/shutterstock.com

P. 45 Newlyweds in front of the altar during the wedding ceremony. © wideonet/shutterstock.com

P. 47 Baptism ceremony in Church, blessing with water. © sweet marshmallow/shutterstock.com

P. 48 St. Thomas Aquinas. Public Domain.

P. 49 © Restored Traditions. Used by permission.

P. 50 Wheat field. Ears of golden wheat close up. © Subbotina Anna/shutterstock.com

P. 52 Alone broken sullen young teen sits looking on light white gloomy city in window. © ArtMari/shutterstock.com

P. 54 Cute portrayal of a range of different emotions. © Rawpixel/shutterstock.com

P. 55 Bronze statue of the Roman war in a chariot with two horses. © GrashAlex/shutterstock.com

P. 56 Mother Talking With Teenage Daughter On Sofa. © Monkey Business Images/shutterstock.com

P. 58 Young girl screaming in front of police riot, during ecological protest against construction work at the Bulgarian sea coast-Sofia, Bulgaria-June 14, 2012 © Tramvaen/shutterstock.com

P. 59 The capture of Christ. Public Domain.

P. 61 PHILADELPHIA-January 28, 2014: Temple Owls guard Will Cummings (2) Hangs in the air taing a shot after contact on a fast break in an AAC basket ball game © Aspen Photo/shutterstock.com

P. 63 Young woman giving money to homeless beggar man sitting in city. © Halfpoint/shutterstock.com

P. 64 The Civil Rights Movement. Public Domain.

P. 66 Chocolate cake with a cut piece and blade on gray background. © Africa Studio/shutterstock.com

P. 68 Vertical shot of beautiful cheerful female student enjoying studying with her male friend at the library. © Nestor Rizhniak/shutterstock.com

P. 70 Rio de Janeiro-Brazil-October 18, 2011 Show of BEYONCE, Hsbc arena. © A. RICARDO/shutterstock.com

P. 73 Overweight woman eating junk food. © suparat wanpen/shutterstock.com

P. 74 Mr. and Mrs. cardinal on berry branches. © Bonnie Taylor Barry/shutterstock.com

P. 75 Man eating hamburger with two hands into mouth. © karanik yimpat/shutterstock.com

P. 76 Lovely interracial couple having lunch at restaurant. © Luck Business/shutterstock.com

P. 77 Young couple carrying a seedling to be plantedd into the soil in the garden. © Freedomz/shutterstock.com

P. 79 Mother and father holding hand of sleeping baby. © O_Lypa/shutterstock.com

P. 80 Student celebrates graduation with parents. © Monkey Business Images/shutterstock.com